The Education
of a 90-Year-Old

Youth,
Experience,
Fulfillment.

Life teaches:
  It is never too late
    to learn,
      to live, and
        to love.

The Education
of a 90-Year-Old

**Youth,
Experience,
Fulfillment.**

Life teaches:
It is never too late
to learn,
to live, and
to love.

Roger Turner

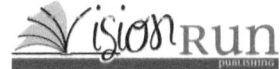

The Education of a 90-Year-Old
by Roger Turner

Copyright © 2023, Roger Turner

ISBN: 978-1-954509-13-9

Scripture taken from the New American Standard Bible®
Copyright © 1960, 1962, 1968, 1971, 1977, 1995 by The Lockman
Foundation. Used by permission. Also the RYRIE STUDY
BIBLE, NEW AMERICAN STANDARD TRANSLATION,
Copyright © 1976, and 1978 by the Moody Bible Institute of
Chicago. Used by permission.

Printed in the United States.

Text and cover design by visionrun.com
Photography by iStock.com, MarkD800

Dedication

*To those I have always loved,
Ruth, Anne, Sarah, and Dean.*

About The Author

Roger Turner is a graduate of Duke University and The University of Texas School of Law. He also earned a diploma from the Episcopal Lay School of Theology, Alexandria, Virginia. He is a member of the Texas State Bar. During his 35 years of service with the United States Government, he worked for both the U.S. Department of Commerce and the U.S. State Department. After retirement from government, he became a full-time chaplain for the Good News Jail and Prison Ministry. He is now fully retired and lives in Falls Church, Virginia with his wife, Ruth.

Other Books By Roger Turner

Love and Forgiveness,
  A Christian's Journey in Prison Ministry

An American Heritage,
  Chronicles of Our Family, 1640-2012

No Life Is a Failure,
  Provided the Will to Contribute Lives

America's Fragile Experiment and The Patriots Who Helped Preserve It

Architects for Religious Freedom –
  The Puritans, Thomas Jefferson, and the Supreme Court

What Makes a Good Father

Acknowledgments

This memoir could not have been made presentable without the marvelous help of my gracious editor, Susan Ward, and the efforts of my friend and publisher, Debbie Patrick. Thank you both so much!

Table Of Contents

Author's Note

New Year's Day, January 1, 2022, presented a challenge. It was not only the start of a new year, but it was also a year in which I anticipated reaching my ninetieth birthday, a milestone for old men. Those who approach such an advanced season in life often ponder what their future might hold. They may ask themselves the age-old question: *What should my purpose be in the time I have remaining?*

Then I reasoned. Provided my health permits, my response must be to emulate St. Paul's perspective. For a time he questioned whether it was better to die and be with Christ or to continue serving our Lord's purposes on earth. Paul chose to remain in order to serve Him. He explained, "To live in the flesh requires fruitful labor in support of others."[1] I chose to follow his approach of service to others in whatever manner I am able. Even though it had never been my intention to accomplish this by writing a book, surprisingly, that is what I have done. It is based upon a weekly compilation of reminiscences or essays to leave for my children and their descendants.

They recount family memories, personal beliefs, and a few political opinions. My hope is they might provide friendly insight as to how one might deal with the challenges and opportunities we all face in life. Invariably their content will reflect past joy, success, failure, and mere idle contemplation. Yet my primary criterion for their inclusion is whether I

1   Philippians 1:22

was able to learn from them. As the theologian Oswald Chambers once said, "God allows the memory of our yesterdays to be turned into a ministry of spiritual growth for the future."[2] I am persuaded that there is potential for such growth within each of us, especially where there remains a desire to encourage others in need. I am hopeful my choices will prove to have that effect, or at least they will reflect a humble attempt to offer my appreciation for the gift of life itself.

---

2   Oswald Chambers, *My Utmost for His Highest* (New York: Dodd, Mead & Company, Inc., 1935), December 31st entry

Introduction

Unsurprisingly, in the preparation of many of my essays, I had no choice but to reminisce. In many instances I discovered these musings tendered me some useful, even painful insights into my forgotten past. At times that past still weighs heavily on my conscience. Because it reflects how often I failed to put to proper use the wisdom that had been lovingly imparted to me as a youth, especially by my kind parents. I confess this because as I began to enter manhood, I encountered a strange idol. Increasingly, it appeared to promise a future filled with success and achievement, yet without concern for the need to live a righteous life. Eventually I discovered these promises were a chimera, an illusion. Today I would characterize them as resembling the false pride and hypocrisy of the ancient Pharisees described in Matthew's gospel.[1]

It is quite clear to me now that for many years I was ineffective at practicing the second great commandment: to "love your neighbor as yourself."[2] I confess this because of the many things that I failed to do or should not have done. My shortcomings here were largely the result of a consistent lack of concern for the interests of others, especially where mine were involved. Strangely, however, there were times when I felt confused by this attitude. There were moments when I acted or thought out of real concern for others. On those

---

1   Gospel of Matthew, Chapter 23
2   Matthew 22:39, New International Version

fleeting occasions I often experienced a surprising and uplifting sense of humility. It seemed as if I was acting in accord with some higher purpose. I believe the following Scriptural passage reflects the purpose underlying such occasions: "To the extent that you did it to one of these brothers of mine, even the least of them, you did it to me."[3]

Despite my youthful, naïve hopes of staking out a highly successful course to my life, I confess to having often fallen short of such an objective. As earlier expressed, this was the result of false pride or doing my own thing. Another way of explaining it might be that my feet were not firmly planted; it took me a long time to truly mature. I credit any such maturity I may have finally achieved primarily to God's patience with me, and to the love of family and friends.

Most assuredly, I will always be grateful for my good fortune in having been blessed with my dearest friend, my loving wife Ruth. For over 52 years she has remained faithfully by my side, guiding me, encouraging me, and sharing with me, even when I failed to reciprocate, as thoughtless husbands so often do. Our marriage has helped turn my focus from the shallowness of prideful self-centeredness to the joy and truth of learning how to share. Ruth's love and God's patience with me have opened my heart to the essential need of learning how to love. The result is that I can now better appreciate St. Paul's admonition: "If I give all my possessions to

---

3   Matthew 25:40

feed the poor, and if I deliver my body to be burned, but do not have love, it profits me nothing."[4]

Whatever modest yield I may have accomplished in life has largely been the result of accepting the authority of God's word. This has prompted me to attempt living a life in obedience to it. Often I have fallen short. It was not fear of the grave that prompted my acquiescence, but my desire for true repentance. This is why I have spent much of the past thirty years ministering in jails and prisons to those who had also lost their way. In truth this mission was never something that I would have even contemplated had I not felt called to undertake it. Until that momentous occasion in mid-life, I was too focused on worldly success and career. Only when my heart and ears were sufficiently opened to hear and internalize the wisdom of God's word was I able to respond to His call to serve. Indeed, my nearly 35 years of U.S. Government service were immensely challenging and rewarding. But once the call came, there was never any doubt in my mind that I must respond to it. I yearned to do so. The result has been that the last quarter-century of my life has been more fulfilling than I could ever have imagined.

To some degree, my late maturity enabled me to appreciate Henry Adams' thought in his highly acclaimed autobiography, "Boys never see a conclusion; only on the edge of the grave can man

---

4   1 Corinthians 13:3

conclude anything."[5] Historians suggest Adams expressed such belief at a moment of disillusionment, shortly after his wife's suicide. His attitude differs from mine, however, in that he seemed to be disappointed with his life, whereas I feel grateful for mine and inspired by my hope for the future. Unlike Adams, my spirit is at peace. It is this attitude of encouragement which I have sought to portray in this collection of essays. They reflect the truth of the life I have lived, as best as I am able to recall.

It took me some time to reach a level of maturity whereby I was able to enthusiastically accept the responsibility of being a man of faith. It wasn't until that point that I was able to appreciate that in searching for a path to fulfillment in my life, it was essential for me to listen and to learn about truth as presented in Scripture. Until then, my access to its wisdom was limited. As the great theologian, St. Augustine once explained, "Good men make use of the world in order to enjoy God, whereas the bad [try to] make use of God to enjoy the world ... For the path of virtue starts from humility and rises to higher things."[6]

---

5   Henry Adams, *The Education of Henry Adams* (Boston& New York: Houghton Mifflin Company, 1918) p. 88
6   Augustine, *The City of God* (AD 426) p.71

Chapter I

Youthful Endeavors

One of the challenges of youth is that we have yet to realize who we really are or what will ultimately fulfill our greatest needs. We spend a substantial amount of enjoyable, seemingly frivolous time, simply exploring for answers. These youthful endeavors begin to take on a sense of meaning once the nexus between our natural maturity and our varied experiences is formed. The meaning we seek is most satisfying when that nexus brings wisdom and especially a sense of purpose. Those who accomplish this early in their lives are truly fortunate. It gives them a head start on finding fulfillment.

Some of us allow our youthful tendencies to linger and consequently our paths toward maturity and acquiring wisdom tend to wander aimlessly. At times this applied to me. I knew I was growing both mentally and physically, but I lacked the wisdom to internalize my growth, to take the best advantage of it. I tended to hang on to my self-indulgence rather than concern myself with the needs of others.

As I began to mature, I remember hearing my father say, "Life should begin in old age and run downhill." I presumed what he meant was that if we were born with the wisdom of past experience, we would make fewer mistakes. It would be much simpler to chart a course for our lives. We would know a great deal without having to go through the peaks and valleys of life.

Today, when I attempt to revisit what motivated my youthful years, one word stands out: *enjoyment*. There were games of hide and seek, hop scotch, and marbles, which later gave way to sports. I thought little of my future, as each day presented me an opportunity to have fun exploring my surroundings. My family lived in a rural community some 20-25 miles outside New York City. So I often walked in the nearby woods behind our home. As I look back on that period in my life, I recall how enjoyable it was, especially my escapades in learning about nature.

Both high school and Sunday school were important for my future maturity, even though they didn't seem very important to me at the time. Unfortunately, there were few books that caught my imagination (unless they had pictures in them). Clearly, the nexus between maturity and wisdom was forming slowly. I hadn't begun to really take life seriously. Later on I would pay the price for such prolonged indifference. As the following essays may suggest, I believed in what the poet Longfellow once said, "Youth comes but once in a lifetime." Yes, and I was determined to make the most of it.

My Birth

I was born at an early age, some eight months and twenty days into 1932, during the midst of the Great Depression. Had I been born in China, I would have been considered older. The Chinese tradition is that a child is considered to be a year old at birth.

Regardless of such cultural differences, I believe every culture would agree with Webster, that one's birth is best described as the emergence of an infant or youth from the body of its mother. There is also a second and equally valid definition of a birth, such as the beginning or coming into existence of something, including an idea, a belief or a civilization. The writer Victor Hugo liked this latter definition, based upon his famous quote: "Greater than the tread of mighty armies is an idea whose hour has come."[1]

My emergence, however, was not an idea but a fact, as I was born in White Plains, New York, some 25 miles northeast of New York City, not far from where Washington in 1776 once had his headquarters during the Revolution. The records show that I weighed nine and a half pounds and was 21" inches long. While these dry statistics didn't mean much to me at the time, I was told later that they indicated I had been well nourished and that I would probably have

---

1 Victor Hugo, *The History of a Crime* (1877)

good height. The records also reflect that I was born at 4:15 in the early morning after my mother had been in nearly twenty hours of labor.

In describing the obstetrician who brought me into the world, my father, for some reason, often mentioned that he was from Spain. Apparently, earlier in his medical career he had also been a physician to the Spanish Royal Family. Fortunately, he arrived in America in time to help usher me into the world.

My birth did not attract much attention, as I was only one of over two million children born in the United States during 1932. So with the exception of my parents, the doctor, his nurse, my grandparents, and an aunt and uncle; no one else was present. I always took great satisfaction in the knowledge that my grandparents had been there. It seemed to make it more of a family affair.

Once, years later, when I was going through some old family scrapbooks, I spied an announcement card my dad had printed for the occasion. It depicted a wolf cowering away from a large stork. This big bird was holding a diaper with a baby in it. Further, the card read: *It's not the wolf, but the stork, announcing the arrival of Roger James Anderson Turner.* Apparently, the name James was added to avoid my initials being RAT.

With the exception of the aforementioned attendees, I do not believe that the world at large knew or cared that I had been born. That is the way it is with most births. Other more dramatic events always seem to occur. In 1932, for example, Amelia Earhart made the first woman's solo flight across the Atlantic; Mohandas K. Gandhi began his hunger strike to protest the British Government's decision to separate India's electoral system by caste; and Babe Ruth called his home run shot in that year's October World Series. Fortunately, the Yankees won, defeating the Chicago Cubs in four games.

Upon further reflection, however, I do believe that our Father in Heaven cared. For He knew that several years later I would prove useful in helping to bring three new lives into this earthly kingdom, two daughters and a son. Like many parents today I am confident they will help to make this world a better place. Mine have certainly done their best in this regard, especially where love, family, and respect for others are concerned.

To be honest with you, I do not remember anything about the actual birthing process, except that I was moving, as I left the comfortable home of my birth mother. Probably, I was otherwise unaware of what was happening until that mean Spanish doctor whacked me on the backside to make certain I would begin to breathe. But three characteristics of mine today were certainly in evidence at that time. When I was hungry, I made it known. When I was sleepy, I simply fell asleep, regardless of the time or place. And finally, when I felt pain or discomfort, for whatever reason, I would let others around me know it by crying out.

Today my wife Ruth might say that when I am hungry I still make it known. And when I feel sleepy, I still fall asleep without asking anyone's permission — usually in front of the TV after dinner, but I guess that is one of the privileges of old age. However, one thing has changed since my birth: when I am in pain I tend to groan sometimes, rather than cry out.

The aforementioned discussion records all that I can say about my physical birth. But it does not address Webster's second definition of birth mentioned earlier. If you will recall, it described birth as the beginning or coming into existence of something such as a belief. In my case, the belief I refer to is the belief that God exists and that He sent his Son, Jesus Christ to earth to urge us sinners to repent so as to achieve forgiveness and the promise of eternal life.

This, of course, is a new birth in the spirit, which Jesus said was critical for us to see the kingdom of Heaven. Those familiar with the Scriptural references in John 3:3 and 3:5 will recall that unless one is born of water and the spirit he or she cannot enter the kingdom of Heaven. While my original, physical birth is what gave me life, it was my spiritual rebirth many years later that gave my life a sense of meaning. It convinced me that God had a purpose for me and that by obediently following the teachings of His Son, I could live a life in accordance with God's word.

How did this second or spiritual rebirth occur? Has it truly accomplished its purpose? Answers to those questions are for later chapters in this book.

Wild Pets

In my youth, I was fascinated by the exploits of the fearless big game hunter, Frank Buck. Beginning in the late 1920s and early 1930s, he was famous for his daring capture of wild animals in the jungles of Asia, Africa, and South America. He sold these wild beasts to zoos in America for viewing by the public. *Bring 'Em Back Alive* was his motto. He took movies of his hunting expeditions, and it was one of these that first caught my attention.

His exploits, coupled with a ten-year-old boy's normal curiosity, inspired me to consider becoming a wild game hunter myself. What I needed was experience. So, for a few summers I fearlessly sought my quarry by exploring the 'jungles' around Hartsdale, New York — its nearby fields, ponds, creeks, woods, and estates, even my own back yard. I imagined myself being fearless, unconcerned with any dangers I might encounter or strangers that I might meet. Unlike Frank Buck, I carried no rifle or capture nets, nor did I have a crew of local natives to assist me. Occasionally I was accompanied by my trusty, nine-year-old native guide, Billy, a helper. But my only weapons were my mother's kitchen strainer and an old water bucket.

My quarry included the vicious snapping turtle, the wild duck, the elusive wild carp, the sharp clawed crayfish, and the noble bull frog. I refer to it as noble because of its majestic posture as it sits patiently on the embankment of large ponds, waiting to shoot out its laser-like tongue at the next passing insect.

As well as I can recall, Billy's and my hazardous travels began one day when we were tromping in a local swamp. It was infested with the fierce, deadly mosquito and the stinging bumble bee. Suddenly I said, "There he is Billy. The one we've been looking for." It was a huge, 14-inch snapping turtle sunning himself. Cautiously, I circled behind him and motioned Billy to be still. Then from behind I lifted the turtle up and put him in my bucket. Calmly, I ignored his displeasure at having had his nap interrupted, as he hissed at me angrily.

That night my father gently placed the turtle in his bench vise to drill a small hole in the hard lower part of the turtle's shell. Dad then put a small rope through it. Next, I tied the rope to a stake by one of our small ponds in the back yard and lowered the snapper into the water. My zoo had begun. Now I could pull up my prize and show it to other kids in the neighborhood.

I should add that we had two spring-fed ponds in our back yard. The large upper pond was fenced in as my father kept two pet ducks in it. The lower pond was about ten feet long and quite narrow. Just below the water level was juicy sediment that wild ducks occasionally came to feast on. They did this by seemingly standing on their heads, webbed feet completely elevated, as they sifted through the dark mud in search of a meal.

Being a wise hunter, I quietly observed the ducks' foraging technique and realized that I could approach the pond without the ducks being aware of my presence. On one occasion a duck stayed under water so long that I was able to reach over and grab his feet. He quacked, screeched, and flapped his wings furiously, but I held on, putting him in a cardboard box until my father came home. He then clipped the duck's main wing feathers so he couldn't fly away immediately, and we put him in the upper pond to keep our white ducks company.

On another occasion Billy and I invaded the small lake on the Warburg Estate, the property of a wealthy banker. It was teeming with fish, frogs, Canadian geese, and wild ducks. This abundance made it seem like a big game hunter's paradise. We each caught a few bull frogs, but our prize catch was a sixteen-inch carp. We accomplished this by quickly dropping a bucket over its body and sealing its escape route with my mother's trusty kitchen strainer.

The following summer Billy and I discovered what looked like another small lake, but our access was denied by a lengthy, six-foot-high cement wall surrounding three quarters of the property. The other portion of the lake was fronted by a large house, a garage, and a mews which housed two horses. Today the property is home to the Episcopal Church in Hartsdale. But during our visit it was home to the retired head of the Salvation Army in America, General Evangeline Booth.

Her father, William Booth, had originally formed the Salvation Army in England in the mid-nineteenth century. Of course, I knew nothing of this at the time of our trespass. I was only interested in what wildlife existed at the lake. Although Billy left to run an errand, I courageously decided to explore. To do so I climbed a nearby tree, jumped down onto the top of the wall, and then leapt to the ground on the other side.

The view would have stimulated any great hunter, as it did me. There were two beautiful white swans, one gliding gracefully over the water and the other sitting on a nest that had two large eggs in it. I had never seen such enormous eggs before. Each was larger than a softball. Boldly, I drew closer. I was within a few feet when the mother swan began to hiss at me sternly. I stopped in my tracks.

As I pondered my next move, it seemed as if some wild creature had leapt on me from behind. I felt the sting of its claws on my back. No, it wasn't a tiger, it was an angry father swan fiercely attacking me from behind. It hurt. So despite my fearless nature, I decided it was time to exit. But then, *what to my wondering eyes should appear?* — not a reindeer, but rather a stately, elderly woman, dressed in riding attire, her hair covered with netting. It was none other than General Booth.

She greeted me with the obvious question, *What was I doing there?* I sheepishly explained I was admiring her swans and also looking for my guide, Billy. She may have smiled at my comment, but a few moments later she ushered me out a side gate and probably suggested that I should not return. I never did.

At the time, I was unaware that General Booth was world-famous for her past humanitarian efforts, having been awarded the Distinguished Service Medal in 1919 for her humanitarian work following World War I. Years later, after her death in 1950, then-President Truman commended her for her great service to America.

I would love to tell you how I became a noted frog whisperer, but that tale will have to wait for later in this chapter.

Unexpected Events

Many of us may have experienced circumstances where we could have been seriously injured or worse, had not unexpected events occurred. I must confess that I had only given this subject a passing thought until I recently read a new book entitled *When Animals Rescue*.[1] One story in the book particularly fascinated me. It described how a swimmer was saved from drowning by a group of sea lions that succeeded in buoying her up until she reached shore and finally emerged from frigid waters off the coast of Scotland.

No, my story today is not about being rescued by animals. Rather, it is how several times I seemed to have been saved from serious injury or worse, had it not been for what some would call good luck, mere chance, or happenstance. In fact, that's what I used to think. The best way to convey the purpose of my story is to describe four brief tales for you. Three of them were personal experiences and the fourth was related to me. I begin with the following tale.

On a cold winter afternoon in lower Manhattan, New York, in early 1935, my young mother was walking beside her nearly three-year-old son who was enthusiastically peddling his tricycle along the sidewalk near Washington Square in lower Manhattan. As we proceeded up the sidewalk passing many apartment buildings, I suddenly began to cry. My

1   Belinda Recio, *When Animals Rescue* (New York: Skyhorse, 2021)

concerned mother immediately looked down at me and was startled to see a 14-inch iron curtain rod sticking out of my right arm. According to what my mother told me years later, the rod had slipped out of a repairman's grasp while he was trying to hang some curtains in one of the third-floor apartments.

If you can picture a small child on a tiny tricycle, you can appreciate how close his arms would be to his head. Maybe an inch or two further in and the rod would have pierced my skull. Yes, I would call it good fortune or luck that the rod hit my arm instead. Could this result have been part of a plan to save me from serious harm or death? Depending on how one reads Psalm 139:15-16, it may well have been. But let me continue with my second story before I attempt to address such considerations.

When I was around nine or ten, I was given a new Schwinn® bicycle for my birthday. As you can imagine, I couldn't wait to ride it. This was in the early 1940s, and our family lived in a rural area, some thirty miles east of New York City. The streets in my neighborhood were generally empty of cars and trucks during the day. And with one exception, you could always see whether the street ahead was free of traffic. The one exception was Lakewood Drive, where it crossed Jane Street. As one headed south on Jane Street, toward Lakewood, on the left there was a long, high hedge that blocked one's view of traffic coming down Lakewood toward Jane Street. So, any car (or bicycle) traveling down Jane Street had to stop at the stop sign to make certain no cars were coming.

In my youthful exuberance, with the wind at my back, I completely ignored the stop sign and kept going. Almost immediately, I heard a screeching of tires skidding on the pavement. As I turned to see what the noise was, I saw a neighbor's car had come to a halt, its bumper almost touching my bike. Had the neighbor not stopped, her car would have run directly into me. Had luck saved me or was it merely a safe driver?

My third tale took place in the autumn about five years later. A teacher had asked me if I would climb up her thirty-foot apple tree and shake down some ripe apples which had yet to fall. I loved climbing trees, so I readily agreed and climbed up to the top, where the ready fruit dangled invitingly. The limbs immediately below me were less full of fruit, but appeared sturdy enough to hold me. Rather than shaking them with my foot, I went out on a limb, the very thing the old saying says not to do.

Suddenly I heard a crack as the limbs I was standing on began to break off from the trunk of the tree. There was no doubt I was going down with them. The only question in my mind was, would I survive? At that moment, all I thought about was missing my parents and my brother. We often hear of people thinking in that manner when they believe they are facing death. I believe that there must be some truth to it. Fortunately, the broad limbs and their leaves had cushioned my fall. I stepped away from them and began to pick up the apples that had fallen. Was it luck again?

My fourth and last story occurred in the mid-1950s, on the Los Angeles Expressway. Two sisters and the eight-year-old daughter of the driver, her mother, were traveling home. Cars in those days did not have the secure safety latches of today, nor the all-important seat belts. Unfortunately, the child in the back seat was fiddling with the safety latch of her door. She accidentally opened it, and immediately fell out onto the highway, where she began tumbling toward oncoming traffic. Fortunately, the driver was able to stop the car while her sister hurried out and raced to pick up her niece. Once back in the car they got the child to a nearby hospital.

After about a half-hour of being examined by two doctors, the child was given back to her mother. She had suffered a few scrapes and bruises, but otherwise was declared uninjured. The young girl seemed extremely excited as she said to her mother, "Guess what Mommy? I just saw Jesus! When I fell out, He stepped in front of me, held out his arms, and all the cars stopped." This story was told to our congregation some fifteen years ago by John Yates, our Rector.

I also recall a recent sermon about our identity by my current Rector, in which he clearly said that God is in control and knows how our lives will turn out. At once, his statement raised in my mind the question of how God influences certain events. Psalm 139 certainly suggests that He does.

Psalm 139:15-16, says: *My frame was not hidden from Thee, when I was made in secret… And in Thy book they were all written, the days that were ordained for me, when as yet there was not one of them.* This suggests to me that there was more than luck or happenstance involved in the events just mentioned. Further, it says in Isaiah 55:9, *For as the Heavens are higher than the earth, so are My ways higher than your ways, and My thoughts than your thoughts.* Yes there are some events that occur that seem to defy explanation. Maybe we aren't supposed to know how to explain them.

How I Became A Frog Whisperer

As a young boy, frog whispering was challenging to me, possibly because I learned how to do it well. At an advanced age, I even astonished my son when demonstrating my smooth technique. But I'm getting ahead of myself. First, let me provide you some background on frogs.

Research suggests several reasons why the British demean the French by sometimes referring to them as "The Frogs." In history, the two countries have frequently been enemies. Then, there is the claim that the French were the first in Europe to eat frogs. Finally, there is the amusing story of how Queen Elizabeth I often referred to one French embassy official as "My little jumping frog." Apparently, she enjoyed watching others dance, especially when the dance required quite a bit of leaping. The French official in question was quite good at leaping up.

Archaeologists estimate that frogs as a species probably existed as much as 265 million years ago. However long they have existed, I believe that the Lord may have actually chosen them to survive the flood. For in Genesis 7:23 it reads: *Thus God blotted out every living thing that was upon the face of the land, from man to animals to creeping things, and to birds of the sky, and they were blotted out from the earth.*

This suggests to me that God may not have intended for

frogs or other aquatic animals to enter the ark. He knew they could survive in the water, at least for forty days. Also, some frogs have ingenious methods of surviving under severe weather conditions. Take, for example, the Australian water-holding frog. It dwells in the desert, and can wait up to seven months for rain by burrowing itself underground in a self-made cocoon.

You may wonder whether there is a significant difference between a frog and a toad. The answer is, not really. Both belong to the same species. Frogs have longer hind legs and live by the water, while toads are found in gardens or on forest floors. Toads are accustomed to making short hops, while frogs are noted for their long jumps. The record for the longest frog jump is 33.5 feet. Both these amphibians are valuable as environmental bell-weathers. For if their population seems to suddenly be in decline, it's an early warning sign of environmental damage.

In my youth, I had no knowledge of a frog's relationship to our environment, but I did notice the difference between a frog's jump and a toad's hop. So, when I was eleven, I immortalized my findings on toads with the following words:

> *As I was walking home one day, I saw upon the road,*
> *A funny little hopping thing that was a little toad.*
> *Now every little toad you know always likes to hop;*
> *But when you ask him if he'll start, he always likes to stop.*

Now that you are familiarized with the nature, importance, and durability of the species, I need to explain how the existence of these amphibians caught my interest. It happened one summer day when I was about seven. I was walking by a stream near our home when I spotted another boy about my age on the opposite side. He pointed to some small frogs nearby and explained why they always jumped into the water when I approached.

He explained that when a frog sees you coming, you have to freeze and make eye contact with it. A moment later kneel down, but never raise an arm or hand or show upper body movement. Then, slowly move to within arm's length of the frog and stop. This approach allays the frog's fears that you might be a threat, causing him to jump into the water. Most importantly, maintain eye contact, as a frog's eyes move around the top of his head so he can always see you. His eyes operate much like an owl's head, which can move in any direction.

Upon kneeling, lower one arm to ground level and slowly push your hand through the grass toward the frog's back, until you are only an arm's length away. Now begins the final test for all would-be frog whisperers. Can you launch your hand over his body and grab him before he sees your hand?

It took me a while to master this technique, but after several failed attempts I finally was able to gauge the critical arm distance necessary to make a successful launch. I guess you could compare it to a boxer learning how to gauge an upper cut before striking. Eventually, even the largest frog was unable to escape my grasp. I had become a certified frog whisperer. When I reached my teens, however, I retired and began to pursue more wholesome pursuits.

After 40-some years of retirement I had a unique occasion to once more demonstrate my skills. It occurred at a large family gathering in Connecticut, at my father's home. After dessert was served, I excused myself and motioned to my ten-year-old son to join me outside. It was dark, but a spotlight illuminated the large fishpond behind my father's home. As we approached, the area echoed with the sound of croaking bulls calling to their mates. Once I spotted my quarry, I quickly motioned to my son to be still. Slowly I knelt down, as my eyes locked in to those of the big bull. Gradually, I lowered my arm and slid it through the tall grass behind him, while he continued croaking to his lady friends. Then, like a shot, my arm sprang forth and my hand clasped him. My young son Dean looked on in amazement.

We then returned to the dinner table, but not before I placed our catch in a large soup tureen and put the lid on. It was Father's Day and I wanted to surprise Dad. So once seated, I placed the tureen in front of my father and said: "Here Dad, I want to give you one additional present for being such a good father." As I lifted the lid, all eyes became fixed on the tureen, as Dad viewed his gift with a startled look. At first nothing happened. Then, like a jack-in-the-box, the frog jumped out and onto the floor. Huge outbursts of laughter followed. My first cousin Delsa laughed so hard, tears began to roll down her face and she turned beet red. My daughter Sarah couldn't stop laughing.

Now the secret is out concerning my unique talent. Fortunately, our son became an excellent tennis player instead. But in closing I must leave you with the following thought:

> *Now I have told you all that I know,*
> *about this funny hopping thing that always wants to go.*
> *I hear my mother calling; I know I cannot stay;*
> *I wish I was like that little toad that always hops away.*

Youthful Years

The years from August 1932 until August 1950 carried me from my first glimpse of life at a White Plains, New York hospital to my entrance into college in Durham, North Carolina. In the following text I will relate certain events I experienced along the way. One was quite painful, others quite eventful, and another quite amusing. Their variety enabled me to appreciate how life offers us a natural pathway toward maturity, provided we have the interest and wisdom to learn from our experiences. Unfortunately, there were occasions when I failed to learn a great deal from them.

Though my memory can be somewhat faulty these days, I distinctly recall when I first learned what it's like to experience physical pain. At three years of age, as related earlier in this text, a repairman accidentally dropped a small curtain rod from a building while I was riding on my tricycle three stories below him. I don't remember any pain when it entered my arm, although I must have cried out. But I distinctly remember what it felt like when the doctor stitched up my wound.

In my youthful brain at the time, the pain must have been so excruciating that it seemed like a flaming hot needle was touching me every time he added another stitch. Apparently, he had no local anesthetic. Years later my mother was astonished that I could remember such an early event in my life. She was correct. I didn't remember the event until she talked about it years later. But I could still remember the severe pain I felt when the 'hot' needle entered my arm. As a result, even today, I tend to wince whenever I have to have an injection; I always close my eyes to avoid seeing it.

My father grew up in Georgia, but never spoke with a Southern accent when at home, except when reading me certain stories about the South. When I was age six or seven, he would read to me stories taken from African American folk tales or Uncle Remus. In 1946 the tales were made into a popular movie by Walt Disney. I enjoyed listening to one story in particular. It told how a clever fox was outsmarted by a wise rabbit, who avoided being eaten for the fox's dinner. Br'er Fox, as he was called, had built a tar baby to catch Br'er Rabbit. And the rabbit felt insulted when the tar baby didn't acknowledge him. So, he proceeded to strike him several times while getting himself more stuck in the process. Building to a climax, after each strike, my father would read the following words: "Tar Baby he don't say nothing, and Br'er Fox he lay low." It thrilled my youthful imagination just to hear him say this. Once the rabbit was captured, he managed to trick the fox into throwing him into the briar patch, where he escaped. The story taught me not to panic when disaster threatens but to reason out your difficulty.

After I became a proficient frog whisperer, our family joined a swim and golf club. In a stream near the swimming pool, I spied several frogs of various sizes. Remembering my frog whispering training, I caught several of different colors and sizes. My father let me bring some home and keep them in the tub in our guest bathroom. I made certain of course to provide them water and rocks to sit on. Unfortunately, it never occurred to me to supply them with food, other than breadcrumbs. I didn't realize that frogs ate mosquitoes and other insects, none of which I could have brought into the bathroom.

After two weeks, several of the smaller frogs began to disappear, yet none were able to jump out of the tub. Where did they go, I wondered? Then one night my Dad walked into the guest bathroom and suddenly called to me. He had found the answer. There in the middle of the tub the largest frog sat with the legs of a much smaller frog sticking out of his mouth. The next day we took the remaining frogs back to the club and released them. I had learned a valuable lesson. Frogs don't eat people food.

My youthful experiences with pain, bedtime stories, and frogs may suggest my broader education was somewhat restricted. The contrary is a more accurate account of my upbringing. My father saw to it that I was given good training in religion, education, and patriotism, especially the importance of presidential leadership. He would often regale me with stories of our family in America's various wars and the heroism of some of our greatest presidents.

In the early 1940s, I was aware that America was at war with Germany and Japan, and I wanted us to win. Accordingly, it was both exciting and reassuring to actually hear President Roosevelt on the radio. I looked forward to those occasional Sunday evenings when he spoke to the nation during his famous fireside chats. He encouraged all Americans about the progress of the war. I certainly don't remember exactly what he said, as I was only ten or eleven at the time. Yet I always felt encouraged after listening to him. Just hearing his voice gave me a sense of assurance we could count on his protection. It was my introduction to patriotism and the importance of having a president who could lead a united nation.

During my early teenage years, 1944-1947, I attended a nearby private school. One class experience during that period forever changed my attitude toward famous people, especially entertainers. It occurred when our class attended a play in New York City. Once the final curtain came down my classmates and I were allowed to line up to get actress Celeste Holm's signature on our programs. After about twenty minutes standing in line, I reached to within one or two persons of Ms. Holm. Unfortunately, at that very moment she excused herself. I was quite disappointed at the time and made a vow.

I vowed never again would I ask someone to give me their autograph, especially someone I didn't even know. Only twice did I break my vow, but in each instance, it was not for me but for someone else. The first was to get Perry Como's signature in 1954, after I sang with our Duke Glee Club on the Perry Como TV show in New York City. My purpose was to send it to a girl I was dating. The second exception was to get the signature of the Hall of Fame baseball player, Stan Musial, of the St. Louis Cardinals. I had promised to do it for a young boy when I attended a game in Los Angeles. Mr. Musial kindly obliged my request.

When I think of people I did not really know, I will always remember our Chinese laundryman, Harry. When I was about nine years old, men's permanent-press shirts had yet to be marketed. Consequently, there were many Chinese in the New York area who ironed shirts for a living. I would often join my mother when she dropped off a load of my dad's shirts at Harry's Chinese Laundry. The small shop was divided into two small rooms. The front room was where he ironed and met his customers, and the back room was where he slept. It was that room that truly fascinated me because it only contained a small cot on which he slept and a gas stove where he cooked his meals and where he heated his hand irons to iron his customer's shirts. I always managed to peek into his bedroom area and wondered what it was like to sleep seven days a week in the same small quarters, on such a small bed.

For some reason he felt flattered by my continued interest in his lifestyle and asked my mother if he could take me with him to New York's Chinatown to celebrate the Chinese New Year. She and my father agreed. So, on the appointed day my Chinese friend and I took the train to New York City and a cab to Chinatown. Outside of San Francisco, it houses the largest Chinese population in America. I remember watching the parade there, but the most interesting thing to me was lunch.

Following the parade, we lunched in the kitchen of a large Chinese laundry. We were joined by four or five of Harry's friends. There we were seated at a large round table. It was covered with all kinds of interesting dishes I had never seen before and plenty of chopsticks. When one of the men showed me how to use them, I was able to eat until I had a sufficiency. Afterwards, Harry and I returned home.

It would be another fifty years before I again ate with chopsticks. It was during my visit to Hong Kong in 1993 with Charles Colson. On that occasion, the local Chinese were amazed that I could handle them well enough to eat my meal without using a knife or fork. I never told them that I had learned as a boy, from my friend Harry, the Chinese laundry man. My experience as a boy in Chinatown had taught me how to clear my plate of food. More importantly, I had learned something that would help me in the future. It is always nice to take an interest in other people. For as our Lord once said, "If you love those who love you, what reward have you?"[1]

---

1   Matthew 5:46 (New King James Version)

Learning from Man's Best Friend

"Where is Bip?" I asked my mother. "I want to play with him." I was about five years old at the time and Bip was my little pet dog. He was probably a mixture of bull dog and terrier. When Mom informed me that he had to be given away, I burst into tears. Unbeknownst to me, Bip had bitten the mailman and later threatened a neighbor who came to call. These details seemed beyond my understanding. All I wanted was my dog. I had become more attached to him than I realized. For several days following his departure, I would stand by the window looking out at the street, hoping one of the passing cars would soon return Bip to me. It would take many years and several dogs before I truly learned how integral my relationship to a dog could become and how greatly I would benefit from it.

Four years after the loss of Bip, I was playing baseball with my grandfather. Then I hit a ball across the street and into a neighbor's yard. It had landed near where their Spitz dog, Fritz, was tied up. As I ran over to retrieve the ball, Fritz broke loose from his rope tether, charged me, and bit me in my left leg. My grandfather chased him away and my mother then drove me to a nearby doctor to be treated. Fortunately, no rabies shots were required. But as a result of the episode, I began to beg my father to get us a St. Bernard, a big dog who could protect me.[1] But with World War II in full swing there were simply no breeders nearby who could supply such a puppy.

Eventually my father located a three-year old, full-grown, Newfoundland dog that a nearby priest needed to find a home for. He was being transferred and couldn't take the dog with him. My new dog's name was Babe, and as characteristic of his breed, he was quiet natured and good around children. Unfortunately, he didn't like cats. Despite this, I took Babe and our young Persian cat Rusty into a small room to make them respect one another. I truly had no idea how to accomplish this, except my determination to do so. But somehow I got it done. Whenever one would seem to attack or threaten the other, I would whack them with a stick. Eventually, they got the idea they needed to respect one another. Later, during that winter, they could be seen resting beside one another in front of our fireplace, next to a glowing fire my father had set.

According to family legend, Babe was a good watch dog. In a supposed effort to keep strangers away, he would follow my younger brother Heyward around our yard. One afternoon Heyward wandered off, but he didn't appear when my grandmother called him for dinner. As the story goes, she then ordered Babe to find Heyward and bring him home. A few minutes later Heyward appeared, somewhat reluctantly, with Babe pulling him along by his pants strap. This story sounds a little unreal, but my father always maintained it was a true story. His mother would never lie about such things.

Unfortunately, this happy ending was followed by a sad

---

1   During my married and family years, I have actually had four St. Bernard dogs, but was unable to keep them for various reasons, including health and housing.

one. One day Babe managed to break loose from his tether and killed our next door neighbor's cat. The neighbor, a somewhat stiff-necked bank manager, carried his dead cat over to our house and asked my father what he planned to do to remedy the situation. Being a gentleman, my father agreed to give Babe away to a business colleague living in California. I never saw Babe again, except in the occasional photograph dad's friend would send us at Christmas. I was now in my early teens, so I wasn't as emotionally saddened as I had been over the loss of Bip. Still, the loss of a second dog kept me from learning more about how a dog could be my best friend.

It was over 30 years later when I first was able to raise a dog from the cradle to the grave. Ruth, the children, and I were based in Sydney, Australia at the time. She considered they needed to have a pet. So she purchased an Australian Silky Terrier pup and called him Fair Dinkum, a local term which means that when everything is okay it's fair dinkum.

We kept her with us when we returned to Washington and she became a real pet. She was a more gentle, intelligent, and faithful dog than any we'd ever had. She even took a semester at the University of Virginia, rooming with our son Dean. Unfortunately, we lost Dinkum to old age, but she will always have a place in our hearts. At times she almost seemed like a person, a member of our family. I still miss her jumping up into my lap as I sat down to read or watch TV. She made me wonder whether dogs have feelings like humans, as strange as that may sound. When she passed away I felt resigned to not having another dog that we might lose. I was traveling overseas frequently so that seemed the wise plan. Fortunately, Dean and Ruth thought otherwise.

Dean felt that a home is not a home without a dog, and Ruth agreed. Together they conspired to present me with a unique birthday present the August after Dinkum died. After their returning from a drive in the Virginia countryside, Ruth and Dean arrived at our house. Ruth then told me to close my eyes. Then she gently placed a beautiful, tiny black Labrador retriever puppy in my arms. At that moment I had no idea how much this present would soon mean to me. It enabled me to experience the full sense of what a loving relationship between a dog and its owner can really mean.

My sister-in-law was visiting us at the time and suggested we name the pup Winston. So we did. During the first few months after Winston's arrival, I was truly amazed at how attached I had become to him. He was so gentle and loving. Whenever I would pat my knees while seated, he would place paws on them as I praised him saying, "You're the last best doggie. There's no doggie as loving as you." Literally, I couldn't wait to get home at night just to be with him. Dean often took him to bed with him on the floor of our porch. In reality, Winston's influence seemed to pervade our home with a sense of caring that was reassuring. But the best was yet to come, as I will now explain.

Two months after Winston arrived, I was again scheduled for travel to South America on government business. On the day of my departure, Ruth brought me home at lunchtime so I could pack for the trip. Upon our arrival, Ruth exited the car, intending to let Winston out into the back yard. A few moments later I heard her cry out, "Winston is gone! He's been stolen!" Immediately, I rushed to see what I could do. As I looked at the dog run where we had left Winston, I saw it was empty with the gate wide open. Where was Winston?

For several minutes Ruth and I thoroughly searched the back, front, and side yards while calling his name, but he was nowhere to be found.

Ruth then said, "I'll get in the car to see if he has gone out into the nearby streets. Possibly he is injured. Meanwhile, please call the police to ask them to come and investigate." As Ruth left, I went into the house and called the police station. A friendly, understanding sergeant answered the phone and promised to come by to investigate. Then, as I hung up the phone, the possible loss of Winston, and how much he had meant to our family, truly hit my emotional chord. Overcome, I fell to my knees and began to pray. As best I can remember, I said, "Lord, you know how much this little dog has meant to us as a family, the power his love has helped to inspire in us. If it is your will, Lord, please allow him to return to us. If this is not to be, Lord, it will in no way lessen my love for you. I will love you all the more."

With tears welling in my eyes, I then gathered myself sufficiently to walk back outside to survey the dog run, hoping I might find Winston. It was a beautiful fall day, with the leaves in the trees fully green and yet completely still. There was no wind. As I surveyed the empty dog run and Winston's overturned water bowl, I felt devastated. It was as if I had lost my best friend. For a moment all was quiet and still, with only the birds breaking the silence. Suddenly, I began to hear the sound of wind and looked up at the trees to see if the leaves had begun to sway. Yet they remained completely still, even as the sound of wind began to increase.

For a few moments I was confused. Yet the sound kept increasing, when suddenly it seemed to be right next to me. When I looked down at my feet, there was Winston looking up at me as if to say, "I've been waiting for you." Immediately I knelt down and grasped him with one hand, while using the other to balance myself on the gate. As I did so, I remember saying, "Thank you Lord for answering my prayers." A moment later Ruth returned and began to say, "I couldn't find—" Before she could finish the sentence, she spied Winston and her expression quickly changed from sadness to joy. Then I said to her, "Let's take him inside and say a prayer of thanks for his safe return."

Barely a week later, my work in Chile was finished. But on Saturday, I addressed some 300 young inmates in Santiago, Chile's largest prison. As I finished my remarks, I mentioned my experience with Winston as proof of God's answer to prayer. Barely was I able to finish telling the story before a tremendous sound of elation suddenly echoed from the young inmates. Startled at first, then I started to realize that they had understood what I was just now beginning to appreciate. It was likely the presence of the Holy Spirit who had announced Winston's return. Didn't Jesus say, "The wind blows where it wishes and you hear the sound of it, but do not know where it comes from and where it is going; so is everyone who is born of the spirit."[2]

Several years later, Winston passed away at the age of 12, as subsequently did a successor, named Joshua, our first chocolate lab. We are now blessed with our second chocolate lab. His name is Duncan. And we enjoy our time together. I have learned that I can talk to him, as I do every day, sharing with him what's on my mind at the time. Sometimes it is about issues of the day; sometimes it's about him and what

---

2   John 3:8.

a wonderful dog he is. Frequently he just sits and stares at me intently, as if trying to comprehend what I'm saying. At other times he simply runs to get his bone or a toy to give to me so we can play together. When Ruth and I take an afternoon nap, he curls up at our bedside and sleeps. Or when I may be reading, he often lies down by my feet, his head resting on my toes. I feel reassured that he wants to be with me. Yes, I have learned what it means to be loved by man's best friend.

Chapter II

The Importance Of Family

The family is one of nature's masterpieces. As Pope John XXIII said, "Family is the first essential cell of human society." Other than the Creator's gift of life itself, nothing can surpass a home where parents' love and encouragement enable a child to thrive. Unfortunately, when such attention is lacking or misapplied during a child's youth, it can cause an emotional burden which may weigh heavily on the child's emotions, causing the child to feel rejected.

It's not hyperbole to claim that the family is the fundamental building block of a strong society. This assertion correlates with the belief that parents' love and interest in their children is crucial to their children's emotional, spiritual, and mental development. Raising a child with the assurance that he or she is loved and considered worthy is an invaluable gift. Such parental support helps to nurture a child's sense of confidence as they begin to mature. In turn, a child's confidence helps to nurture his or her sense of responsibility, with the result being the child will be more inclined to embrace morally responsible values along the road to adulthood.

Conversely, when a child is raised in a dysfunctional family environment where love and the confidence it creates are lacking, it hinders the child's motivation. If a child feels denied parental love and lacks a sense of worth, it can cause resentment, rebellion, or anger in the child. The child may be inclined to take out his or her feelings of rejection on innocent people or even turn to crime. My experience working in jails and prisons in America and offshore underscored the critical need for loving parents. A large percentage of inmates I met had been raised in dysfunctional families. By dysfunctional, I mean any circumstances which prevent a child from growing up with the loving care and emotional support of both parents. Most commonly this occurs in single parent families.

As I reflect on the importance of my own family upbringing, there are those tender moments when I wish my parents were still alive. That I could talk with them, express my love for them, and tell them how much I appreciate what they did for me. I long to tell them how wise they were to try to teach me the importance of such things as obedience, faith, learning, and consideration for others. I wish they could see how I have finally matured in my old age. My guess is that such reverie is not unusual. It confirms how important good families are, especially in this modern age of children wanting complete independence to live their own lives, as they determine what is best, often disregarding the wisdom and useful values of their parents.

I Remember Mother

Those who knew Clara Marie Anderson Turner would agree that she was an extremely attractive and gracious person. In appearance she was tall for a woman (5'8") with lovely auburn hair that would later turn a soft white. A most endearing feature, however, was her beautiful, loving smile as she greeted you. When considered along with her jovial personality, it is easy to appreciate why she made friends so easily. While always conservative in manner and dress, her loving, friendly nature was yet another beautiful feature. Characteristically, she would express sincere interest in learning about others' needs, rather than focusing on her own. At heart she was a people person. This is how I remember my mother.

Born in Sandusky, Ohio in 1904 into a relatively poor family that included two sisters and one brother, Clara grew up with few luxuries. Her father, a hard-working railroad worker from Sweden, and her mother, the daughter of an Indiana school teacher, provided their children with the basic necessities of food, shelter, and clothing. Her family encouraged her appreciation of music. As a result, Clara became proficient at both the cello and the piano.

When her father's work caused him to move to Cincinnati, Ohio, Clara attended a year of college at the local university before moving to New York City. There she lived with her older sister who was an accomplished harpist with a New York symphony orchestra. Clara went to work as a secretary for a local business, until she met my father. After their marriage, he encouraged her to take classes at Columbia University until I was born.

My earliest recollection of my mother is from April 1937, four months prior to my fifth birthday. The occasion was my father leading me upstairs to see her. She had just returned home from the hospital after giving birth to my brother. I definitely recall her loving, welcoming smile as she greeted me while she continued nursing her newborn. I then remember my father lifting me up so I could see my brother. I was curious as to what a newborn really looked like.

During the ensuing years, I began to learn what it was like to have a loving, concerned mother. Daily she would sing or read to me melodies or stories stemming from her own youth, including *The Tale of Peter Rabbit*[1] and *The Bobbsey Twins*[2]. She was also very frugal and made certain that I cleaned my plate at every meal. Having grown up in a family of limited means, she was taught not to waste food.

I remember her saying, "You need to eat all the food on your plate if you want to grow up to be strong and healthy; it will put hair on your chest." Her concern for my brother's and my health didn't make our vegetables taste any better. And I truly did not enjoy eating potato skins, beets, or liver and onions. But at breakfast there was always fresh squeezed orange juice and brown sugar to go with my cream of wheat,

1   Beatrix Potter, *The Tale of Peter Rabbit* (London: Frederick Warne & Co., 1902)
2   Laura Lee Hope (pseudonym), *The Bobbsey Twins* (Newark: Stratemeyer Syndicate, 72 novels 1904-1979)

oatmeal, or Ralston® cereal. Her concern for our health must have worked as we grew up quite healthy. And today I really love eating beets and other vegetables. While I do feel humbled in admitting it, Mother did know best.

As I grew older, I remember observing how kind and concerned my mother was toward others. Whether it was during shopping at the greengrocer, leaving a check at Christmas for the postman, or discussing her purchasing needs with store clerks at Macy's or Lord and Taylor, she always made others feel good. As Dad always used to say, "Your mother has the unique ability to strike up a conversation with any stranger and make them feel that she is a good friend."

During my early teens, my father had become quite successful in the business world, so my parents frequently entertained or were entertained, sometimes with my brother and me included. It was during these gatherings when I was introduced to many interesting people, all of whom enjoyed meeting my mother. As one lady said to me during a social affair, "Your mother is the kind of person I can always talk with; she's interested in you as a person."

Partly because of her family's limited financial means, my mother had learned to become skilled in performing domestic chores, especially the ability to knit and sew. My father claimed that she was such a skilled seamstress that she could earn her living at it. Whether it was adjusting trouser waist bands, making curtains, or shortening a skirt, she saved us many dollars by doing the work herself rather than farming it out to a professional. I can still remember marveling at how rapidly she peddled her old Singer® sewing machine without missing a stitch or allowing the fast-moving needle to strike one of her fingers.

Mom also became involved in community affairs as an officer with the local PTA, a volunteer with the Red Cross, and a member of the altar guild at our local Episcopal church. These activities also resulted in making acquaintances with many interesting women and their families in our community. She enjoyed playing cards and took up bridge. She eventually became so proficient that she was in frequent demand when bridge groups were formed.

After my parents divorced, my mother moved to Atlanta to be near her brother. I visited from Washington as often as possible. When I arrived, Mom would always greet me with her beautiful smile and a kiss. Not long into my visit, she would ask me what I would like for dinner. Then she would insist on taking me shopping with her for our meal. I must confess that grocery shopping was never of great interest to me. I much preferred to eat the food rather than shop for it. Yet I always obliged her. It was such a small thing when I considered all the wonderful things she had done out of her enduring love for my brother and me. Little did I realize how much I would miss such outings after she passed away at eighty-nine years of age.

I well remember my last visit to her home. After the funeral, it was time for my brother and me to clean out her apartment. As I drove there, I began to weep. The realization truly hit me that our wonderful, loving mother would no longer be there to welcome me at the door with her loving smile and embrace. I began to realize how easy it is to take for granted these little joys of life, until they are no longer available. Oh, how I wished that I could have had just one more visit to the grocery store with her, just to have her with me.

One thought gave me peace. It was my belief that she was now in an even better home where her love, sweetness, and enthusiasm would be greatly appreciated. In her new home the love and concern that she had always shown others would be reciprocated as never before.

Family Reunions

The coming together of families and relatives has been encouraged throughout recorded history and is often noted in Scripture, especially for such occasions as worship, weddings, and funerals. Family reunions are an apparent offshoot of this process of honoring, maintaining, and renewing relationships. Such reunions can offer special benefits. Foremost among them are the opportunities they provide for different generations to build or to renew close ties, to meet relatives they have only heard about but never met, and to learn about the origins and accomplishments of unknown ancestors. What makes these occasions fascinating is that the participants usually have a keen interest in their family's history.

I was extremely fortunate to have been raised by parents who believed in strong family ties. They instilled in me the importance of knowing about my family lineage. For example, at one family reunion I learned that a first cousin of my mother's was Lt. General Harry H. Schmidt, who commanded the Marine recapture of several islands in the Pacific (including Iwo Jima) from the Japanese during World War II. I had previously enjoyed reading the history about our troops in World War II and had seen this man's name, but had no idea we were distantly related.

My father often spoke of his distant cousins, great grandparents, and other ancestors from earlier generations. He stressed the importance of knowing about them and keeping in touch with their descendants. Often, he would remark, "At reunions, you gain a greater appreciation of how people with roots related to yours set out on different paths to accomplish things in life. You can also learn of relatives who might otherwise remain a mystery." It is largely owing to this frame of reference that I am able to relate to you a few snippets relative to my own family lineage dating as far back as the American Revolution.

My focus on such family history probably began in 1936, when I attended my first Dowling Family Reunion in Hampton, South Carolina at four years of age. While I personally do not remember the occasion, I do recall watching some old black and white films of the event taken by my father. In one segment, I am pictured wearing a sailor hat with ice cream sliding down my chin as I tried to eat my first ice cream cone. Other shots showed cousins, uncles, aunts, some of whose faces were known to me, as well as others whom I had never met.

At the 1940 reunion there was another young boy who attended with his parents. His name was Richard Riley, and he was only two years old at the time. I actually met him forty years later at our 1980 reunion when he was then Governor of South Carolina (1979-1987). Only by attending our 1980 reunion did I learn of our distant relationship, although I may have seen his name in the *Washington Post*. The following year, he graciously hosted our reunion at the governor's state house in Columbia.

My father's interest in family heritage was largely

influenced by his mother, Maude Dowling Turner. She was always proud of her family's history, dating from before the American Revolution until just after the Civil War. Consequently, in the late 1920s, she and one of her first cousins decided to begin an annual family reunion, bringing together as many lines of their respective families as they could. Today it is known as the Annual Dowling Family Reunion, held in alternate years in either Hampton or Beaufort, South Carolina.

Maude came from a family of eleven children, six girls and five boys. Her mother, my great grandmother, Clara Louise (Ruth) Dowling, had once passed on to her a saying that had its origins several generations earlier, "Behind every great man there stands a great woman." During the 1980 reunion I learned the origin of that saying and why it had been passed down to Clara Louise from her own great grandmother, Christina Bridenger Ruth. Here is some of that background on Christina, my great grandmother four times removed.

She was born in 1731 in a principality in southern Germany. At the time of her birth, Germany was comprised of several small principalities or states. Each was ruled by some local prince or princess. It wasn't until the 1870s that the Germany we think of today was actually united. Until then, each principality had its own royal heritage. So, family lineage was extremely important in determining one's standing in the local community. As the family story goes, Christiana fell in love with a young German suitor named Adam Ruth. Apparently, he was handsome and manly, but was only a blacksmith by trade. Consequently, her family did not approve of him as a future a son-in-law.

But the young lovers were not to be denied, so they eloped on a ship headed for America, arriving in Philadelphia in 1764. From there, they migrated to Charleston, South Carolina, where they eventually purchased farmland near Beaufort. In time, they raised several children. Equally significant, Adam earned quite a reputation for himself during the American Revolution. He joined General Marion's brigade. The British referred to Marion as "The Swamp Fox," as he led a group of guerilla patriots who harassed British Troops under General Cornwallis and the infamous Colonel Tarleton.

Marion's brigade was comprised of untrained patriots, who customarily had to supply their own weapons and food. They avoided capture by hiding in South Carolina's swamps and forests, hence the nickname 'swamp fox.' Although greatly outnumbered by British regulars, the group was successful in disrupting British supply trains and killing British soldiers. Mel Gibson's (2000) movie, *The Patriot*, is loosely based upon the exploits of General Marion. He and others succeeded in harassing the British, following them from South Carolina toward North Carolina, and eventually to Yorktown.

Under Marion's leadership they had an uncanny ability to elude capture and to outsmart even Colonel Tarleton. I must confess a certain pride in knowing that a great grandfather, four times removed helped to defeat the British. When I visited Hampton for the 1980 reunion, I noted the following inscription on Adam Ruth's tombstone:

Adam Ruth, S.C. Regiment, Revolutionary Patriot, Marion's Brigade, sponsored by Beaufort Chapter of the DAR-1937.

When I last attended a reunion in 2012 in Beaufort, I

learned more about Christina and her husband. Some years after Adam had died, Christina (who lived to be 100) was celebrating her ninety-first birthday. On that occasion, she was asked if she ever regretted giving up the luxury and status she would have been entitled to had she not eloped. According to family legend, her reply was quite insightful. Even though seated and normally stooped with age, Christina suddenly assumed a most regal, upright bearing and replied, "My dear, Adam Ruth was a monstrous, pretty man." Apparently, she coined the saying concerning great men and great women.

I believe family reunions support a great American tradition — a sense of history about one's family and equally vital, the importance of family itself. It all goes back to that seventh commandment: *Honor your father and your mother.*[3]

---

3   Exodus 20:12

A Childhood Mentor

Our earliest mentors are customarily our parents. We are fortunate if we have had loving parents who take a genuine interest in our emotional and intellectual growth. Accordingly, our chances of pursuing a fulfilling or rewarding life are greatly enhanced. One might easily equate a loving parent with a fine teacher. Both possess the ability to encourage a child by expressing a sincere interest in his or her personal growth and welfare. And like a fine teacher, such a childhood mentor will consistently demonstrate a capacity to inspire the child, both by example and instruction.

Of course, childhood mentors are not limited to parents. They can also be other family members, teachers, or good friends. But all share an important characteristic: they manifest a genuine interest in the child's development and happiness. Sometimes a child's future happiness requires a mentor who will teach the importance of wise discipline. Here are a few examples from my own experience.

As a boy, I would announce to my father when Luis, our yardman, arrived. My father would then walk outside to greet Luis and begin chatting with him. As I accompanied my father, I noticed he would always greet Luis in a friendly manner. During these friendly encounters Dad would always ask how Luis and his family were faring. For a few minutes, they would laugh and chat with one another. It was apparent to me that they were talking like old friends, not like master and servant. Right away I began to see the beauty and the importance of taking an interest in other people, regardless of their professional or personal relationship. While it never occurred to me at the time, my father was mentoring me in how to deal with people. Today, I try to emulate his example.

When I was a young boy, my father would sometimes come in and read to me prior to my going to sleep. And as I mentioned earlier, since he was from the South, he would often read from the now-banned classic, *Uncle Remus*[4] (later made into the movie *The Song of The South*), about Uncle Remus, Br'er Rabbit, and Little Black Sambo. As I grew older, the quality of the reading matter greatly improved. He would talk with me about Revolutionary and Civil War heroes such as Washington, Hamilton, and Lincoln, and the importance of Jefferson's *Declaration*. Needless to say, he did not raise the issue of slavery for bedtime conversation. What he did do was to inspire me to learn about our nation's history and to pursue my interest in it by reading more. At my advanced age, I must confess that I continue to enjoy reading about our nation's history. I had a good mentor to inspire me.

My father's mentoring where character-related issues were concerned was somewhat more subtle. This was especially the case where truth and determination were concerned. But it wasn't until I became an adult that I began to realize how wise and effective his mentoring of these two virtues had been. For example, on one occasion he had asked me

---

4   Joel Chandler Harris, *Uncle Remus: His Songs and His Sayings* (Boston: D. Appleton & Co., 1880)

to read and comment on one of his speeches, but I failed to do so. When he later asked me what I thought, I had to admit I hadn't read the speech. But rather than indicating any displeasure, he praised me for telling the truth. In fact, truth always seemed so important to him that rather than punishing me when I did something wrong, he would often say, "Just tell me what happened and we'll see if we can't help you to improve." Ever since those wonderful moments from my youth, truth has always been important to me.

Hard work was not something that ever seemed to deter my father. When faced with a task that appeared too difficult to accomplish, he would always say, "You have to keep on keeping on, and eventually you will find a solution." I greatly admired his ability to solve problems that seemed beyond my ability. I attributed this to the fact that he was an engineer. But as I grew older, I began to realize that no matter how difficult a problem might be, I could work to find an answer. While it might not be what I had hoped, it still proves that you don't give up until you have done all you can, as well as you can.

In many ways my mother was also a fine teacher, especially where music was concerned. She had played the cello in her high school orchestra, and she sometimes sang duets with her father (who had a marvelous tenor voice). Even before I could talk, I am told that she used to sing to me. And even before I could understand the meaning of the lyrics, I could remember tunes. I always urged her to repeat them over and over again. I believe this gave me an ear for the sound of music and a sense of rhythm. From grade school through college it seemed as if I was always involved with singing, either in school operettas or college choirs. Eventually I learned to play the coronet and later in life taught myself to play the guitar, primarily so I could sing different folk tunes. Whether she realized it or not, my mother was a wonderful mentor in helping me to love music.

As I suggested at the start of this essay on mentoring, it is critical for a child to learn the reason for discipline and its importance at an early age. In this context, many will remember the Biblical saying that urges, *Train up a child in the way he should go. Even when he is old he will not depart from it.*[5] From my late childhood and through my early teenage years, I fell far short of obeying wise parental guidance. I said and did foolish things that caused me trouble. One of the prime causes was that my parents were too forbearing, especially where discipline was involved. Yes, they told me when I did or said something improper, and why I should not repeat the same mistake. But when I continued to repeat my mistake, they failed to discipline me for doing so. I was terribly spoiled.

Possibly my father was overly concerned with the Biblical warning, *Fathers do not exasperate your children, that they may not lose heart.*[6] He often said that he wanted to raise his children in ways that would not restrict their emotional growth. Unfortunately, his approach and my attitude enabled me to believe that there were no real consequences for improper conduct. I tended to do pretty much as I pleased. Despite my parents' loving and wise counsel, this

---

5   Proverbs 22:6
6   Colossians 3:21

lack of discipline haunted me through much of my early adult life. The amazing thing was that I often felt that I had acted properly, when in reality I was simply doing what I wanted to do, without regard as to how it might adversely affect others.

It was only when I came to the realization that I needed to attend the funeral of my own independence that my attitude began to change. I could no longer reason as a self-centered child. I would have to give up childish ways. One might ask how I was able to change my way of thinking in mid-life. And my answer would be it wasn't possible until I turned my life over to Christ.

As Scripture urges, *Trust in the Lord with all your heart, and do not lean on your own understanding. In all your ways acknowledge Him, and He will make your paths straight.*[7] I had taken advantage of the leniency of my childhood mentors. But once I saw the reflection in the mirror of my wasting life, I had to change. My only recourse was to seek a spiritual mentor, and God answered my cry for help. Christ, the eternal mentor, truly entered my life.

Once I grasped the need for this mind-altering transformation, my entire life began to change. Thereafter, for the last quarter-century of my life, I have felt a sense of fulfillment that I never before envisioned.

---

7   Proverbs 3:5-6

Remembrances of my Father

In my grandmother's dining room in Atlanta, Georgia there was a beautiful, mahogany sideboard, approximately seven feet long and five feet high. Normally it was used to store Maude's dishes, cutlery, and table linens. But it also served another purpose. It proved to be the secret hiding place of three-year old Willie Turner, Maude Turner's youngest son, and my future father. And it was usually around bedtime when Willie would hide from his mother, by crawling inside the sideboard so he wouldn't have to go to bed. Born in October 1904, William Heyward Turner was frequently called Willie by his father. As he matured, he soon learned never to hide from the realities or challenges of life. He courageously faced them. So eventually, he would grow up to become an accomplished, respected, and gracious man. The following are a few of the fond memories I have of our relationship.

As previously mentioned, my earliest recollection is from April 1937, when I was four. On that occasion my father led me upstairs to see my mother. She had just returned home from the hospital where she had given birth to my brother. My father lifted me up so I could see my new brother. I had no idea where new babies came from and was curious to see what one looked like. My brother's eyes were closed and he seemed to be asleep. Apparently, my curiosity was satisfied.

Like most sons, from that day forward until my father's death in October 1997, my relationship with my father remained extremely important to me. I must confess that sometimes this importance affected me negatively, because of our seeming lack of closeness and my sense that he did not truly approve of me. At other times, however, there was a closeness that gave me cause to rejoice, to believe that I was loved by him. The reason for this seeming contradiction in our relationship was never fully clear to me until late in my adult life. He was then advanced in age and I was in mid-career.

At that point I began to fully appreciate not only his kindness, generosity, and caring toward me; I realized how fortunate I was to have had such a good father. What helped me to finally appreciate him fully was that I began to realize how positively he had affected my life. What also helped was I was better able to understand the importance to him of his desire to succeed in life, how motivated he was by ambition.

It was largely because of his ambition that my brother and I received many wonderful experiential, financial, and educational benefits that we would otherwise have missed. In effect, Dad made the choice that to be successful he would have to sacrifice time with his sons. In my teens I can often recall him saying that, "When you are young you sometimes feel like the world is your oyster, but as you mature you recognize that success in life requires hard work and determination."

Dad characterized these qualities. So, from the time I was a young boy and later as a teenager, whenever he saw that

I was not always actively doing something constructive or intellectually challenging, I felt his displeasure. His manner toward me, while gentle, made me think that I was wasting time. The result is that today, even in my late season of life, I become concerned if I am not doing something useful.

This awareness is the direct result of his example, but it took me many years to realize its importance. I only wish I had listened to him as a teenager. At that time, he made a conscious effort to be more directly concerned with my future. Often, he would try to encourage me by explaining, "You never get much further in life than the dreams of your youth." His purpose was to try to get me to think more in terms of what I wanted to do with my life.

Frequently he would try to inspire me to give greater thought to my future by saying, "Your salad days are almost over." His meaning was clear. If you want to get ahead, you must realize that you only have so much time early in life to plan for your future; don't spend all of it on such things as sports, comic books, or playing games.

As I look back wistfully on those years now, I realize how wise my father was and how foolish I was in not being more mindful earlier of his sage advice. Ironically, what contributed to my mental laziness was my reliance on his kindness toward me; if there were problems, I considered he would always be there to help. Instead of trying to forge my own way, I relied too much on his support.

He was too lenient toward me as a boy and as a teenager. I repeat, I was spoiled. There were never any penalties or punishments when I failed to follow his advice. His manner was always kind and forgiving. The fact that he did not have a great deal of time to share with me may be true, but his example of ambition was always there for me to learn from, and eventually I did. I must also confess that early in our relationship there was resentment on my part. I resented that he did not share more of his time with me. Nonetheless, his examples of determination and ambition were ever before me.

The ambition that my father tried to instill in me was, I believe, the direct result of his heritage. Born to lower middle-class parents in Atlanta, Georgia, he came from a strong southern heritage, including a grandfather who was a prominent Baptist clergyman, admired public servant, and former Confederate soldier from South Carolina. Dad's ambition had begun to surface early in his college years. Despite being only 5' 8" tall, 140 pounds, and with limited physical skills, he tried out and made the freshman football team at the Georgia Institute of Technology.

Following graduation three years later, he began his career as an engineer in Florida. Some thirty years later he ended up as the Vice President and Executive Director of the United States Steel Foundation. To accomplish this career rise, Dad devoted his life to hard work, courtesy toward others, and many, many days and nights of formal post-graduate study. The latter included a degree in journalism, two law degrees and a Ph.D. candidacy. But despite his many professional accomplishments, my father remained humble concerning them.

I distinctly remember those occasions when he indicated he had made a mistake. He admitted it. Smilingly, he would often recite Mark Twain's famous comment concerning his father:

"When I was a boy of 14, my father was so ignorant — I could hardly stand to have the old man around. But when I got to be 21, I was astonished at how much the old man had learned in seven years."

In closing this essay, I am reminded of the old saying that what goes around comes around. Eventually it was that way with my relationship with my father. For example, I remember one summer afternoon in August 1991. At that time my eighty-seven-year-old father and I sat on the patio at his suburban Stamford, Connecticut residence. He and I reminisced about family and spiritual life, while all around us seemed oblivious to our presence save for a refreshing breeze.

At one point I asked, "Dad, considering your extensive career and experience, what advice would you recommend I impart to my young children? Something to help them appreciate the challenges in today's surprisingly challenging and changing culture?" My sage father pondered the question for several moments before replying in his calm, almost whisper-like voice. "There is good and evil in this world, and my efforts have always been directed toward doing as much good as I could to help balance out the evil that exists."

While his answer surprised me at first, I realized that he and I were on the same wavelength. Certainly, we both recognized the need to use our talents wisely; and that the desire to succeed is an integral part of any such endeavor. But the critical thought he kept in mind was not what he could do for himself, but what he could do for others. For only then are we fully making our unique contribution to the world around us. As a noted sport's writer once wrote:

> "For when the great scorer comes to mark against
> your name,
> He writes not that you won or lost, but how you
> played the game."[8]

---

8   Grantland Rice, "Alumnus Football," in *Only the Brave* (New York: A. S. Barnes & Co., Inc., 1941)

An Open Door Which Cannot be Shut

The process begins in our youth and continues until we have breathed our last. It is called learning. Regardless of whether one's attention is on the secular, the spiritual, or some combination, we continue to be confronted with a surfeit of learning experiences, especially in the form of opportunities, joy, challenges, and pain. Provided the doorway to our mind and heart remains open, we gradually learn how to relate to these phenomena. The better we do this, the greater our chances of reaching a stable, mature adulthood.

Conversely, if we consistently close the doorway to openness because of prejudice, indifference, pain, or suffering, we severely limit our capacity to grow intellectually and emotionally. The result is that one's potential capability is stunted. Accordingly, the person is restricted in how to respond effectively to their world. The following examples of openness, or its lack, are used to indicate how they can affect a person's way of thinking.

It was late fall in 1949, on a Saturday night at the Turner household in Hartsdale, New York. Having finished my supper, I was preparing to attend a high school dance. I had taken great care to dress appropriately. My blue pleated slacks were nicely pressed. Under my tan checkered sports coat I wore a pink dress shirt and a garish tie, which was nearly four inches at its base. My tie of choice was splashed with a mix of yellow, pink, and orange colors, and had drawings of birds on it. Loud ties were the fad in those high school days, and this particular tie was as loud as any I possessed. I was particularly proud of my sartorial choices.

As I bid goodnight to my father, he looked at me, smiling somewhat discerningly, and remarked, "When you become older and go into business or a profession, your taste in ties will change. You won't want to wear such a colorful tie." My immediate, defensive response was what one would expect from a typical teenager who believed his parent's taste was behind the times. I said, "Dad, I will always want to wear this bold type of tie. It looks great. I will never change my taste in ties."

Within a year I was off to college, all my garish ties having been replaced by narrow, conservative pinstripes. They made me feel more mature. My acceptance of this sartorial change had opened a door to a new perspective I had presumed was shut.

But one such enlightening change was insufficient to overcoming my general resistance. Technology intervened. For example, my mother made me a present of a battery-driven toothbrush. Almost immediately, I gave it to a good friend. My reasoning was that using such a device would demonstrate weakness on my part. I was wedded to the traditional hand-method of brushing my teeth. It took me many years to surmount such prejudice. Today, I am embarrassed to admit that I not only use an electric toothbrush, but find it cumbersome and old-fashioned to occasionally have to use the old hand-driven method.

Opening the door of my mind to modern hygiene appliances was not my only concession to advanced technology, but the second took a lot longer. I was well into married life and fatherhood, and pleased with the "technology" of my electric Smith-Corona® typewriter. Then a 1970s article in *Time* magazine predicted that within 2-3 years, every home would have a personal computer. I remember remarking to my wife, Ruth, "Why would anyone want a home computer when they already have an electric typewriter?" A year later, when I began writing my first book, we purchased a home computer. Over the ensuing thirty years we have made several upgrades to more advanced computers. The door to modern technology is now completely open in our home, including the use of several iPads and smart phones.

While openness toward new technology is certainly commendable, for me the most important area of openness has to do with human relations. Many of my preconceived attitudes toward others badly needed improvement, occasionally, even during this, my last season of life. This shift began to occur as I finally realized that as a man of faith, I needed to change my way of thinking if I were to attempt living a righteous life. For far too long, I had considered my needs paramount, as earlier explained, and the needs of others usually less important.

Part of the reason for this was I had been raised to think this way. My parents spoiled me by seldom disciplining me when I was clearly in the wrong. Why this occurred is another story, but it led me to think that I was always right. This was a difficult mistake for me, as Scripture points out, *A child who gets his own way brings shame to his mother.*[9] The

9 Proverbs 29:15

result was that I foolishly shut doors that were essential to my ability to practice good human relations. Certainly, I was taught proper manners, the importance of respecting others, and not being rude. But the old idea of self-righteousness kept my heart and mind closed for far too long. Then I met a woman at work. Her name was Susan.

At the time, I was working in government and needed some advice on completing a recent travel voucher. Susan was a young, Special Assistant to a Deputy Assistant Secretary in the United States Department of Commerce.

Like all special assistants in government, she was overworked and was expected to do everything for her boss on a short timeline; otherwise she would not keep her job. It was late on a Friday afternoon near closing time when I asked to see Susan. She agreed and we met in her office. Because of the pressure she was under, she almost immediately expressed frustration in having to see me. In a disapproving voice she asked, "So what is it Roger? I'm very busy." My reply didn't help her mood.

I said, "Susan, if you want people to be nice to you, you should be courteous to them." Immediately she replied, "Get out of my office! I'm not going to help you." At once I left, trying to conceal the heat of my displeasure at being so summarily dismissed. At another office I did get the information I was seeking, but when I returned to my office, I could barely control my displeasure. But as I sat down, I recalled a passage from Scripture that I knew I must follow. It says, *If you are angry with another ... first be reconciled to that person or you will be the one to pay the penalty.*[10]

Still seething with displeasure and barely able to hold

10 Matthew 22:26

my pen, I wrote the following note, *Susan: I now have my answer to the travel question, but I want you to know that you are doing a terrific job, despite tremendous pressure. Thank you for seeing me.* Almost instantly, before I set down my pen, my displeasure dissipated. No longer did I hold feelings of resentment toward Susan. The door leading to my anger had been firmly shut, or so I thought. Almost immediately it again opened wide. After putting my note in the inter-office mail, I left for the day. But over the weekend, I continued to re-read another passage from Scripture. It read: ... *first be reconciled to your brother...*[11].

On Monday morning, after arrival at my office, I once again prayed the aforementioned passages. Then work began and I thought no more about Susan. During the afternoon, I stepped into the hallway adjoining my office and headed to the water fountain. But a few paces outside my office door there was Susan. She was conversing with three other women. I waved a hello and continued my walk to the fountain. Then Susan called out to me, "Roger, please forgive me for how I acted toward you last Friday. I was terribly wrong."

I walked up to Susan to reassure her and said, "When we have a moment, I want to tell you a story." The story I intended to tell her is the one I have just related. It was the story of how I was able to open a door that had seemed to be shut.

Susan and I had done what was necessary to emphasize the importance of never shutting a door that should remain open. As I recall this episode, there may have been another force that facilitated our reconciliation. It reads as follows:

---

11 Matthew 5:24

"*I know your deeds. Behold I have put before you an open door which no one can shut, because… you have kept My word and have not denied My name.*"[12]

---

12 Revelation 3:8-9

The Missing Photograph

In 1921 an advertising executive authored the now familiar adage that, "A picture is worth a thousand words."[13] A picture provides you a sense of your subject (e.g., the Russian atrocities in Ukraine that we see nightly on the TV as I write this). But the same is not necessarily true of family photographs, several of which hang on various walls or rest on tables in our home. A stranger entering our home can learn very little about the individuals depicted in the photos. The following essay is about a framed photograph that hung in my grandmother's living room in San Antonio, Texas, a place I used to visit frequently during my law school days. It depicted her father, The Rev. William Hamilton Dowling.

I remember frequently gazing at his photograph, wondering what kind of a person he actually was. His daughter made him sound so heroic, and I often asked her about him. She obviously loved and admired him greatly. His colored photograph is of a distinguished-looking man in his early sixties, still with dark hair, a strong looking face, with the faint hint of a smile. He also sported a neatly trimmed Van Dyke beard and mustache. He is wearing a black frock coat over a slim vest. An elegantly tied bow tie can be seen around the collar of his white shirt. But none of this tells us what sort of man he was.

---

13 Frederick R. Barnard, in *Printer's* Ink (December 8, 1921)

Hamilton was born in August 1842 at his home in what is today Hampton County, South Carolina. As the eldest of nine children of a Baptist minister, he was raised on a large family farm along with some slaves. From an early age, he learned to love and respect the Bible, give assistance to the poor, and to help work the family's farm. By the time he reached his late teens, he had also become a skilled horseman. Yet he felt no calling to the military, despite the fact that several of his ancestors had fought in either the Revolutionary War or the War of 1812. Instead, he planned to attend seminary. However, in 1861 those plans were put on hold after the outbreak of the Civil War. Therefore, at the age of nineteen, he volunteered to serve the Confederacy as a member of the cavalry.

Over the next four years he was involved in 25 military engagements and had several horses shot from under him; yet Hamilton was never wounded. However, his outer military breaker or coat revealed a several bullet holes. Years later when he posed in his Confederate uniform for a 50th wedding anniversary photograph with his wife and ten children, she volunteered to repair his coat. He refused her by saying, "Daughter, I want my descendants to know that I fought hard for the South."

By the time the war was ending, Hamilton had risen to the rank of Captain and was fighting in southern Virginia. In late October of 1864, he was engaged in a Battle called Burgess Mill near Petersburg. There, another horse was shot from under him. He had to engage in hand-to-hand combat with Union soldiers. Ammunition was running out, so soldiers attacked each other with knives and sabers. Hamilton's courage and his compassion were both on display as his following account of the battle demonstrates. He said:

"I had just knocked a Union soldier to the ground and was about the run him through with my saber when he suddenly looked me in the eye and made the sign of the cross. This suggested he was willing to surrender. Instinctively, I held back and started to take him prisoner when suddenly he came at me with his knife. Fortunately he merely tore my coat and I was able to subdue him and finally make him my prisoner."

At the conclusion of the war in April 1865, Hamilton returned home and was faced with restoring his family's home, while also studying to become a Baptist minister by 1867. A month after graduating from seminary, he married my great grandmother, Clara. Following the ceremony, he preached his first of many hundreds of sermons. He told Clara of his belief that God had spared him from serious injury in the war so that he could serve the greater cause of sharing God's Word. Each of his five sons would later claim, "For Father, Christ was the greatest friend of all because Christ loved every person." Evidence of Hamilton's dedication becomes apparent in the following story told to me by his daughter Maude, my grandmother:

"During Reconstruction I once accompanied Father when he ministered to some nearby neighbors who were extremely poor. All seven of their children were ill with measles, but their parents had no money for a doctor or even medicine and scarcely any food. That very day my father had just received his full year's salary as a minister. It was only $5.00, as there was little money to pay ministers during

Reconstruction days. Despite the needs of his own family, he immediately turned over his salary to his neighbors in need.

"The very same day, as Father and I were returning home on horseback, we met a young couple who were planning to elope, but needed a minister to marry them. Father agreed, and he asked a neighboring farmer and his wife to be witnesses, essentially marrying them in the middle of the road. Afterwards, the excited bridegroom paid my father ten dollars, double his annual salary. At dinner that evening when asked why he had given away his annual salary, Father would only say: 'I believed it was my duty to give all I had to those poor people and their sick children. And I had faith that God would provide in some way for our family's needs'."

The remainder of Hamilton's life would be a testimony to his devotion to helping others. He recognized the most important task before him was not vengeance, but to repair the damage his community had suffered from the war. He made this a component part of his spiritual journey. During his sixty years of service, he was twice elected a local probate judge, served as Superintendent of Education for Hampton County for over 25 years, and was a founding member of the Savannah River Association of Churches. His great concern for the underprivileged and his recognition of the importance of education inspired him to arrange a dozen or more small school rooms to be set up throughout the county and he arranged for volunteer teachers to staff them.

In September 1924, the local paper said Reverend Dowling was laid to rest at 82 years old after a service attended by seven to eight hundred mourners. His son Joel said the following words at the service, "Father believed that whatever duty he faced, he could perform it if he claimed the help of the Lord."

My own father has told me that the Reverend Dowling had freed his slaves and actually given parcels of land to some of them. He was also one of the first persons in South Carolina to help establish schools for Negroes, which several of his former slaves were able to attend. This being the case, I consider my ancestor to have been a good, courageous, and compassionate man, as befits a devoted Christian leader. Metaphorically speaking, he was a man who at times actually stood above others, but never considered himself better than them. So why is his photograph missing from a place on one of the walls in our home?

The best answer I can give is his participation on the wrong side during the Civil War. This is not something that I would like to be reminded of each day as I head to breakfast. I truly believe that he was a God-fearing servant of our Lord, and I am proud of his wonderful contributions. I simply don't want to be reminded, or to remind others, that he fought for an unrighteous cause, a defense of slavery.

Chapter III

Life Changes – the Weight of Experience

Julius Caesar, the famous Roman warrior and political leader of ancient Rome once claimed, "Experience is the best teacher."[1] The question I often ask myself is why did I so often remain ignorant of the purpose of experience? It was only after many failures or mistakes that I began to realize that many of my painful experiences in life were not caused by my ignorance, but instead, by my stubborn indifference to learn from them.

Change is part of life, how we react to it greatly determines the course our life will take. In the essays of this chapter the reader will be able to discern a person whose life was often troubled. I am that person. Despite having the benefits of a good education, a loving family, and many opportunities to succeed, I could never truly rid myself of a sense of insecurity. This is not unusual— many successful individuals experience such concerns, regardless of their successes. In my circumstance, I needed to strive for something more lasting than mere worldly success; I needed to find a true sense of meaning and purpose to my life.

Ultimately, I was able to accomplish this, but it took a change in my way of thinking. I learned to cease simply seeking what I could get out of life and sought to determine what I could give to it. My essays in this chapter and

1   Julius Caesar, *De Bello Civili* (c. 52 B.C.)

elsewhere reveal that my early indoctrination in religion at best only served to make me a nominal Christian. Until I was able to internalize the significance of religion, and until I was able to become a man of faith, religious matters had little meaning for me. The effect of my change from a nominal or indifferent attitude to one of deep faith is best described by the philosopher William James, "The sense of God's presence makes one sensibly conscious that, no matter what difficulties, for the moment, may appear to be, one's life as a whole is in the keeping of a power that one can absolutely trust."[2]

The following essays depict my response to changes I have made. The story about COVID-19 is included to illustrate how rapidly our lives can be affected by changes in circumstances, especially during wartime and the spread of disease. The topic of gardening is included not only to reflect the changes that are required during a time of war, but also to encourage others to enjoy themselves by learning how to begin something that is both personally useful and appealing to others. Some people are unfortunately reluctant to respond effectively to change. They find reasons to resist it. But I have accepted that change provides an opportunity to learn and to grow.

---

2   William James, *The Varieties of Religious Experience* (New York: Longmans, Green, & Co., 1902)

A College Education

The hour had finally come; it was time for me to board the train for my overnight trip to begin college. As my dad held my hand to say one last goodbye, I could see tears in his eyes. "Goodbye guy" he said, as I boarded the train. For the first time in my life, I was essentially on my own and would have to make decisions accordingly, especially if I was to gain a college education. What was I expecting?

Most young men, as they head for their freshmen year in college, consider they are taking advantage of an opportunity which will enable them to better prepare for their future life. And there is ample merit in such a belief. In America, an advanced education is considered essential; it is often heralded as the first hesitating step one takes on the ladder to a satisfying career. Because of their youth, however, many young men have yet to appreciate that gaining a college education involves a great deal more than merely selecting a course of study, attending class lectures, successfully passing a number of exams, all ultimately leading to graduation and a diploma. Overnight, they are exposed to many of the vicissitudes of college life, for which they have no real frame of reference. They are on their own.

The most perceptive of these young men will eventually begin to adjust and mature. Their decision-making will become less of a challenge. Others who are less flexible or less perceptive may fail to envision the broad scope of this new and exciting learning experience until much later. And only then will they be able to discern how they actually profited from it. The following essay describes my experience upon entering Duke University in September 1950, which was considered one of America's best universities. There were times when I could not fully absorb and or clearly internalize what I was learning, but that paradox was destined to be part of my college education.

From the first day I arrived on campus, I was brought into contact with a group of other young men and women of similar ages, usually with different cultural values and backgrounds than mine. The sooner I began to recognize these differences and adjust to them in a responsible manner, the sooner I would begin to form relationships. (And a limited few of them actually still exist, some 72 years later.)

While this learning process is repeated on almost every college campus in America, it is not listed as one of the courses in your typical college catalogue. This may strike the reader as somewhat strange, because the ability to meet new people in college is merely illustrating what will occur throughout a student's future life. In college, if you are successful in forming relationships with others of different backgrounds, you are practicing a virtue which must rise to a higher level in the future.

For example, in my freshman year at Duke, I was housed with two roommates, one an athlete from New Jersey named Blair, and a second named Stanley, the son of a Methodist minister from Henderson, North Carolina. My being from New York meant Blair and I probably had a similar frame of reference concerning the Civil War. However, that was not the case with Stanley. While I didn't recognize this at the time, Stanley harbored resentment over the South's loss of the Civil War. It caused him to express his disapproval of Yankees if they did or said things he wasn't familiar with. For example, one day when he saw me cutting a hangnail with a nail clipper, he said, "I cut mine with scissors; I've never seen those." He seemed to be looking for an opportunity to prove himself to me.

Had I been more sensitive to Stanley's feelings of resentment, he and I might have become good friends. Unfortunately, that never happened; my cultural education had not progressed sufficiently. Coming from the North, for me, the Civil War was over, and the right side won. But for the South, the loss of the war was still a burden that many of its young sons seemed to harbor. Almost every week around bedtime, one particular freshman would poke his head out of his neighboring dormitory window and holler, "All Yankees eat…" At first, I was amused by such verbal assaults, believing them to be in good-natured jest, but in time I grew to feel sorry for the classmate who felt the need to utter them.

I came to college to gain knowledge, not to re-fight America's historical cultural battles. And when I think of battles, I am reminded of the 16th century European history class I took. The professor who taught our class made it extremely interesting. I soon realized that not all professors were able to do this. But there were times in class when I felt he was mixing in details about religion and the invention of the printing press that seemed peripheral to military battles. What did religion have to do with war? As I look back on that class, I now realize how ignorant I was about the historical period in question, and especially the importance of a German monk named Martin Luther.

This courageous monk helped the Reformation to succeed and thus freed Western Europe from the yoke of Roman Catholic hegemony. And his challenge to the Holy Roman Empire helped to firmly establish Protestantism in many European countries, including Germany, where previously only Roman Catholicism was permitted. Our professor further explained how the invention of the printing press enabled Luther to get the Bible printed in the vernacular. This enabled many in Germany and other European countries to read the Bible for the first time. Gradually, I began to realize how conflated politics and religion were in 16th century Europe, and still can be today, even in America. (Supreme Court decisions are a case in point.) Slowly, I was learning how broadening a college education could actually be.

While I continued to be pleased at how much I was learning about European history, there were other things that I was also learning, especially about people and their sincerity. My gradual discernment in this regard was not strictly textbook-related. For example, on one occasion a classmate and I were chatting in the college souvenir shop. I had mentioned that I would like to learn how to do a particular dance step so I could better enjoy dating. Unbeknownst to us, our conversation was being overheard by a large fellow student standing nearby. He was a starting tackle on the Duke football team; after graduation he would go on to star for the Chicago Bears in the NFL. His name was Ed Meadows and he offered to teach me the dance step, but I would have to pay him for the service. Fortunately, I had already learned how to recognize a slick salesman when I met one. So, I declined Ed's interesting offer.

One of the temptations college students may confront is the temptation to cheat on an exam or to get someone else to do their term papers for them. In either circumstance, I can honestly say I never gave in to those temptations, even when opportunities to do so were present. In Spanish class, where I was an A student, I was startled during one exam when I realized the student sitting next to me was copying from my paper. His name was Paul, and we were friends, so I said nothing. Although I was quite surprised at his conduct, I did not allow it to affect our relationship.

By the time of our graduation, four years later, Paul had actually become one of the most honored, respected students in our graduating class, earning several student awards. At first this seemed a little incongruous to me in light of our Spanish class experience. But as I recall this episode today, I realize I was being given an opportunity to learn something invaluable. Actually, it was a lesson that took me years to fully appreciate. No, it was not about Paul's failure to refrain from dishonesty, although that would characterize his surprising conduct. Rather, it was something I would have to learn about my own conduct. In life everybody makes mistakes, but it is the ability to repair them that matters. Paul had certainly made the essential repairs. And in future years, I would have to repair several of my own.

One decision that I made turned out to be a wise one — I

joined a fraternity. Until presented with the opportunity, I had never given it much thought. But eventually I decided to join because many in our freshman class were doing so. It proved to be a wise choice because, for the first time in my life, I was able to bond with a group of young men. The experience taught me to appreciate true fellowship, and to gauge how I was measuring up to older men, including men from different backgrounds. Again, I should confess that at the time, I was not consciously aware of what prompted me to make my decision to join. But as I look back on it today, it was a part of my college education that I will always treasure.

After four years, I graduated. What had I learned? Here are a few things I consider it wise for a student to practice, not because I always did them, but because when I did, I learned the benefit of doing so. They were part of my college education. Obviously, a student should try to capitalize on every opportunity his classroom offers and avoid the typical distractions that prevent one from doing their homework thoroughly. By homework, I include reading books occasionally recommended by one's professor. I have since learned that such books will greatly expand a student's perceptions in college and certainly later in life. Should the student fail to develop such habits, he or she is likely to have to make up for that failure later in life. I speak from experience.

Don't overdo your free time; you will always have sufficient time for parties, sports, or mere pleasure; just don't overdo them. And always take advantage of chances to learn from others, especially where good habits and good human relations are concerned. People will always be a major part of your life.

Yet, there remained an important goal I still had failed to achieve. Simply put it was: *How can I become a better person; someone I would be pleased to know?*

This left a gap which no college education, regardless of its curriculum, is fully equipped to address. The personal nature of each student is simply too unique.

Mere self-interest further restricted my research. For at the time, unfortunately, I was incapable of internalizing why the personal virtue I sought was dependent upon humility, a word that had little meaning for me then. But as the great theologian, St. Augustine once remarked, "The path to virtue begins with humility and rises to higher levels."[3] So, it was only after I perceived the wisdom of forging such a path, that I began to realize how this gap in my college education could be reduced.

---

3   *The City of God,* by St. Augustine, p. 71.

Learning to Yield

In our writing we often use a word that can have different connotations, depending on the context. Take, for example, the verb *to yield*. With good soil and good weather, a farmer can expect the soil to yield a good crop. Or, take the driver who obeys the yield sign when making a turn, giving way to avoid an accident. A timid person will often yield to his or her fears. And a person may yield or surrender to a temptation.

When the latter occurs, a person essentially yields control or authority over their thoughts or actions at a particular point in time. When one yields to improper emotions, self-interest, or reckless actions, they can expect to be burdened or to suffer. Conversely, if one chooses to yield to a firm belief in a loving God, their life can be brightened.

The negative effect of yielding to reckless self-interest was dramatically brought home to me when I was a teenager of nearly fourteen. It happened in January 1946, when I was returning home from school. Driven by my desire to get home quickly, after exiting the bus, I yielded to my desire to cross the busy thoroughfare rapidly. My quick glance at the road suggested it was clear of oncoming traffic, so I ran in front of the parked bus. At once I was struck by a speeding truck that tossed me to the curb. The bus had blocked the truck from my view. Had I not yielded to my careless impulse but waited for the bus to move away, I would have been saved from the pain of two weeks in the hospital with a compound fracture of my left leg.

Unfortunately, I had yet to truly learn how and when to yield, as the following episode will illustrate. It occurred around seven in the morning on a rainy spring day in 1961. I was driving home from North Carolina to New York. The highway was deserted, save for a single large truck far ahead of me. My speeding soon enabled me to overtake the truck in my reckless, foolish attempt to pass it. But as I began to do so, the truck driver suddenly turned his wheels toward my car, threatening to run into me.

I had to make a split-second decision — either to hit my brakes and risk skidding and turning over, or to turn off onto the muddy embankment, hoping it would slow me sufficiently to avoid hitting an oncoming telephone pole. My decision to turn off may have saved my life, but it didn't slow me down. The mud acted like a banana peel to my car, so within moments I crashed at high speed into the telephone pole, breaking it in two before coming to a stop. Surprisingly, there was no broken glass, and I was unhurt. Did I thank God? No. Instead, I immediately yielded to my anger and cried out, "God why did you let this happen to me?" Was He to blame? Today, I would have bowed my head and thanked Him that I was still alive, despite my impetuous conduct of trying to pass the truck.

After graduating from law school and passing the bar, in the fall of 1960 I began working full time in Manhattan, New York City for General Motors Overseas Operations. Much like the prodigal son we read about in Scripture, I was also enjoying my off-hour pleasures, partying, and relishing the company of other young people. I actually told myself that I would serve the Lord later, when I wouldn't have to concern myself with making a living or when I had more spare time. But He seems to have had other plans for me.

My parents lived about an hour's train ride from New York City. One winter night, in February, 1962, after joining them for dinner and pleasant conversation, I retired to my boyhood room and quickly fell fast asleep. Some fifteen minutes later I was startled awake by a voice calling my name. Initially, I wondered if it was my father needing my help, but he did not appear. Still, the voice persisted, so I cautiously turned over in bed and looked toward the doorway to my room about ten feet away. I was stunned by the sight of a tall figure standing in the doorway, hooded in black. Although its facial area glistened brightly, it was devoid of all features. Suddenly, one arm of the figure pointed at me as a voice said, *Roger unless you change your way of living there, will be no hope for you. You have only one choice.* Shivering with fright, I wanted to ask the figure if it was the Virgin Mary, but before I could utter a sound it slowly dissipated before me.

The next morning, heading back to Manhattan on the train with my father, I related my experience to him. He good-naturedly said it was only a dream, nothing to concern myself with. Thus reassured, and for some thirty years thereafter I forgot all about it. I had yet to learn how to yield to reality. Self-sufficiency remained my true god.

By 1964, I was working in Washington, DC, and envisioning an exciting career. Increasingly, however, I suffered from a sense of emptiness and lack of purpose. It was as if I were on a roller coaster, as I continued to experience success and failure at work. I had yet to realize what was causing my life to seem without meaning. The truth was there was no room for God in it, only my idols of career and accomplishment. I meandered on without Him.

There eventually would come a time when I would rethink that evening at my parent's home in 1962. And I pondered whether it was merely a dream, or rather a Heavenly messenger trying to awaken me from a sinful life? Still, I continued to push aside any real thoughts about that experience and continued to focus on my career and family.

But in February 1991, another experience finally awakened me. It happened early one morning before dawn. I had been unable to sleep and felt that I had been throwing my life away in selfish endeavors. I was almost sixty and realized that I could die at any time. Increasingly at that difficult emotional moment, I began to feel helpless. Humbly I threw myself on the mercy of our Father in Heaven. How I was able to express this, and the specific happenings at that electric moment I describe in Chapter VII, in my essay on Satisfying a Need at Christmas. I finally understood why yielding, in my case, meant yielding to our Father in Heaven.

Suffice it to say, from that moment forward, my life began to change. I no longer yielded to my pride of self-sufficiency, but humbly turned to Christ. I began reading the Bible and increasingly sought for ways in our local church to serve Him.

It was during this period of spiritual transformation that I chanced to hear Charles Colson speak at the Columbia Baptist Church, in Falls Church. He was a former White House aide and convicted felon, who by then had formed Prison Fellowship. He spoke inspirationally of his travels to India to encourage the thousands of inmates there. Never before had I been the least bit interested in working with inmates, much less sharing the gospel with them. But after listening to Colson, something in me changed. I actually wished that I had been with him on his trip. I now felt the need, the desire to find a way to also serve prisoners. What I didn't realize it at the time, and only later came to believe, I was answering a Divine call.

What is still amazing to me is that only two years later, I actually accompanied Colson and some businessmen on a similar visit to Southeast Asia, where we toured several jails and prisons. And, upon my retirement from government, I became a prison chaplain at the jail where I had previously been a weekly volunteer. Thanks to my call, I had at last learned how to yield. Life now offered me a sense of meaning and purpose. I began to see the light of life of which Jesus spoke when He said, "I am the light of the world. He who follows me shall not walk in darkness, but shall have the light of life."[4]

---

4   John 8:12

Changes in my Life

Many will recall the old maxim that only two things in life are certain: death and taxes. This wisdom is incomplete, however, unless the reality of change is added. In truth, change is an integral part of every life, whether it is self-induced or precipitated by events beyond one's ability to control.

The Greek philosopher Heraclitus understood this, when some 500 years before Christ he said, "You can't step into the same river twice." He reasoned that a river is constantly changing as it flows, whether or not the change is perceptible to the naked eye. The same can be said for changes in our lives. Whether we recognize them at first or not, they are ongoing. Examples can be anything from aging to new taxes. In the following essay I describe a few instances of how such changes have impacted my life.

I begin with a story that occurred when I was barely three years old. My mother took me to visit with her parents in Ohio. I quickly became attached to my grandmother and began to follow her as she went about household chores. One day after breakfast, I accompanied her to a washroom where I was startled to see her remove the teeth from her mouth, brush them in the sink and replace them. My attitude towards my teeth was forever changed. Thereafter, I became concerned that I might lose mine. Later, I followed her to the laundry and watched as she filled an old-fashioned wash tub with water and proceeded to submerge some small cages in it. They cages were not special except for the fact they each contained a live rat, which she proceeded to drown. For the first time I realized that rats are bad. I remember nothing else from that visit, but somehow these two events had changed me. Each new experience has the potential for doing that.

When I was almost eight years old, my family joined a golf and swim club. Like most boys, I found playing around water was always great fun. At the beach I had gone wading in shallow water near the shore but had yet to learn how to swim. Now, watching the people swim at the club pool made it seem easy to do; you merely had to jump in and move your arms and legs. So, when I saw a friend of mine swimming, I decided to jump in and join him. Moments later a lifeguard had to rescue me by lifting me out of the water in response to my cries for help. For the rest of the summer, I took lessons, determined to become a good swimmer. In time I became quite proficient and swam in races at nearby clubs. Had I practiced more, I was told by my coach that I could earn a college scholarship to help pay for my education.

Speaking of education, in high school, I enjoyed learning about America's history. I was a proud young patriot, pleased to learn that we had bested the British in our Revolutionary War. In fact, I was quite angry with the British for trying to keep us from becoming independent. When I later learned of the Spanish Armada and Spain's attempt to invade the British Isles, I was disappointed that its Armada had been destroyed by a storm. Naively I thought that if the British had been defeated it would have served them right. But further along in my high school history classes, I began to realize how fortunate it was for America that the Armada failed. Spain was ruled by an oppressive monarchy, whereas Britain's monarchy believed in many of the individual rights and freedoms that we Americans enjoy today. As colonists, we had inherited them. If Spain's Armada been successful, that might not have happened. My appreciation of world history had changed for the better and my appreciation of the British grew accordingly.

Studying history in college further broadened my understanding of world history. But that was not the case where religion and faith were concerned. My feelings about them were, at best, ambivalent. My parents had never discussed how to internalize their purpose. My father simply required that I attend Sunday school and later church, so as to learn about the Christian message and become a good person. While these experiences did plant the seeds of my belief in Jesus' resurrection, I still couldn't understand why that was significant for me.

In college, in order to graduate, we were required to take a semester course in religion. I postponed fulfilling this requirement until my senior year. I did attend chapel all four years, but that was because I enjoyed singing in the chapel choir. I also hoped to learn how to become a better person by listening to the sermons, but they didn't seem to help. This was primarily because their life application had little meaning for me. At that point in my life, I had very seldom read the Bible. I had no idea of how or why prayer was important. My life's sole purpose was to be successful. Service for God and the Golden Rule were fine things, but I would have time to focus on them after retirement.

Once I entered the workplace, my concentration was on my future. Service to God could wait. I was, young, single, working for a large corporation, driving a sports car, and living the life of a carefree bachelor in New York's Greenwich Village. As the saying goes, I considered the world my oyster. Looking back, I realize that I was living a singular life of self-sufficiency. Regardless of the occasional benefits, I now recognize that such a life leads one to a sense of emptiness, but I lacked the ability to appreciate such reality. There were times, however, when my conscience began to bother me. And as I related earlier, I had been warned of the damaging direction my life was headed during my 1961 visit to my parents' home.

My father's reassurance following that visit seemed to dispel its significance, so for the next thirty years I forgot all about my visitor. Unlike the penitent Isaiah of Scripture (who answered God's call to serve),[5] I resembled the Ancient Israelites of that epoch. *Listening I did not perceive; seeing I did not understand; my heart was rendered insensitive.*[6] Over the ensuing years, marriage, children, and work experiences caused changes in my life, but not in my attitude toward faith and religion. I had yet to alter my reliance on my own self-sufficiency. The need for God's presence in my life still eluded me.

This meant I remained unaware how the spiritual seeds sown early in my life had begun to take root. Ultimately, they, along with the emptiness I felt, caused me to literally cry out to God for help. Yes, my cry was answered, as I will shortly explain.[7] And now, thirty years later, I recognize my

5   Isaiah 6:8
6   Isaiah 6:9-10
7   Psalm 107:28

earlier mistake in failing to heed the warning in 1962 of my unique visitor.

Why I was given this second chance to repent I can only attribute to the healing nature of God's forgiveness. Its effect on me was so overwhelming, so awe-inspiring, that its infinite nature surpasses description. I was humbled thereby, overcome by the truth of a Divine presence, blessed by the majesty of God's grace. It forever changed this recreant sinner's life.

Washing Dishes —
Little Things Can Mean a Lot

After dinner my mother would often say, "Put on your apron and help your grandfather wash the dishes." This was probably one of the least interesting things I was ever told to do as a boy, only slightly less displeasing than making my bed or brushing my teeth. This kitchen responsibility was bestowed upon me around the age of eleven, or 1944, near the close of World War II. Coincidentally, it was also the same year that Spike Jones and his band came out with a song that had the following chorus:

> "Leave the dishes in the sink Ma.
> Leave the dishes in the sink.
> Each dirty plate will have to wait.
> Tonight we're going to celebrate.
> Leave the dishes in the sink."

The celebration the song alluded to was a response to the expected return from the war of some of our servicemen and women. Of course, I was delighted that the war was nearly over — it would be in August 1945, to be exact. But my main reason for celebrating Jones' hit song was that it supported my desire to leave the dishes in the sink for someone else to wash. Unfortunately, my mother didn't see it that way. Thus, my heart jumped a beat when I learned that my father had purchased an electric dishwasher. Once it was installed, I believed my dish washing days would be over. Sadly, I was mistaken. Once again, Mom didn't see it my way.

She said the dishwasher took too much water to clean the dishes and that raised our water bill. She also claimed it didn't do a good job of cleaning the dishes unless they were first scraped and lightly rinsed prior to placing them in the washer. So why waste all that time and money using a machine? Sadly, we mostly continued to wash dishes the old-fashioned way. My dreams of liberty and justice for all — freedom from this kitchen chore — were scrubbed away. Unless my grandfather or an aunt were visiting us, I was also expected to help dry the dishes after washing them. This seemed to be such a useless waste of time. Why not just place them in the dish rack and have Mother Nature dry them overnight by evaporation? But Mom didn't agree. My only reprieve from washing and drying occurred when my parents entertained, and the dishwasher was actually used. I made sure on those nights that I got to bed early so I wouldn't have to help clean and rinse.

In my early childhood years, washing dishes was not something that ever occurred to me. I was enjoying a child's carefree world. At that time, I am confident that if someone asked me, I'm sure I would have said, "Why does a dish have to wash itself, does it get dirty playing outside?" In fact, I may have thought dishes actually had fun and took care of themselves. I guess this came from reading too many nursery rhymes as a child. Here's one that I always thought was fun to imagine.

"Hey diddle, diddle the cat and the fiddle,
The cow jumped over the moon.
The little dog laughed to see such sport;
That the dish ran away with the spoon."

Whenever I opened my *Real Mother Goose* nursery rhyme book, I would always chuckle and enjoy looking at the plate, smiling and holding hands with the spoon as they ran. It fascinated me to see such a wide, happy smile on the face of the plate and the spoon's spindly legs. It did wonders for this child's imagination. But of course, I had no understanding of the bacteria that can stay alive on a dish, up to four days apparently. And that the longer dishes sit in the sink the more time bacteria has to multiply. It can then attract fruit flies, mice, and cockroaches.

So, if you use a dishpan, don't soak the dishes, wash them quickly. And make certain to rinse them with very hot fresh water. Should you plan to continue using the same dish cloth for the next load of dishes, you should first microwave it for one minute before doing so. These steps help to avoid any concern about food poisoning or related digestive issues.

But I'm getting somewhat off track here in terms of how I came to terms with dish washing. I must confess that when I reached adulthood, I recognized the need to clean dishes after every meal. But I did so more out of a sense of responsibility than enjoyment. And I didn't want to resort to extreme measures like those a European friend of mine did. As a bachelor, he was out on a dinner date and was asked to help wash the dishes; he must have experienced cultural shock. So, he devised a scheme to avoid doing them. He simply made sure to drop one occasionally so it broke. In no time at all, his date refrained from asking his assistance. I was never so heartless, especially after I became a father.

Faithfully, I attended to my fatherly domestic duties, and responded to requests for kitchen help whenever asked, but I seldom volunteered for dish washing duties. One thing that helped was that the quality of dishwashers had greatly improved since 1944. They required less pre-rinsing. Nonetheless, I soon became disenchanted with automatic dishwashers.

My reason for this is that once they have finished a particular cycle and have cooled, it's usually too late in the day to be emptied and the dishes put away. That responsibility is usually left until the next morning. Unfortunately, that coincides with finishing breakfast, getting to work, or running an errand. At that time of day, who wants to take time to empty the dishwasher? And it is always frustrating when your favorite cup or plate is still in the dishwasher, and you have to go rescue it. You're reminded that you have yet to put the clean dishes away. Wasn't washing them enough? Why do dishes keep bugging me?

Despite the foregoing, I have actually come to look forward to washing dishes the old-fashioned way after every meal. Sometimes Ruth even jokingly accuses me of depriving her of an opportunity to do them. There is a reason for my change of attitude. As time has gone by, my thoughts have fortunately turned to the dangers of living a sinful, self-centered life. I have learned to appreciate the application of the Golden Rule in Scripture. *Do unto others as you would have them do unto you*.[8] It makes no difference, in God's eyes, how minor the task may be.

---

8   Matthew 7:12

Putting this another way, I have come to realize that by being obedient to it, we are being obedient toward our Lord Himself. For as He explained to His disciples, "The Son of Man did not come to be served, but to serve."[9] Often, in my counseling with prison inmates, I explain how my dish washing has helped my obedience. To date, no inmate has laughed or mocked me, and I actually believe they are helped by this illustration of the importance of obedience to our Lord.

In closing, I am reminded of Jesus' response to the lawyer who asked him how to inherit eternal life. Jesus responded by asking him what the Scripture required. The lawyer's answer was to recite the two Great Commandments. Then Jesus' answer to him was simply, "Do this and you will live."[10]

Yes, little things can mean a lot.

---

9   Matthew 20:28
10 Luke 10:25-28

A Fresh Start

Conventional wisdom suggests that by making a fresh start we have recognized the need for improvement. Possibly an earlier effort or experience was not completely satisfying. And to improve upon it will require our renewed effort, a new response to our circumstances. I speak from experience. For example, in my early boyhood years my mother tried to teach me how to tie my shoelaces. After closely observing her demonstration, I succeeded in tying my right shoe, but failed at tying my left. In boyish frustration I untied my right shoe and had to make a fresh start on both. It took time, but I am happy to report that eventually I did succeed and am highly accomplished at this task today. I have made a fresh start.

New starts are certainly not limited to success in dealing with one's footwear. But the motivation behind any fresh start is often the same — the prospect of future success. Such motivation can be constructive and is applicable to almost any circumstance in life. For example, it can be the start of a New Year, a change in a person's spiritual beliefs, or even a nation's actions in world affairs. Concerning the latter, I am reminded of Winston Churchill's comment during World War II, following the British Army's success at El Alamein in North Africa. It was a success that followed on the heels of earlier British Army failures. After the victory, Churchill said, "Now this is not the end … but it is, perhaps, the end of the beginning."[11] He was looking forward to a fresh start in the war against the Axis.

When I think of fresh starts, I often recall my annual New Year's Day greeting to my father. Customarily, I would begin by saying, "Happy New Year Dad! Tell me about your New Year's resolutions." He would pause for a moment and then usually reply, "I'm going to be more positive. It makes life so much more interesting." We would then laugh together and begin talking about family matters. Yet, the more I think back on those fun conversations, the more I realize he had a valid point. We need to remain positive even when facing difficult circumstances, especially if we plan to make a fresh start.

It is likely each of us has faced such circumstances at some point in our lives, and consequently wish to avoid them in future. A fresh start is often the best way. When I received a note from a friend during this past Christmas week, my belief in this approach was reaffirmed. Apparently, a good friend of his had just been convicted of a felony and sent to Federal prison. Owing to my years of experience as a prison chaplain, my friend asked for some advice on how to best visit with his friend, so as to help him. Our busy Christmas activities prevented our making contact by phone, so I sent him the following note:

> "Many thanks for your note concerning your friend's circumstances. Here are a few thoughts that, in my experience, have proven helpful in reaching

11 Winston Churchill, *Speech at the Lord Mayor's Day Luncheon*, November 10, 1942

out to inmates. When you visit with your friend, you might wish to consider the following virtues — forgiveness, encouragement, and hope. Allow me to further clarify their possible use by starting off with an example of how I sometimes used them in tandem when counseling an inmate who was facing difficult circumstances.

"The case in question occurred one morning during my first few weeks as a Chaplain at the Fairfax Jail. I suddenly received an urgent call to counsel with a mother who was awaiting trial for intentionally setting fire to her daughter's room, killing the daughter in the process. The mother herself nearly died in the fire that she had intentionally started. The case was mentioned in the local papers a few years ago. When we first met that morning, her appearance startled me. Burnt, dead skin, caused by the fire, was still peeling from her face and her badly burnt hands were still bandaged. She appeared truly shaken. Since she spoke no English, we conversed in Spanish.

"After I began with a prayer for her, something I would recommend when meeting with any inmate, I reminded her of the biblical story from 2 Samuel 12:1-24. It addresses David's great sins of murder and adultery. God was greatly displeased with David. So, despite David's beseeching God to spare the life of his sick, infant son, the boy died. In effect, God held David accountable for Uriah's death and David's adultery with Bathsheba. Later, because of David's repentance, God forgave him. Eventually,

God blessed David with another son, Solomon; he was to become an important biblical figure. If you recall, it was God who commissioned Solomon to build the Jewish temple, even though David had hoped to do it.

"My purpose in using this example was to emphasize to the mother that while God does hold us accountable for our misdeeds, provided we repent, He is a forgiving God. And through our humble belief in His grace, we can attain forgiveness. The mother in this case was given extensive spiritual counseling and it appeared to help. Two months or so later, she gave a tearful, moving witness before a women's prayer group in the jail. It reflected her sense of hope. She confessed her misdeed and thanked Christ for dying for her. Her repentance, I believe, expressed her sincere belief that God had forgiven her.

"This story may help to instill new hope in your friend's heart, especially in the authority of God's forgiveness. It is important to encourage such hope; it is something most inmates yearn for. I'm confident you can appreciate this. This is where your friend comes in. As in the case of the aforementioned mother, he is likely both confused and full of remorse over his action(s). It is fortunate that you already have a relationship with him and are bringing the authority of the Holy Spirit with you. This gives you a vital entre to address your friend's feelings of unworthiness. Because he can trust you, he will be more inclined to listen to you. This is so helpful in such circumstances, especially if your friend is a believer. Provided he is, it will help him to make a fresh start on his future.

"When counseling inmates I sometimes try to illustrate a point by describing an example from my own past failures. I find this helps to personalize the important elements of forgiveness, encouragement, and hope. In other words, after expressing how I failed the Lord in some instance, I express how my faith in Christ and true repentance brought me the hope and forgiveness I had sought. This expression of vulnerability helps the inmate to have greater confidence in the authority of Scripture. It is a further way of explaining St. Paul's belief that God's power is perfected in our weakness.[12]

"I hope that these comments are helpful when you visit your friend. I would be pleased to learn how he is faring. In expressing these suggestions, I feel somewhat like I am preaching to the choir, considering your wide experience in the spiritual world. Your strong faith should be of immeasurable help to your friend. Provided he is willing to express comparable belief, he can become another example of how, through prayer and faithfulness, God can heal us despite our failures. This is what Oswald Chambers probably meant when he said: "God does not give us overcoming life. He gives us life as we overcome."[13] Once a similar attitude abides in the heart of your friend, I am confident he will truly be

12 2 Corinthians 12:9
13 Oswald Chambers, *My Utmost for His Highest* (New York: Dodd, Mead & Company, Inc., 1935), August 2nd entry

prepared to begin a fresh start. I wish you and your family a very Merry Christmas."

Vaccinationʓ anƌ COVID-19

Ever since the COVID-19 virus became a concern for Americans, circa February 2020, three issues have become conflated which have disrupted the way most of us normally conduct our daily lives. Such conflation has disrupted relationships, spread disinformation, and distorted our customary hygiene practices. Of course, individually, each of these can be disruptive of a person's daily activities but combined they have caused extensive consternation throughout our nation. In the following essay I will attempt to elaborate on these charges, after first providing some recent statistical insight into this deadly pandemic.

COVID-19 first surfaced in Wuhan, China in late 2019. But there is still a lot we do not yet know about the COVID, because of our lack of information, especially from China. At first, it was considered to be a previously unknown strain of pneumonia, an entirely new version of a Corona virus. By March 2020, the World Health Organization had declared it to be a pandemic, in that it affected the entire global population. As of November 2022, some 636 million cases have arisen worldwide, and 6.6 million have died as a result.[14] Since it first struck America, there have

---

14 "WHO Corona virus (COVID-19) Dashboard," (accessed November 27, 2022),https://covid19.who.int

been 98.5 million cases resulting in 1.08 million deaths.[15] Much of the American economy had to temporarily curtail normal business operations and many small businesses had to shut down completely. It is estimated that 80 percent of our population has had the COVID-19 virus (many asymptomatic)[16] and most are expected to eventually become infected. How has the virus directly affected a large majority of our personal and professional relationships?

One response is that to avoid spreading COVID-19, many relationships have been greatly curtailed or suspended entirely. Extended families that customarily get together for special occasions or holidays have had to cease doing so. Instead, many have relied on communicating via ZOOM, email, letter, or phone. Travel, entertainment, and the movement of goods and services have at times been severely restricted or eliminated entirely. The result has been a shortage of goods and services and a disruption in all types of relationships being conducted normally. Masks have been recommended and something as natural as shaking hands is considered unhealthy unless you immediately wash your hands.

Over the last several months of 2022, restrictions on relationships gradually eased, as vaccines and related health protection measures began to limit the spread of COVID-19. Since then, however, new variants of the virus have begun to surface. Depending on the case load in a given area and our own health status, we are advised to wear masks, regularly wash our hands, and avoid large public gatherings. These

15 "CDC COVID Data Tracker," (Accessed November 27, 2022),https://covid. cdc.gov/covid-data-tracker/#datatracker-home
16 Yasmin Tayag, "America is Running Out of 'COVID Virgins,'" *The Atlantic*, July 22, 2022, https://www.theatlantic.com/health/archive/2022/07/never-had-covid-infection-avoidance/670620/

precautions imply that human relationships come with a risk. For example, the elbow press is recommended in lieu of shaking hands. When someone sitting behind you in church or on the subway sneezes or coughs, you wonder if they're infected or unvaccinated. The circumstances can be somewhat unsettling, especially when one realizes how essential good, friendly human association is to the human psyche.

One result of the pandemic was an increase of disinformation; we can certainly appreciate that in more normal times it would be far less. Such disinformation has acted as an irritant to human relationships and proper hygiene practices. COVID-19 has changed the dynamic of receiving medical advice. Take President Trump's wild suggestion that common laundry bleach had the ingredients needed to cure the virus. Then there is the ever-present question of whether the vaccines have been proven safe. Therefore, only 80 percent of our populace has taken some form of the vaccine; 68 percent have received the initial recommended doses and only 34 percent are boosted.[17] The rest remain unvaccinated for reasons including religion, ongoing health issues, and the makeup of the vaccines themselves. Disinformation may be largely responsible, as supposedly reliable authorities in the field of vaccination often claim it is risky.

My oldest daughter is an expert nurse, but she and her immediate family have declined to be vaccinated. Wisely, she has studied the issue carefully on the internet and elsewhere. And her sources tell her it is not safe, not fully tested, and that it may have negative after effects, including

17 "See How Vaccinations Are Going in Your County and State," *New York Times*, Updated October 20, 2022, https://www.nytimes.com/interactive/2020/us/covid-19-vaccine-doses.html

death . However, when I asked my doctor, an internist, about these concerns he explained that many of these so-called experts are simply not addressing the facts. He, by the way, is fully vaccinated, wears a special mask, and doesn't shake hands any longer.

Furthermore, there is some discussion on the internet that the vaccines may contain the remains of fetal cell material; or that there has been insufficient testing to prove the vaccine's reliability; or that the pharmaceutical firms have a vested financial interest in urging their use. There is even the claim that the Centers for Disease Control and the FDA experts have been too hasty in fully testing the vaccines. And remember that Dr. Fauci of the NIH, when first discussing a new vaccine, claimed that it customarily requires at least a year and a half to two years to come up with a reliable vaccine.

Of course, some of these naysayers simply do not believe in the use of vaccines. And I admit that I would prefer not to take them, even though I have done so. I have relied on the advice of my physician. Of course, many naysayers are unaware or unconcerned about the important and effective history of vaccines, especially for the likes of smallpox, tuberculosis, and polio.

In 1800, for example, many experts doubted that Edward Jenner had truly established the protective powers of cowpox, the non-lethal cousin of the smallpox virus; or that in 1874 Louis Pasteur used chicken cholera inoculation with pus from cowpox sores to save lives of chickens, leading to the resistance of the deadly smallpox in humans in the early 18th century. Do they forget that George Washington had his troops inoculated against smallpox, and that was toward the end of the 18th century?

As a young man of nineteen, George Washington survived smallpox while visiting Barbados. This made Washington immune to the disease. During our Revolution, his experience prompted him to inoculate new soldiers into the U.S. Army upon their recruitment. Despite receiving significant criticism for intentionally giving the troops a mild version of the disease, Washington persevered. Eventually his decision saved the bulk of his army, despite a 1% mortality rate, and was critical in enabling him to carry out America's fight for independence.

It was also news to me that there are records of smallpox insufflations — the snorting of powdered smallpox scabs — from China in the 1500s, and 18th century accounts from India suggest needle-based inoculation had already been in use in parts of the subcontinent for hundreds of years.

Disinformation certainly has become conflated with respect to hygiene, as I mentioned at the beginning of this essay. Initially, President Trump, as many will recall, certainly did his best to confuse the issue. Webster's definition of hygiene is, "conditions or practices conducive to maintaining health."

In early 2020, Dr. Fauci and other public health experts advised that until a vaccine is discovered, the best way to avoid catching the COVID-19 was to wash your hands regularly, avoid being in groups larger than fifteen people, and to wear a mask. Initially, Fauci said a mask was not essential, but later the head of the CDC contradicted him, and Fauci agreed. My mother might turn over in her grave if she believed that I was not washing my hands after playing outside, especially before dinner.

In my judgment, hygiene is an essential key to everyday good health, and especially to avoiding the COVID-19 virus. Washing one's hands remains a wise plan. In fact, I must thank the COVID-19 experts for reminding me of this. For example, my church (The Falls Church Anglican) was packed when the new sanctuary opened in September 2019. As a result, I must have shaken hands with at least 50 old friends and acquaintances, and even given a few *abrazos*, or hugs, to some. Three days later, I came down with a severe sinus infection that lasted almost two weeks.

At that time, I gave little thought to how frequently and instinctively I put my hand to my face. Many of us do this without thinking about it. While COVID-19 apparently doesn't travel by touch, you can still run a risk of meeting someone who has the virus and whose hands have been near their face, mouth, or nose. When you shake hands with that same person you are running a risk that you will catch the virus.

I have remained relatively healthy since September 2019, and COVID-19 has made me more alert as to how best to avoid becoming infected. Here is the pattern that I have followed since then. I took the initial two Pfizer vaccines, followed by two boosters, but none since then. What I have also done is to wear a mask whenever I am shopping, getting a haircut, participating in church, or riding the subway. I have avoided large gatherings elsewhere. In church, I have developed the elbow knock to avoid shaking hands. And whenever I return home from an outing, including walking the dog, I always wash my hands. Whether my good fortune will continue remains to be seen. But I'm praying that it will, the good Lord willing[18].

---

18 https://www.merriam-webster.com/dictionary/hygiene

Confession: My readers should now know that my good fortune finally ran out in late 2022; I caught the COVID virus. Thanks to my earlier vaccinations and boosters, however, it was not too severe. I was essentially recovered within a week and tested negative, although I continued to experience significant fatigue for over six weeks.

Gardening

Surprising as it might sound to the uninitiated, to garden can be an extremely satisfying endeavor. Foremost is the nourishment to be derived from the many foodstuffs to be harvested. There is the esthetic reward to be derived from watching colorful flowers grow and blossom. But there is also the personal satisfaction derived from creating something that provides ongoing pleasure to others. And anyone who has gardened, or intends to do so, is carrying on a rich tradition.

In fact, it all began some 23,000 years ago when hunter-gathers in various parts of the world decided to give up their nomadic lifestyles and began to establish centers of civilization like small communities. They used Mother Nature as their example by deciding to plant seeds themselves, so as to grow their own food rather than having to continually search for it.

Then, as population centers grew into larger kingdoms, such as Persia, Egypt, and Babylon, their wealth allowed for esthetic displays, such as the hanging gardens of Babylon. Hundreds of years later, many stunning displays of beautiful gardens were developed outside the great palaces of Europe, such as Versailles outside Paris, France and the Schonbrunn Palace by Vienna, Austria. Regardless of the scale of one's gardening activity, every gardener can be proud of carrying on an important tradition. The following text describes how the Turner family has participated in this tradition.

My earliest recollection of our family's gardening for food occurred in 1943, in the midst of World War II, when I was about eleven. At that point, the federal government had instituted food rationing to reduce the demand for commercially grown vegetables, packaging materials, and shipping. These were urgently needed to supply our troops and to conserve our resources. Many American families, including ours, not only grew much of their own personal food needs, but also learned how to can and preserve their surplus.

I recall helping my parents dig up about a quarter-acre of our back yard to plant corn, asparagus, lettuce, tomatoes, carrots, cucumbers, string beans, beets, cabbages, and other less well-known vegetables. We also planted potatoes and even some strawberry plants. The asparagus and potatoes required a year's growth before yielding much. As I remember, however, our harvest was somewhat limited. There were extensive woods directly behind our new garden, so squirrels, rabbits, and deer often helped themselves.

The squirrels especially liked the corn, and the rabbits ate much of our lettuce. To address that problem, my father and I encircled the vegetables with wooden stakes and chicken wire. Unfortunately, squirrels are good climbers, so they continued to enjoy our corn. Nonetheless, I do remember how satisfied I felt while hammering in the wooden stakes as my father held the wiring. I probably blackened two or three of his fingers inadvertently, but he smiled, and we continued working. We also erected a scarecrow, but it only seemed to be useful during Halloween, by which time our harvest was over for the year.

Some of our harvest, including peaches from the local farmer, was to find a temporary resting place in the many glass jars stacked up in the kitchen, waiting to be boiled and then sealed. I still remember seeing jars of peaches in our cellar years after the war was over. Some had turned quite dark after their lengthy storage and eventually had to be thrown out. Once the war ended in 1945, canned goods, especially fruit were much more readily available.

Despite the occasional invasion of unwelcome wild animals, all was not lost. There was a large farm nearby which grew great quantities of all sorts of produce. Trips to the farm with my mother were always a treat, since she would customarily pick up ears of corn, strawberries, and honeydew melons. My mouth would start watering before we got back home, as I envisioned another delicious summer dinner. That would mean corn on the cob and strawberry shortcake with real whipped cream for dessert. Mom was such a great cook.

My mother was also an expert at growing things, especially our tomatoes and her roses. The former were always so juicy and plump. In my opinion, nothing tastes better than a fresh summer salad with home-grown tomatoes. Mom also knew about certain greens that were nourishing. She often reminisced about going into a field near her home in Ohio, when she and her sisters were young teenagers, to pick some large dandelion leaves for their salad.

While I don't believe I ever sent our children to pick dandelion leaves for the day's salad, I have earnestly tried to emulate my mother's ability to grow good tomatoes, even at

90 years of age. I have been growing them for over 50 years, except when living or traveling overseas. I have been less successful in growing beautiful roses, however; they never seem as lovely as Mom's did. Her multicolored varieties were always so lovely that I am confident they would have looked perfect fronting some European palace or even the Hanging Gardens of Babylon. Her secrets in growing them, as best I can remember were to always mound the roses, cut them back as least twice a year, and spray them to keep the insects from infiltrating the buds.

These days I sometimes reminisce about summer and gardening at the Turner household in Hartsdale, New York. Almost magically, my thoughts drift back to my wonderful parents and those heartwarming, reassuring times of watching them, and learning from them on beautiful, warm summer days in our back yard. For a nostalgic moment I can still see them smiling and helping to beautify our property. Truly, these were some of the most enjoyable times of our life together. Everything seemed so peaceful, as if the Lord Himself was blessing our day.

Gardening lessons were not the only ones I carried with me when I moved to Falls Church, Virginia, just outside our nation's capital. There, my wife and I bought our own home and raised a family. The inclination to garden still existed. I was reminded of my father's frequent comment that there is always something to do or fix around one's house. This is certainly the case when it comes to gardening and related yard chores. There are bushes to be trimmed, flowers to be watered in dry weather, flower beds to be weeded, and of course, tomatoes to be nourished twice a month to encourage additional growth. I must confess that one of a homeowner's most burdensome chores, time wise, is mowing the lawn. It is terribly repetitive and time consuming.

In my 90th year, I still enjoy tending to my roses and tomatoes, but I leave the weeding and mowing to our gardener. My back no longer enables me to bend over to do an adequate job. In between planting seeds and later harvesting their fruit, so much happens that is beyond my control, especially severe storms. Yet I will always remain hopeful that the seeds planted will have fallen on good soil, later yielding a crop some thirtyfold. It is similar in a way to what our Lord explained in His "Parable of The Sower."[19]

---

19 Matthew 13:23

What Scripture Doesn't Tell Us

The Bible states that the first man, Adam, was made in the image of God. Sadly for mankind, Adam was disobedient. He ate from the tree of good and evil and was summarily thrust out of the Garden of Eden by God, predestined to be a life-time commuter.

Since that eventful moment, Adam's descendants have been forced to till the fields by the sweat of their brow. Over thousands of years of time and distance, we have been condemned to commute to work, from the farmyard next door to the distant cities. Whether by foot, bike, car, bus, train, or subway, this bondage of commuter servitude continues.

Yes, I genuinely believe the judgments of the Lord are true and righteous altogether, including his purpose for our bondage — I'm assuming there must have been a purpose.

Customarily, one man's bondage begins each Monday when his alarm rings. Half-asleep, he treks into the washroom for a quick shower and shave. After dressing, he must hurry into the kitchen for that soothing cup of coffee or tea, some fruit, and hot cereal. Simultaneously he bemoans, "Oh why can't this be Saturday when I could enjoy a leisurely breakfast with some tasty hot cakes and bacon and a leisurely second cup of coffee?" Reluctantly, resigned to his fate, and with coat, hat, and briefcase in tow, he heads to the garage and mounts his trusty bike for a mile ride to the bus stop. At least this gives him some exercise. But half-heartedly he wishes the pandemic had arrived sooner so he could work from home.

Once the bus arrives, he enters and pays his fare. His hope is that he's caught the early bus so he can find a seat and read his paper, thus avoiding another scenic, bumpy ride to Constitution Avenue near his place of work. When evening rush hour arrives, the weary commuter resigns himself to reversing his morning commute. His bus is again jammed with standing commuters all homeward bound, some retaining that posture for up to 30 minutes. Soon our morning biker will begin peddling his way home to the joys of household responsibility. Friday night at home finally allows our weary traveler to breathe a sigh of relief. For the next 48 hours he is released from his commuter bondage.

The poor karma of commuter-hood does have its own uniqueness. Daily, there is the opportunity to meet many probably interesting fellow passengers. However, most are as wearied as you are and thus only offer a meek grin or nod, while mulling over their own day's concerns. Occasionally, you marvel at the agility of the standees, as they use one hand to keep their balance while attempting to read with the other. Five o'clock shadow suggests some men are now ready for another shave. Always welcome, of course, is the sweet smell of perfume. Occasionally you are greeted by the anguished grimace from a passenger whose foot was too close to the aisle, and inadvertently trodden on by you.

Of course, all commuters don't take the bus. Other methods of commuting largely depend upon one's geographic location. Take for example the commuter who lives in the bedroom communities surrounding New York City, such as Westchester County, or Greenwich, Connecticut. At these locales, both the New York Central and the New Haven trains offer the luxury of early morning, one-stop travel from point to point until reaching the great working hub of New York City. During one's relaxing ride of anywhere from a half-hour to over an hour one gets to admire the same scenery week after week: the traffic jams on the highway, children headed for school on yellow buses, even the window clothes lines filled with the day's first wash as you approach the outskirts of New York City.

When longer distances are involved, going by train is preferable. There are separate rail cars for smokers; you have time to master the art of the commuter fold of your newspaper, so as to avoid it brushing against the passenger seated next to you. Seats can be folded to face each other, thus allowing card games to be played; and, of course, there is an opportunity to gain a few extra moments of sleep by dozing off for a short nap. Then suddenly the serenity of the rail trip changes as the conductor cries out, "Grand Central — the next stop."

Ah yes! Grand Central Station during rush hour is like a bustling community with a variety of fast-food counters, a busy shoeshine stand, and the famous oyster bar. If you have time for a donut and a quick cup of coffee, you feel replenished and ready for the next challenge of your commuter odyssey — the infamous New York subway system.

When following the signs to the appropriate subway entrance, you must remember to secure your wallet or purse to avoid pick pockets, and then be prepared to push your way forward toward the subway that will take you to your destination.

At morning rush hour in New York City, catching a subway train is seldom a problem — they run almost continuously. The challenge is positioning oneself sufficiently close to the incoming car to allow being pushed into it. Accordingly, during rush hour, you need not fear your ability to enter a stopped subway car provided you're within five feet of it. I say this because during rush hour hordes of other commuters, anxious to get to work, are continually pushing you forward. It is the poor man's way of fulfilling the Golden Rule, "Do unto others!" In Japan "pushers" are actually hired to load subway cars during rush hours.

Seating between 7:30 AM and 9:00 AM is problematic. Usually, you are pressed shoulder to shoulder with your fellow passengers, hoping against hope to reach a ceiling strap to hold on to. The jostling back and forth in the cramped car is good training for those who visit Times Square on New Year's Eve. The secret is to learn how to push without offending. You see all types of races, nationalities, distinctive dress, and the latest hat and hair styles. It's really a bird's eye view of your world en route to the office. Should you be fortunate enough to find a seat, be alert to the distinct eating habits of New Yorkers.

New York is famous for its excellent variety of cuisines, which many of your fellow passengers enjoy. But the aroma of their choice may cause you to give up your seat to the passenger breathing over you. I must admit, I enjoy the pungent taste of garlic and spices. But I simply don't like to inhale either right after breakfast. Many times, I have been thanked for my kindness in surrendering my seat, when, in reality, I was merely seeking breathing room. Advice on how to exit a crowded car is also essential. The sardine-like positioning requires you to position yourself reasonably close to a door. Failure to do so may mean you are pinned in and unable to exit at your intended stop.

Driving one's own car may be a commuter's best option. Of course, your first concerns are timing and traffic. You need to schedule your departure from home to avoid traffic. Cities like Washington, D.C. offer several access routes. Sometimes I forfeit the joys of bus riding to enjoy a free trip with my wife on Route 66, over the Memorial Bridge, and then onto Constitution Avenue. She rents a monthly parking space under her building at work. Unfortunately, the IRS doesn't allow a tax deduction for parking. When driving home, unless you purposely start late, you will enjoy traffic jams exiting the city.

In closing, there is one question I have often wanted to ask the Christian commuter. What would the Good Samaritan have done had he been facing the challenges of today's commuter traffic? If you recall the story from the Bible, a commuter on his way to work in Jericho was set upon by thieves and left for dead. On two separate occasions, an official from the temple passed him by without stopping. But the Good Samaritan did stop, aided the man, and took him to a local inn to recover. Clearly, that ancient commuter went out of his way to help someone in need. Would today's commuter do the same?

Before you answer, fast forward some 2,000 years, and pretend you are a commuter, driving in heavy traffic, on your way to an important meeting at work. You consider your meeting critical in terms of both time and career. Then you're nearly at your destination when suddenly you spy an injured person lying by the roadside. The police have yet to arrive, and no one seems to be attending him. Will you be the first commuter to stop and offer aid, or will your work appointment take precedence? I am confident I know what all of you would do. Maybe that's why God needs Christian commuters and why He made so many of them.

Chapter IV

The Two-Sided Coin

Every coin has two sides with its value clearly indicated on the coin itself; those particulars do not change. I also consider that education and character can form a unique value. It is taken from the bank of one's experience and, once deposited, it continues to increase in value.

The educational side of this coin is the process whereby we acquire knowledge, a benefit that enables us to develop skills essential for our daily living, including social norms, judgment, and reasoning. In addition, formal education provides people the opportunity to live better lives. Ideally, the more education you attain, the better your potential ability of gaining rewarding opportunities in life. Of course, a key ingredient here is a person's ambition and their willingness to work hard.

Likewise, the character side of this coin, and by this I mean good character, is an essential requirement to living a fulfilling life. Character determines how we think, which in turn determines how we speak and act, which can certainly affect the results we get in life. Provided we develop good character, we give ourselves the best opportunity to relate effectively with our fellow human beings.

Properly understood, education is our mind's ability to move beyond mere knowledge of facts and figures to their application. Education is comparable to travel, or the reading of a good book — once it is finished, the joy or wisdom gained from the experience remains. Sometimes it opens entirely new vistas, not just for individuals, but for humankind itself.

A case in point would be July 20, 1969, when Neil Armstrong was the first person to set foot on the moon. As he stepped out of his moon capsule and set foot on the moon itself, he uttered the famous words: "That's one small step for man; one giant step for mankind." Since that time, space exploration has expanded. Humankind has learned more about the universe and space than when the astronomer Galileo first wrote in 1610 that the earth revolved around the sun.

I am convinced that the two-sided coin of education and character is essential to add value to every person's life. It teaches us that together there is great potential benefit that can be derived. Where the good character side of the coin is not present, however, its value is greatly diminished.

Collecting Things

Have you ever considered how often you have repeated sayings to fit real life situations? The sayings seem to remind you of some truth or reality at a given moment, or better still, truth itself. For example, have you ever said, *Many hands make light work; Never put off till tomorrow what you can accomplish today; or, Do unto others what you would like them to do unto you* — ? Over the years, I have tended to collect such sayings either because they make life more real to me, or because they cover important moments that may have changed history.

My reasons for this are quite simply that my mind and heart enjoy listening to the truths these sayings are intended to convey. Frequently, they provide subtle wisdom that I find stirring, inspirational, or useful. Such as, *Not even when one has an abundance does his life consist of his possessions.*[1] Often, they express something about life that is encouraging or challenging. In this essay I share some of my collection, while also adding some background on their authors.

Let me begin by repeating a thought from the great French poet and writer of the 19th century, Victor Hugo. "Greater than the tread of mighty armies is an idea whose hour has come."[2] To Americans, Hugo is probably most famous for his

---

1   Luke 12:15
2   Victor Hugo, *The History of a Crime* (1877)

prose, as he authored *The Hunchback of Notre-Dame* and *Les Misérables*. I like Hugo's thought because it suggests how the power and authority of an idea can surmount even mighty forces aligned against it. The quote also suggests that an idea can overcome evil or despair. Take for example, the Civil Rights era of the 1960s. Despite the cultural and political forces aligned against him, Dr. Martin Luther King, Jr.'s words concerning the need for the freedom and equality of Blacks helped to eliminate the Jim Crow era in America, resulting in the first effective Civil Rights legislation in a century. Better still, consider the 2,000-year-old message of forgiveness and salvation, "I am the resurrection and the life; he who believes in Me shall live even if he dies."[3]

Another quotation that truly speaks to me was apparently authored by the Chinese philosopher and mystic, Lao Tzu, who is said to have lived in the 6th century BC. He wrote, *"Life is like a cookie jar. It would soon grow empty if we continued to take the good things it offers without putting back something good in return."* This thought reminds me of the true insight in his words, especially when I consider the gracious, generous people I have met over the years. They each possessed a special trait in common. They made it a point to concern themselves with the needs of others, rather than focusing attention solely on themselves. I am reminded of such a person every time I think of the "Parable of The Good Samaritan."[4]

During my high school graduation ceremony in June 1950, we were privileged to have as our speaker the then-President of America's Professional Baseball Association, Ford Frick.

---

3 John 11:25

4 Luke 10:25-37

Of course, he gave us the customary encouragement expected by young graduates starting out in life. But in his closing statement, he quoted from William Shakespeare's *Hamlet*, a passage that has always rung true to me where human relations are concerned. In reality, it was an essential point of his advice to our class. "This above all, to thine own self be true; and it must follow as night the day, thou canst not then be false to any man."

Some may recall that this quote was from the First Act of *Hamlet*. In it, there is a scene where Polonius, the Chancellor, is advising his young son, Laertes, on how to conduct himself in Paris as the son prepares to depart on his first trip to Europe. As I recall Mr. Frick's use of this saying, it seemed as if he were advising us of the following, if a person is honest with themselves, as to how to comport themselves responsibly in life, they will then be genuine and honorable in their dealings with others. I still believe this to be sound advice.

For my next quote, I have Cal Berlin to thank. Not only was he the best boss I ever had, but he also had great wisdom. Occasionally, I would get down on myself for my mistakes. It was then that he admitted to similar experiences when he was starting out. For example, he described how he had paid his way through college and graduate study by working as an apprentice carpenter. He claimed that he would often make wrong cuts in the wood he was attempting to shape or smooth. This made him frustrated. His boss, a master carpenter, recognized his predicament and gave him some sage advice to encourage him. He said, "Everyone makes mistakes. It is the ability to repair them that counts." Whenever I make mistakes, and I frequently do, I try to remember Cal's wise counsel and adjust. It always helps.

Abraham Lincoln's Second Inaugural Address is considered by historians to have been his greatest, or second only to his Gettysburg Address. In the former, Lincoln describes the horrors of the Civil War. He relates these to the suffering, death, and destruction brought on by the offense of slavery. In fact, he implies that God may be punishing both the North and the South for the conflict, especially the injustice of slavery. He clearly believes that God has his own purposes as to why the war and suffering have continued. He believes the final result of the conflict is in God's hands regardless of its outcome.

Lincoln then appears to explain, and possibly justify, the circumstances surrounding that terrible conflict by repeating a passage from the Old Testament, *The judgments of the Lord are true and righteous altogether.*[5] It is hard to disagree with Lincoln's logic, especially for people of faith who are familiar with the major cause of the Civil War. We acknowledge that God is in control, and His purposes are His alone.

Switching to another forum, I want to give credit to a quotation by one of America's most acclaimed sports writers, Grantland Rice. He was prescient in writing that, "When the One great Scorer comes to write against your name, He marks not that you won or lost but how you played the game."[6] The field of sports was Rice's career, so clearly, he is suggesting that fair play in sports was and is what truly matters, when all is said and done. But I believe that you would agree with me that the meaning of his quote can certainly be expanded to include how we conduct

5   Psalm 19:9
6   Grantland Rice, "Alumnus Football," in Only the Brave (New York: A. S. Barnes & Co., Inc., 1941)

ourselves in life. I certainly subscribe to Rice's belief, and I am confident our Lord would as well. For He once said, "What does it profit a man to gain the whole world and lose his soul?"[7]

It is fitting to close this collection of thoughts with wisdom from one of the 20th century's most respected men, South Africa's Nelson Mandela. He suffered greatly because of his resistance to apartheid. But by the time of his death, he was acclaimed as a great world figure and respected leader. Despite his suffering at the hands of his torturers in prison, he persevered, as great men and women have the determination to do. Their perseverance is consistent with the following words of Mandela, "The greatest glory in living lies not in failing, but in rising every time we fail."

---

7   Mark 8:36

Real Character

The term character is generally understood to reflect the qualities that distinguish us; manners or traits that reflect the essence of our true or inner nature. Yet, to define a person of real or positive character customarily requires more specificity. From my personal experience, I would suggest that such a person is customarily distinguished by how they deal with tribulation; how they handle difficult challenges such as disapproval, disappointment, disrespect, or even despair?

Provided a person responds to any such challenges in a morally responsible or principled fashion, I would define them as having displayed real character. Consistently, they hold fast to what they believe is responsible, acceptable, or righteous conduct. Remarkably, in the process they are modeling for others the character trait St. Paul found helpful in expressing love. *They do not take into account a wrong (or insult) suffered.*[8]

Unquestionably, at birth, few are born with real character. Rather, to acquire it will require learning, especially the mastery of self-discipline. Failure to fully grasp the need for developing such character can adversely affect a person's ability to build and maintain lasting human relationships.

---

8   1 Corinthians 13:5

Consider, for example, the former Governor of New York, who was recently forced to resign. One New York journalist, in analyzing the governor's circumstances, wrote, "Cuomo's comeuppance was inevitable; his high ambition was not matched by high character."[9] The journalist obviously believed that the governor was not a man of real character because of his apparent moral failures. In my judgment, his resignation was definitely called for.

But let me be clear, my intent today is not to dwell on the unfortunate peccadilloes of politicians over their seeming lack of character. Nor am I planning to describe the amusement we get from knowing real characters: persons who can be different or challenging, largely because their manner is characterized by non-conformity toward respected social or cultural norms. In this context, some professional comedians might be one illustration of real characters: persons we do not wish to emulate.

Accordingly, my discussion in this brief essay will be just the opposite. I will attempt to describe persons who are respected or admired for displays of real character as already mentioned. In this effort, I do make a distinction between real character and good reputation. The two can certainly overlap, but it is my belief that real character truly defines who we are on the inside, while a good reputation may simply be how we appear on the surface, especially to others who may not really know us.

Let me begin with an example from my own experience. Several years ago, I went horseback-riding with a friend

9   Michael Goodwin, "Andrew Cuomo is a Heel Who Could Never Fill His Dad's Shoes," *New York Post*, August 10, 2021, https://nypost.com/2021/08/10/heel-could-never-fill-his-dads-shoes-goodwin/

of mine. We arrived at the stables separately, before I had the opportunity to advise him of certain protocols required by the stables' owner. One of these was that no rider was permitted to mount a horse until the owner held the bridle for them. However, my friend is an experienced rider and owns his own horse. So instinctively, he mounted without waiting for the owner's approval.

Barely had he landed in his saddle before the owner began to loudly upbraid him for his breach of protocol. The owner was both angry and rude and, in my judgment, unnecessarily so. Nonetheless, my friend stayed calm, reflecting no observable upset. He immediately dismounted and apologized to the owner. He then engaged her in their mutual interest in horses. Someone suddenly arriving on the scene might have guessed they were old friends.

Some months later I asked my friend how he was able to retain his calmness or self-control in the face of the owner's rudeness. He smiled and said, "Roger, although I was bristling on the inside, that made no difference. Years ago, I had made the decision that I would never allow another person's improper conduct to cause me to act in a manner inconsistent with the person I am. Accordingly, I wasn't going to allow her conduct to alter mine." Without question, his attitude illustrates what I consider an essential trait in manifesting real character: standing firm for what one believes is morally correct.

In Scripture there are numerous examples of persons of real character, certainly Jesus being foremost. He actually described just such a person in His Parable of the Good Samaritan.[10] When I first heard this story as a boy in Sunday

---

10 Luke 10:25-37

school, I was quite upset that two religious officials — first a priest, and later a Levite — would have left an injured man to die by the roadside. Conversely, I was extremely impressed by the third man, the Samaritan, who did stop and made certain the injured man was helped and then cared for.

In ancient Jewish belief, a Samaritan was considered a religious outcast. Yet, the Samaritan went out of his way to aid the injured man, take him to an inn, and pay for his care. From Jesus' telling it was obvious that the Samaritan wasn't concerned about his reputation. Rather, he focused on doing the right thing, even when no one else was watching. He had temporarily interrupted his own activity to help because that is who he was. He displayed why a pure heart is essential to real character.

Many years ago, I was faced with somewhat similar circumstances, while leading a group of CEOs on a U.S. Government-sponsored trade mission to South America. By chance, our stop in Buenos Aires had coincided with the return of the former dictator, Juan Peron, from Spain. Consequently, anti-American sentiment was high. A bomb had actually been detonated in our Hilton Hotel shortly prior to our arrival. Understandably the businessmen were somewhat on edge.

At dusk on the second night, we took off in taxis from the hotel to enjoy some of the famous Argentine beef at a fine steakhouse. En route, I chanced to look out the cab window and saw a man lying on the sidewalk with a knife sticking out of his back. He appeared to be writhing in pain. No others spotted him, and we arrived at the restaurant without incident. It was my professional responsibility to avoid any distraction that might disrupt the mission or cause the

CEOs to fear for their safety. Nonetheless, Jesus' parable caused me to have second thoughts about my decision.

From a State Department protocol standpoint, I probably made the correct decision. When traveling in a foreign country, we are advised to avoid involvement in local criminal or political incidents. Nonetheless, from Jesus' standpoint, I had failed to demonstrate real character. Several months later I had misgivings about my decision. I wished instead that I had acted like the Good Samaritan and asked the cab driver to return to the hotel to call an ambulance. I might add that later in my career, when a similar event occurred in Mexico, I reported it to local authorities. But that's a story for another day.

In summary, I consider that a morally responsible person will always attempt to manifest real character in their own unique manner. Circumstances will determine whether doing so requires great compassion, facing a challenging responsibility, or simply great courage. This being said, I also believe that the essence of real character is not merely an aggregate of positive traits. It must reflect the person's true nature.

The Temporary Resident

In God's great wisdom, He created an amazing universe and the challenging world in which we are temporary residents. As Scripture then explains, God also created other creatures. He said, *Let the earth bring forth living creatures after their kind: creeping things and beasts ... that it was good.*[11] He further blessed us residents with the ability to know and love Him. Possibly He could have saved time and rested on the sixth day, had he never created insects. Had he sought my humble opinion on the matter, my only suggestions would have been to keep the honeybees and eliminate all the blood-scavenging gnats and mosquitoes.

But Scripture isn't always precise as to God's intentions concerning insects, especially in the idyllic Garden of Eden. For example, prior to the disobedience of Adam and Eve, there is no mention of their encountering insects. When Eve walked by the lovely flower beds, she was never stung or harassed by a nasty yellow jacket. And Adam's bare feet were never alleged to have been bitten by a red ant, nor his resting space eaten by hungry grasshoppers, or carpenter ants. Possibly it was God's initial plan to hold off releasing insects until the flood was ended. Noah might have had difficulty housing them on the ark; and they might have been eaten by birds or other animal passengers.

---

11 Genesis l:21-22; 24-25

Yes, I'm speaking about those annoying creatures that are so familiar to us. Especially those menacing wasps that build large gray cocoon nests by a window, the yellow jackets that seem to enjoy stinging human kind for mere sport, all variety of ants who feel no shame in constructing nests of sand and dirt in one's clean mudroom each spring, uninvited flies that want to share our picnic lunches, inconsiderate moths that make holes in new wool sweaters, and spiders that enjoy spinning their webs atop curtain rods or on ceilings where they are hard to reach. And again, there are those blood-scavenging gnats and mosquitoes that consistently harass well-meaning gardeners.

Caution! As we learn in the book of Job, it is presumptuous to even consider that God in His eternal wisdom would require human counsel on any subject. As He asked Job, "Where were you when I laid the foundation of the earth?"[12] Consequently, to better appreciate His purpose for insects, I needed to look to science as well as Scripture. My research has provided some extremely interesting facts. Once more, they highlighted our Father in Heaven's great vision. For through insects, He has not only provided us needed food, but has used them to stress the authority of His word in difficult times.

Entomologists, for example, have discovered that insects are the most abundant life form on earth and are highly nutritious, being rich in fats, proteins, and carbohydrates. Eating insects is common to many cultures in Latin America, Africa, Asia, and Australia. Take caterpillars for instance: they are considered delicacies in southern African countries. Apparently, the best tasting one is the wax worm,

---

12 Job 38:4

which feeds on beehives' wax and honey. I must agree that does sound like a tasty mix. The internet claims that the eight best-selling insects, in order of preference, are: crickets, cicadas, mealworms, scorpions, June bugs, grasshoppers, ants, and wax worms. I must say I was surprised that cicadas were so popular, since in our region they only come around every 17 years. Still, our gourmand dog, Duncan, seemed to have enjoyed eating them during our walks this past summer.

Crickets, in addition to being used for nourishment, have another function. In the Orient, people actually keep them in tiny wooden cages to hear their chirping, much like we do with canaries in America. This may be going a little too far for me. It is difficult to get to sleep while listening to the sound of a chirping cricket. You can put a cover over a canary's cage at night and it will remain quiet. But with crickets you never know when they are going to chirp. Years ago, I remember my brother complaining that a cricket got loose in his motel room one night. Even after an hour's hunting, he was unable to corral it. Ultimately, he had to change rooms.

Speaking of crickets and hotel rooms reminds me of an experience I had with an insect in Costa Rica, where I was on assignment at the U.S. Embassy. The insect was not a cricket but a cockroach. In my hotel room one night I was awakened by one chewing on my big toe. I had been sleeping with my feet atop the sheets, as the air conditioning was not working too well. Needless to say, I slept with my feel under the top sheet thereafter. For those traveling in the southern hemisphere, the term for cockroach in Spanish is *cucaracha*. The Latins have written a popular song explaining its threatening nature. In China, however, cockroaches are not just a threat; they are in demand as a source of both food and medicine.

Even allowing for the beneficial dietary aspects of insects, I am more impressed by how God has used them in Scripture. There, He highlights them to emphasize His disapproval or warning when we tend to be disobedient or otherwise disregard His word. In this context, the following passages help to further illustrate the critical importance of God's purposes for creating insects. To illustrate this finding, I begin with the great passage from II Chronicles, *If I command the locust to devour the land … And My people who are called by My name humble themselves and pray … I will hear from Heaven, and forgive their sin, and heal their land.*[13]

There are also the famous Old Testament passages from Exodus[14] where God sends for gnats and later flies, to harden Pharaoh's heart and punish him for refusing to let Moses and the Ancient Israelites leave Egypt.

In the New Testament, Jesus warned the scribes and Pharisees that their lack of proportion in spiritual matters was as ridiculous as "straining out a gnat."[15] Further, Jesus uses the moth to make His point on our need for spiritual responsibility, as he exclaims, "Lay up for yourselves treasures in Heaven, where neither moth … destroys."[16]

Daily, I am grateful for the benefits of that wonderful insect, the honeybee, and for John the Baptist who also recognized its virtues, "(He) who fed on locusts and wild

13 2 Chronicles 7:13-14
14 Exodus 8:16-19 and 8:21-32
15 Matthew 23:24
16 Matthew 6:20

honey."[17] For each morning, with my first cup of hot tea, I use a teaspoon full of wild honey instead of sugar. Thus, I must humbly confess that I remain awed by God's vision in having created these and other insects. Yet, should I be privileged to gain residence in Heaven, there is one very tiny issue I would like to discuss with God, of course, solely on behalf of my former fellow gardeners. I would humbly suggest that His ridding the earth of all scavenging gnats and mosquitoes would be a Heaven-sent blessing.

---

17 Mark 1:6

Inventions and Innovations

What do Abraham Lincoln, Alexander Fleming, and Thomas Edison have in common? They were all inventors. In 1849, Lincoln became our only president to receive a patent. It was for a device that enabled flat boats to be lifted over shoals or shallow water. Fleming discovered penicillin in 1928, a miracle drug that has since been used to successfully fight a huge number of bacterial infections in humans. In 1882, Edison invented an electric light bulb that would continue functioning. His invention led to a means by which electric power could be effectively transmitted over distances. Over the centuries, these and other inventions have improved life for humankind.

It is my primary intention here to describe additional benefits that resulted from other significant inventions. Second, I plan to share with you an innovation on how to better enjoy your salad days, or rather, how to change your family dinner from an enjoyable tradition to a sumptuous treat. To accomplish these objectives, however, I first need to distinguish between an invention and an innovation. The two terms, while often closely aligned, are truly quite distinct. To invent literally means to create an idea or a product that is entirely new. To innovate, however, is merely to take an existing idea, process, or product and improve upon it.

A useful illustration of this distinction would be the telegraph. It was actually the invention of two Englishmen in the 1830s, but through innovation it was first used in America in 1844. The English invention was primarily used to aid in railroad signaling. But in 1844, it was Samuel Morse's subsequent innovation of the electromagnetic system that enabled the telegraph to be used over long distances. Many of you remember from your history books that Morse's initial message was telegraphed from Washington, D.C. to Baltimore, Maryland. It said, "What hath God wrought?"[18] His invention of the Morse code greatly facilitated telegraph utility.

In addition to some of the inventions already mentioned, there are others that significantly helped to change and modernize our world. One of the earliest and most significant was the invention of the wheel around 3500 BC. Until then, humans were severely limited in the quantity of goods or product they could transport by land or sea. Today, whether the wheel is used in transportation, highly sophisticated machinery, or in the exploration of space, it plays an integral part in the equipment's ability to function. The nail was another valuable invention, first utilized around the time of ancient Rome. Prior to the nail, building materials usually had to be fitted together. Some builders have said that without the nail, civilization would surely crumble.

One of the next important inventions was the compass, invented by the Chinese sometime between the 9th and 11th centuries. It enabled ancient mariners to navigate by day and at nighttime or when it was cloudy. It also facilitated the discovery and settlement of America. Columbus did use celestial navigation, but he also had a compass.

---

18 Numbers 23:33

If we push forward a few centuries, we come to the invention of the printing press by the German printer, Johannes Gutenberg, in the 1440s. His molding technique enabled the rapid use of large quantities of movable metal type to transfer words from the ink to the paper. This facilitated the publication of books and pamphlets in a manner not previously possible. It helped to spread the news of Martin Luther's 95 Theses, thus furthering the launch of the European Reformation and the birth of Protestantism. No longer could the reading and interpretation of Scripture be the sole province of the Papacy. Commoners could now read the Bible in the vernacular and make their own interpretation.

The current pandemic should remind us of the critically important pioneering work done by Louis Pasteur on the use of vaccines in the early 1880s. He pioneered the principles of both vaccination and pasteurization so vital to our health today. In 1885, his vaccination of a young boy who had been bitten by rabid dogs saved the boy's life and made Pasteur a world hero overnight. As with Alexander Fleming, who was mentioned earlier, it is hard to overstate the importance of the contribution these two great inventors and scientists have made to the health of humankind.

More recently, what would we do today without our cell phones? Our ability to communicate instantly with others would be drastically reduced. We have Alexander Graham Bell to thank for inventing the electric telephone in 1876. While many inventors, including Thomas Edison, did pioneering work on electronic voice transmission, it was Bell who received the first patent, calling his device the electric speech machine. Subsequent innovations continue to revolutionize our ability to communicate.

Computer geeks owe a debt of gratitude to Latham L. Sholes. His invention of the first practical typewriter in the 1860s would eventually lead to the invention of the word processor and then the computer. In some form, the latter has become a valuable appliance in innumerable American households. In turn, as a result of the computer, many of those households have benefited from the invention of the interconnected computer network known as the internet. Countless people helped to develop it, but its invention is most often attributed to computer scientist Lawrence Roberts in the 1960s, not former Senator Al Gore. Today, its use is worldwide. Sholes' typewriter was marketed under the familiar brand name of Remington. Thomas Edison did invent the first electrically operated typewriter in 1872, but his application of it morphed into what we know today as the ticker tape printer.

The innovations developed in the computer world lead me to my final discussion point today, the innovation of a better salad dressing. Allow me to explain. For years, my mother struggled to create a salad dressing that appealed to our family. She was otherwise an outstanding cook and superb baker. I still remember her delicious homemade bread, as well as her buttermilk biscuits, the latter covered with melted butter and maple syrup on special Sunday night dinners. Then there were her strawberry short cake and her angel pie. Her recipe for the latter was so popular that when Ruth made it in Australia for a popular restaurant owner we had invited to dinner, he later offered to pay her to make it for him.

Unfortunately, Mom's salad dressing never measured up to her cooking excellence. Occasionally she drowned the dressing in too much oil, diluted its sharpness by using cider vinegar rather than wine vinegar, or dulled its taste by adding Gulden's mustard. During many a vacation from college and later law school, I made suggestions, but all seemed fruitless, until one day, I chanced to eat at a French restaurant near my work. Needless to say, I ordered a salad with French dressing. It was delicious.

Following lunch, I asked my waiter if I could speak with the chef to learn his secret. I explained my hope was to surprise Mom with a new salad dressing. She was due to arrive that evening from Atlanta. At dinner, we had her favorite leg of lamb with Brussels sprouts and mashed potatoes. As a special treat, I asked Ruth to fix a hearty salad while I prepared my innovative French dressing.

At dinner Mom asked, "Ruth, how did you make such a wonderful salad dressing?" My wife turned to me for the explanation. I then repeated what the chef had said, "Begin with the correct proportion of virgin olive oil to white wine vinegar; next add in sea salt and white, not black, pepper to taste; and include a liberal tablespoon of Dijon mustard. Mix thoroughly in a blender and then shake at least one minute before serving." Thereafter, future guests at the Turner dinner table raved about Ruth's dressing. Isn't it amazing how one little innovation can make for a tasty dinner? Try it!

Memorable Road Trips

It was early August, 1954, at Sun Valley Idaho's famous ski resort, nearly two months after my college graduation. Excitedly, my younger brother and I threw our few personal belongings into our car, along with two blankets and two pillows. We ended our janitorial work at the resort and were headed west for a long-anticipated tour of several major national parks. Our final destination before heading back East would be San Antonio, Texas, to reunite with our grandmother, aunt and uncle, some cousins, and to visit the historic Alamo. It would be a whirlwind road trip I would long remember.

Over the next four weeks our travel would include such major national parks as Yellowstone, Yosemite, and the Grand Canyon. With only a limited budget, our plan was to sleep in the car at park sites each night and to eat light. Our morning ablutions were done at the nearest gas station that also had a breakfast counter. With the exception of a two-day visit at an inexpensive San Francisco hotel, there would be no showers or hot water for the next month. We would have only one bath, au natural, in the icy waters of Lake Tahoe. Since it was the heat of summer, light clothing seemed to be all that we needed.

Our first destination was Yellowstone Natural Park in Wyoming, just north of the Grand Tetons National Park. Since first learning about Yellowstone in high school, there were several things that I was eager to see. These included watching the eruption of the geyser Old Faithful, feeding the wild bears, and observing a wild moose in its natural habitat. I had only seen one in a zoo. Almost immediately after we entered the park, we met up with several parked cars. They were all there to watch the feeding of a mother bear and her two cubs.

One eager photographer got out of his car too near the cubs and suddenly the mother charged him. He barely escaped a mauling before jumping back into his car. Later as we took a seemingly deserted road another bear appeared and came up toward our car. I then parked by the roadside, thinking it would be fun to feed it some of Mom's choice, month-old chocolate chip cookies. From the driver's seat I shot a movie, as my brother Heyward cautiously lowered the car window to feed the bear. Its paws and part of its snout hung inside the car window; it didn't seem to want to leave. Finally, my brother threw one cookie out the window to get the bear off the car. It worked. Lesson learned, and we never fed any more bears. Sadly, we were also out of cookies, but it had been for a good cause.

We slept by a deserted road inside the park, something not authorized today. The next morning as the sun rose, we looked over a nearby river and there we spotted a magnificent bull moose with a huge rack on its head drinking from the river. Before leaving the park, we discovered the Grand Canyon of the Yellowstone, a most impressive rock formation surrounding a huge waterfall and a rapidly flowing river.

From Yellowstone we journeyed to Glacier National Park in Montana. It was very scenic and filled with beautiful lakes, but I didn't see any glaciers. So, we headed for Olympic National Park in Washington to see what a virgin forest looked like. While we saw plenty of lush forest, I'm not sure I could distinguish the virgin from the older forestation. We did uncover a roadside stand selling cherries, my favorite fruit at the time. The price was too good to pass up: 25 cents for two pounds. We ate almost all of them that day for lunch, although our meal had a negative effect on my digestion later that afternoon.

From Washington we traveled through Oregon, near Crater Lake, and then on to California. After departing San Francisco, we motored to Los Angeles and slept in a parking lot overlooking the Pacific Ocean. That night a cop or security guard knocked on the front window, probably to see if we were alive. I sat up and explained what we were doing, so he left. But he also left us with a cracked front side window.

In San Francisco we viewed the Pacific Ocean from the Golden Gate Bridge and did some touring. Despite being the middle of summer, it was quite cold and overcast. For two days we actually slept in a cheap hotel, the only time during our lengthy voyage that we deserted our comfortable sleeping quarters in the car. Next, we were eager to move on to Yosemite National Park, where we experienced the breathtaking sights of the Giant Sequoias.

We also experienced the famous fire fall, a man-made event. It takes place near dusk when park authorities spill burning hot embers from the top of a 3,000-foot rock formation to the valley below. With the sun's rays at just the right level, the embers give them the appearance of a glowing waterfall. Later that evening, I witnessed another occurrence, far less enchanting, but almost as breathtaking. It happened when my brother Heyward had to make a quick pit stop before our turning in for the night. He was about 10 or 15 feet from a large trash dump. I turned on the car lights to help guide him, when suddenly a large shadow appeared at the trash dump. It was a large bear foraging for its dinner. I couldn't shout for fear of startling the bear, so I had to hold my breath until my brother returned. Fortunately, neither he nor the bear saw each other; the bear probably didn't even pick up Heyward's scent because he was experiencing the sweet smell of garbage.

A few hours' drive below Yosemite is Sequoia National Park, the home of the magnificent giant sequoia trees. Just to see the size of them is an amazing sight. You feel terribly small standing next to one of these giants. Their width is approximate the length of three SUVs lined up bumper-to-bumper. To give you an idea of their immense size, at one point the park roadway actually takes drivers through the hollowed-out center or trunk of one of these huge trees.

From the Sequoia Park we headed for Las Vegas, about a two-hour drive. Our reason for taking this route was to travel through Death Valley National Park, one of the hottest, driest land locations on earth. It is basically desert, located nearly 300 feet below sea level. In summertime, the temperature can exceed 120 degrees Fahrenheit. We stopped by the sign that said Death Valley National Park, and I suggested we film a brief scene. It shows me in a torn undershirt, weaving haltingly in an effort to shield myself from the hot desert sun while seeking a water hole. The next scene shows my brother picking up the ragged shirt from the desert floor, puzzled as to what had happened to my remains.

In Las Vegas, Nevada, we visited a gambling casino. Unlike today's version of the city, in 1954 it consisted of a few buildings in the desert. It was not the thriving entertainment metropolis of the "Godfather" movies. As we entered the casino, several one-armed bandits, or slot machines, were lined up at the entrance. I actually put a quarter in one of them. And guess what! Five dollars in change spewed out. I tried my luck twice more, but nothing happened. So, I decided to quit while I was still ahead, abruptly ending what could have been a promising gambling career. I had to overnight an extra night in Las Vegas when Heyward discovered that he had left his camera at a friend of our father's, in Portuguese Bend, California, just outside Los Angeles. Even at sixteen years of age he proved to be a good driver, as he was able to retrieve his camera while I waited for his return. When he got back safely, I breathed a sigh of relief; I wasn't sure that I should have let him travel alone.

From Las Vegas, we crossed over into Utah to visit the Great Salt Lake and the Mormon Tabernacle in Salt Lake City. As we approached the lake, the roadside seemed like a solid white crust of salt. My brother got out to try walking on it but found it to be like a quicksand of salt mush. I had wanted to try a swim in the lake to see if I would float, but time did not permit. We were in a hurry to get to Arizona to visit the Petrified Forest and the Painted Desert national parks. At the former, I was amazed to see how once-live trees had been turned into rocks. Some 200 million years previously, these former conifers had been uprooted by floods and were organically turned into stone.

From this site, we motored to the famous Meteor Crater near Flagstaff, Arizona. I had always wanted to see this site, since viewing pictures of it in my high school science book. The crater resembles a huge indentation in the earth, 700 feet deep and 400 feet wide. Apparently, 50,000 years ago a meteor struck this site at an estimated speed of 26,000 miles per hour, leaving this crater. Some scientists have suggested the meteor's landing coincided with the disappearance of the dinosaurs, because of the tremendous heat it generated. Often, I wonder whether another such meteor will strike the earth in my lifetime.

From Arizona, we traveled to New Mexico to view the Montezuma Castle Monument where cliff dwellers of the Sinagua Indian tribe had lived some 90 feet above the ground between the years 1100 to 1400. Apparently, this height enabled them to avoid seasonal floods as well as attacks from unfriendly tribes. Eventually, the arid climate and resultant lack of food caused them to move further south into Mexico.

Our last stop in New Mexico before heading toward San Antonio and family was to the spectacular Carlsbad Caverns, near where the Texas and Mexican borders meet. The caverns' rock formations are strikingly beautiful, as are its huge underground caverns.

From there, it was a day's drive on to San Antonio, family, and hopefully a good hot shower. With Heyward's able guidance, we reached our Uncle Jim's home late at night. No one was up at the time, so we entered the outside porch and slept on the lovely, carpeted cement floor. It had been a great road trip and a summer we will always treasure. After a few days enjoying our family reunion and some good food, we set out at seven o'clock for our 13-hour drive to the environs of Chicago, Illinois. My college girlfriend lived in that area. But that is another story for another time.

European Travel

It was early afternoon on June 12, 1957, when three fraternity brothers, Phil, Ed, and I, disembarked at the Port of Rotterdam in the Netherlands. It had taken nearly four days to cross the Atlantic after boarding the Holland-American Line's student ship at the Port of New York. Our first visit to the old world of Europe had begun. Initially, I just considered it an opportunity to see tourist sites I'd either read about or seen illustrated in textbooks. Yet the visit soon proved to be far more. Not only was I in for some culinary surprises, but I also truly widened my limited cultural education. The latter resulted from numerous visits to the great museums, magnificent cathedrals, and ancient capitols of Western Europe.

In a whirlwind-like two months, we visited nine countries by car. It was tiring but rewarding. What astonishes me today is the realization of how culturally limited I was at the time. Unlike my two frat brothers, art and paintings had never really perked my interest. Of course, I did recognize when a painting looked good or when a piece of sculpture seemed nicely realistic. But that was the extent of my artistic appreciation. This limited understanding began to change rapidly. I was to learn how brilliantly the works of great artists and architects can portray important aspects of life, such as religion, war, faith, and beauty. But I'll begin this story where we first set foot on European soil: in a shipyard.

As we disembarked, I learned one thing right away. Dutch dock workers wear wooden shoes to better protect their feet from injury. Until that revelation, I had assumed that, like American workers, they wore boots to protect themselves from injury. I had incorrectly assumed that the Dutch had stopped wearing wooden shoes long ago, possibly around the time the children's novel, *Hans Brinker, or The Silver Skates*[19] was written.

We had only been off the ship a few minutes when we stopped at a local café for lunch, where we ordered some sandwiches and a drink. As a result, for the second time in only a few hours since our arrival, I learned something else, no, not about European dress, but about European seasoning. It was good. What I am referring to has to do with my introduction to French Dijon mustard. Previously, my mother had always served Gulden's mustard, but it never had much of a bite to it. But the Dijon mustard, wow, it really made for a delicious sandwich. I've used it ever since.

After lunch, we picked up our rental car and drove to Amsterdam. En route, we stopped to take pictures at the Zider Zee and to look at some of the dykes, for which Holland is well-known. That evening, while dining at a street-side table, I was amazed to see many young couples dressed up and riding bikes, not driving cars, to a Saturday night outing. The men were doing the peddling while the women were seated behind them on the same bike. They seemed comfortable enough and it made for far less traffic.

From Amsterdam, we drove northeast through Germany

---

19 Mary Mapes Dodge, *Hans Brinker or The Silver Skates* (New York: Charles Scribner's Sons, 1865)

to Kobehavn, Denmark. That night we ate at the picturesque Tivoli Gardens, while enjoying some fine dinner music. We also were introduced to the velvety taste of the locally brewed Carlsberg beer, which is enjoyed the world over. The next day, we visited the famous Kronborg Castle at Elsinore, Shakespeare's setting for his play, *Hamlet*. We also took the ferry across to Malmo, Sweden, near the Town of Halmstad, where my maternal grandfather Anderson was born.

From Sweden, we spent the next few days traveling south in West Germany to the old city of Cologne. There, we toured its impressive cathedral. Its construction first began in the 14th century, and it is the largest Gothic church in northern Europe. Later, after a quick drive through the Black Forest, we toured the Heidelberg Castle. Supposedly, it was an inspiration for Sigmund Romberg's famous operetta *The Student Prince*. Dinner included some great venison, and roasted wild boar.

The next day, it was south to Mad Ludwig's Castle at Hohenschwangau, located in the picturesque town of Newschwanstein, Bavaria. Many of you have likely seen pictures of the castle's bold architecture in tourist magazines. It was built in 1869 and is often used in movies because of its ornate appearance and surrounding, breathtaking landscape. From there, it was on to Zurich, Switzerland, to view the former League of Nations site and then on to Innsbruck, Austria for the night. The next day we rode on the ski lifts and did some mountain climbing. The following day, we drove to Vienna where we toured the Hapsburg Palace, the Vienna Opera House, and the WWII Russian soldier's monument.

Next, it was south to Venice, Italy, where we toured St. Mark's Cathedral and later rode in a gondola in one of the canals. But the best treat was yet to come, in the city of Florence. There, we visited museums and admired Michelangelo's magnificent sculpture of *The David*. I actually stood for at least a half-hour just viewing this piece of marble sculpture. It was so life-like. Equally impressive was Michelangelo's last *Pieta*, sculpted when he was in his mid-eighties. Despite its somewhat unfinished appearance, it still movingly depicts the Biblical story of Joseph of Arimathea cradling the limp body of the dead Christ.

After Florence, we traveled south to Rome for a three-day stopover. I was particularly impressed by the beauty and enormity of St. Peter's Cathedral, Michelangelo's depiction of the *Creation of Adam* in the Sistine chapel, and the beautiful *Pieta* he created at age twenty-three, now housed in St. Peter's. At another point, we viewed his sensitive painting of the Holy Family. Prior to having observed any of his artworks Michelangelo was just a name to me. After admiring what I was privileged to see in Rome, and later Florence, I quickly began to admire his enormous talent.

From Rome, we headed north along Italy's western coast, stopping only to take pictures of the leaning tower of Pisa. Yes, it was still leaning when I last saw it. From Italy, we traveled through Monte Carlo, Monaco, and southern France, our destination being Barcelona, Spain. After seeing where Columbus embarked for the New World, we made a side train trip to Madrid. There, we attended a bull fight and enjoyed its initial pageantry. But when the killing began, we soon left; it was just too brutal to watch. More encouraging were Spain's culinary treats, including cold vegetable soup (or gazpacho) and seafood paella. Ruth now makes a great gazpacho with my home-grown tomatoes. After Spain, it was on to Paris, the City of Light.

There, we visited the Louvre, attended the Follies Bergère, toured Versailles, and lunched high up in the Eiffel Tower. Phil reminded me recently of an amusing episode at that lunch. He said that when I ordered milk to drink, our waiter was so amused that he and his colleagues all burst out laughing. Speaking of amusement, when I viewed the *Mona Lisa* she smiled at me, just like the song said she would. For me, equally impressive among the artwork at the Louvre was the *Winged Victory of the Samothrace*. Created around the 2nd century BC, it represents the Greek Goddess of Victory, called Nike. Yes, that's the same word used by the company that makes Michael Jordan's sneakers.

After Paris, the last leg of our journey was London. There, we visited Parliament, St. Paul's Cathedral, and watched the changing of the guard at Buckingham Palace. I bought my first turtleneck sweater made of Scottish wool. Occasionally, I still wear it. While it still itches, it keeps me warm. At the boarding house where we stayed, the lady manager was surprised when I asked for milk rather than coffee for breakfast. She fulfilled my request, but upon serving me she said, "And here is milk for the baby." So, when she asked me what we intended to do in London, I tried to sound more British. I replied, "Oh just tis, tat, and tuther." For a moment she seemed speechless, then we both burst out laughing.

Yes, it was an unforgettable experience to visit Western Europe. It certainly opened my eyes to the beauty, sensitivity, and meaning of its art and culture. But as we re-entered New York Harbor in early September and I spied the Statue of Liberty once again, tears came to my eyes. It was good to be home. As a boss of mine, who used to travel the world on business, once said, "There is no place in the world like America." Aren't we fortunate?

Curiosity

Curiosity killed a cat, but satisfaction brought it back.
Sometimes old adages bear fruit — you get to experience
what you think about or what has perked your curiosity. On
two occasions during my early high school years, I became
curious about the origin of different things I had either read
about or seen in pictures. For example, I wondered what
prompted Daniel Defoe to write his famous novel *Robinson
Crusoe*. And I was truly fascinated by the pictures of many
thirteen-foot-tall stone statutes of human-like figures which
appeared in my high school geography book. Apparently,
their origin and purpose had confused historians.

Each figure weighed around fourteen tons and was located
on a strip of land called Easter Island, thousands of miles
from any other land in the South Pacific. Was Defoe's book
based on a true story? And who built those huge statues and
why?

Time and good fortune gave me my answers when I
was working as the Assistant Commercial Attaché at the
American Embassy in Santiago, Chile, from 1967 to 1970.
On a wall map in my office, each day, I looked at the many
islands out in the Pacific and the name of one small island,
nearly 500 hundred miles west of Santiago, always caught
my attention. It was called Robinson Crusoe Island, named

after the story itself. Until the late 20th century, it had been called Juan Fernandez Island. Then its name was changed to encourage tourism. Defoe's famous novel was about a man shipwrecked on a small, deserted island, describing how he survived. The story was inspired by the true-life experiences of a former privateer, later a Royal naval officer from Scotland, Alexander Selkirk, who had been marooned on Robinson Crusoe Island.

Selkirk's experience began when he was forced to leave his ship, the Cinque, and was marooned on Juan Fernandez Island in 1704, for four years and eight months. His abandonment began because Selkirk had initially asked to be left on the island. His reason was he believed the Cinque was leaking and was going to sink. In fact, a few months later, the Cinque did sink off the shores of Colombia, but Selkirk obviously was not on it.

When he was finally rescued, he had actually forgotten how to talk. When marooned, Selkirk had been allowed to take with him only his sea chest which contained the following items: a musket, powder, bullets, a hatchet, a knife, a cooking pot, a Bible, some bedding, and clothing. When Selkirk had a change of mind about being left and tried to re-board, his captain refused to allow him back.

I knew none of this background when I boarded a small two-engine aircraft that flew me for a week's vacation out to Juan Fernandez Island. As I recall, the flight took about three hours and our plane landed on a small mountain some 3,000 feet above the Pacific. A taxi drove me to a small hotel near the ocean. The rest of my stay was spent either sleeping late, swimming, or hiking in the nearby hills. Most of the nearly 900 people living there reside in cottages close to the

Pacific. When hiking in the hills, you frequently run into descendants of the wild goats that Selkirk used for food and clothing. They had been left there earlier by Spanish sailors to be used for food whenever they had occasion to return to the island for food and water.

As I recall, the small hotel where I stayed served good seafood, especially the spiny lobster. Unlike the Maine lobster, the spiny lobster does not have the two large claws, one called the pincher and the other the crusher. Yet they do contain the succulent meat many of us have enjoyed in the States. In fact, the lobster we are familiar with on the northeastern seaboard does not exist anywhere else in the world. Of course, spiny lobsters are found throughout the world.

As I neared the end of my stay on the island, I remembered that within ten days or so I would have to entertain a group of eight to ten American businessmen who were coming to Chile to sell medical equipment and supplies. I thought, why not treat them to a lobster dinner? The problem was I did not have sufficient funds with me to pay what the local fishermen charged per lobster. Then I had a brainstorm. I had been fortunate to remember to bring a couple of bottles of excellent Scotch with me for barter purposes. In addition to the available cash I had, I offered to throw in the Scotch to get twenty spiny lobsters. As I had hoped, the fisherman agreed. Therefore I brought the lobsters back with me to Chile and kept them in water. So, a few days later, I was able to entertain my visitors with an excellent lobster dinner.

As an added treat for the visitors, I had invited a featured guest, Dr. Jorge Kaplan. He was the second man, after Dr. Christian Barnard, to successfully transplant a human heart.

Ultimately, I owe the Scots a debt of thanks for supplying us with such a wonderful dinner.

The mysteries surrounding Easter Island, mentioned earlier, were finally solved to my satisfaction during my vacation in 1968. The island is thought to have been originally settled in the seventh or eighth century by Polynesians but was not discovered by Europeans until the Dutch explorer, Jacob Roggeveen, landed there on Easter Sunday in 1722 — hence the name. Chile annexed it in 1888 but continued to use the Spanish name for the island, Isla de Pascua, or Easter Island. The Polynesian name for the island is still referred to as Rapa Nui.

Rapa Nui is fourteen miles long and seven miles wide and was formed by now extinct volcanoes. It is located 2,300 miles due west of Santiago and 1,100 miles east of the nearest Pacific island. That Island is also well known and is called Christmas Island. It is famous as the final refuge for the Mutiny on the Bounty crew. It is about 2,500 miles from the former French province of Tahiti.

During my visit, I learned that the wide, well-kept runway for planes on Easter Island was partially financed by the U.S. Government. The reason is that when the French were doing their nuclear experiments in the Pacific, our Government wanted to observe French activity and results.

The real mystery of Easter Island has long been, who actually erected the nearly 900 statues, or Moai as they are called, and why? They resemble the upper bodies and faces of humans and have top knots for hats. Supposedly all were erected between 1100 and 1650 and represent spirits or ancestor-chiefs who were considered to have been descended from gods. During my visit to the island, I learned that the statues were sculpted from volcanic rock. They were then pulled by up to 40 men, using wooden rollers, to their temple platforms, or Ahu. I was amazed at how they were able to lift the 10- to 14-ton statues without the aid of a machine. Apparently, the cantilever technique was used.

During my stay, I learned that the first Polynesian settlers on the island had left no archaeological record of their origins or language. As I toured the island, I realized how difficult it must have been for so many men to have pulled the finished statues from where they were sculpted, to their final positioning elsewhere on the island. My tours of the island proved that there were still a few large trees standing, although the original forest-like nature of the island had disappeared. The rocks around the shore formed a private swimming pool for me, one that protected me from any nearby sharks.

On the way back to Santiago, our small two-engine plane flew a few hundred miles above the calm-looking Pacific Ocean. Then suddenly my curiosity hit me. What would be our chances of survival if our plane went down? I asked the pilot what he thought. His reply wasn't too encouraging. Our chances were almost zero. A few moments later, the two engines in our plane stopped for several seconds and then started up again. When I asked the pilot what had happened, he said he was merely switching from one gas tank to the other, nothing to worry about. After that brief experience, I looked forward to our early arrival back in Santiago.

Chapter V

People Are a Gift

As we arrive at our last season in life, we may be inclined to look back over the years to determine what we have learned or to reflect on the purpose of life itself. If we are fortunate, we may realize that age should not keep us from learning something new. This is what happened to me one Sunday afternoon as my wife Ruth and I were enjoying a pleasant luncheon at a local restaurant. I suddenly understood the joy and significance of an occurrence that had repeated itself throughout my life. I began to appreciate why it is so uplifting to be nice to people one doesn't even know.

This sudden awakening surprised me, primarily because its truth had been staring me in the face for many years. Yet until that moment I had failed to recognize it. On the Sunday in question, it happened as I was speaking to our waiter. As we were conversing, this truth about relationships suddenly dawned on me. I am referring to people whom we may meet on the street, on a subway, in a restaurant, or even in church. Our lives are full of such encounters. And now I can fully appreciate why I have always felt so encouraged by them. Simply stated, I finally realized the reason for my sudden enjoyment. I was concentrating on another person's life; my thoughts were no longer focused solely on myself.

However brief those encounters may be, I now realize why they have consistently provided me with a sense of enjoyment. No, it is not the result of my trying to be a good neighbor, as essential as that is. Rather, it is because I am concentrating entirely on the interests of another person rather than myself. Sometimes during these brief encounters, I may even be making a future friend and somehow lifting his or her burdens. I can now go away from these unexpected encounters feeling spiritually buoyed. I believe this buoyancy phenomenon is partly what Scripture was attempting to tell us in Jesus' Sermon on the Mount, where He proclaimed, *If you love those who love you, what reward have you? And if you greet your brother only, what do you do more than others?*[1]

People come in all shapes and sizes. Their attitudes vary depending upon their beliefs, prejudices, or heritage. Consequently, whether we are inclined to agree or disagree with them is not as important as recognizing how empty our lives would be without them. We need to appreciate that without other people, our world would be an empty place. There would be no such thing as human relationships. Furthermore, it is always wise to respect others, to avoid judging them. Provided we bear these thoughts in mind, we are frequently given the opportunity to experience the wonderful richness that can come from new relationships, regardless of their duration. As Scripture tells us, *To the extent that you did it to one of these brothers of mine you have done it to me.*[2]

---

1   Matthew 5:46-47
2   Matthew 25:40

Saying Goodbye

At the close of Act II, Scene 2, in Shakespeare's *Romeo and Juliet*, Juliet says to her loved one, "Parting is such sweet sorrow. That I shall say good night till it be morrow." This past summer provided me more than one occasion to recall Juliet's romantic words. I have said goodbye, sometimes figuratively, sometimes personally, to individuals I greatly love or respect. In different ways each adieu has tugged on my heart strings, yet each has also emphasized the value and integrity of a good relationship. Though many of us have experienced the pleasure of bidding adieu to someone we love or admire, our goodbyes are often accompanied by a sense of sadness; a special feeling that provides a poignancy to the moment. The following three instances from the summer of 2022 helped to remind me of this truth.

The most recent involved the visit of four granddaughters and their mother from Connecticut and my oldest daughter from Virginia, accompanied by her daughter. Unfortunately our son and his family were on a scheduled visit to North Carolina at the time.

COVID-19 had kept the Connecticut crew from visiting for almost three years, while also limiting visits from my eldest daughter. Finally, we all got together. So, for four nights and parts of five days, the Turner household became a women's boarding house for young and old alike. Nonetheless, everyone slept well.

During this period, I was reminded once again of how young women like to stay up late and sleep late. Curtains in their sleeping areas were shut tight most of the morning to avoid any light that might disrupt their beauty sleep. Daytime activities included a morning at our local swimming club, shopping at Tysons Corner, bowling, and side trips to the grocery store. Ruth's delicious spaghetti, my home-grown tomatoes, and even pizza were greatly appreciated at mealtimes. And when the girls were not playing Monopoly®, watching Dr. Pol (the famous TV veterinarian), or merely chatting with their grandparents, computers or iPads were in constant use.

Of prime importance to Ruth and me was the opportunity to once again get to know our lovely granddaughters. Finally, we would have the opportunity to see how much they had developed in mind and spirit over the past three years. All were and are doing beautifully. Two are to enter college this fall, two are about to return to high school, and the youngest, thirteen-year-old Bethany, is a jewel in the making. Her high spiritedness, her grace, and her amazing intellectual abilities charmed us all. She even trounced her sisters and cousin at Monopoly®.

Equally important, Ruth and I had a rewarding occasion to pull down some emotional walls that had developed between us and our daughters. Time, COVID-19, and distance had, unfortunately, raised them. Fortunately, hurt feelings were calmed and loving respect was reinforced. The whole process reaffirmed my belief that provided people love one another and seek to draw closer together, love always finds a way.

As our entire reunion drew to a close, daughters and grandchildren having to return to their respective homes, the sweet sorrow of goodbyes had to be exchanged. When would we be in communication again? My heart weighed heavily on me as that thought continued to pass through my mind. Fortunately, subsequent prayer and reassuring phone talks helped to lift this burden. We have said goodnight until the morrow.

While musing on the subject of saying goodbye, an obituary caught my attention in early August. It was an announcement of the passing of the iconic sports announcer, Vince Scully. For several decades he was the voice of the Los Angeles Dodgers baseball team, as well as other major sporting events. But it was in his work for the Dodgers that Vince became so highly acclaimed. On rare occasions, I listened to him announce Dodger games. In doing so, I was impressed by his acumen, his sincerity, and especially his ability to reach out with his comments to his thousands of fans. He made it seem as if he was actually talking personally with each of them. Dodger fans so enjoyed his ability to connect with them.

Even when they attended an actual Dodger game, many would bring portable radios merely to listen to Vince describe the game. They so welcomed his philosophical way of describing things they could identify with. How does one explain such loyalty, such sensitivity?

I believe his ability to so ably reach the hearts of his fan base can best be illustrated by his manner of saying goodbye. He retired at age 90 in 2018, immediately following his last game as a broadcaster. In his closing remarks, he thanked his thousands of Dodger fans for their support, those at home and those in the stands. Then he offered a prayer even Shakespeare would have been hard pressed to improve upon. Vince said:

> "God give you for every storm, a rainbow.
> For every tear a smile.
> For every care, a promise, and a blessing in each trial.
> For every problem life sends, a faithful friend to share."

My final goodbye of the summer was to my doctor, who is retiring from his medical practice. The following is a letter I wrote to him, thanking him for his wonderful care in our years together.

> "Dear Friend, after 33 years of your wise guidance concerning my health and fitness needs, I must now bid farewell to my grand physician, Dr. Jack! How can I truly accomplish this with grace? How does one suddenly divorce themselves from their reliance on his professional capability and humane concern? Over these sometimes-challenging years, you have demonstrated that you are an accomplished medical practitioner and humanitarian worthy of the highest acclaim. Accordingly, how is it possible for me to permanently remove this vital part of my past life, leaving me with only grateful, respectful memories?
>
> "Your Hippocratic Oath proclaims that, *One who is a physician should devote himself to the benefit of his patient and do no harm to him.* In our experience

together, you have certainly fulfilled this grand commitment. I have always been well advised and cared for throughout our many years of relationship.

"There have been instances where your wisdom was not only timely but essential to my quality of life, especially as I began to age. You have enabled me to retain a continuing, healthy lease on life. How can I possibly forget our relationship?

"There are other fine physicians in the Washington, D.C. area, and I am hopeful of finding one who will take me on, even at my soon to be 90 years of age. The truth is, however, I will instinctively compare them to you, as a wise and perceptive practitioner of medicine. Therefore, the end of our relationship, at least in my mind, can never truly occur. There will be the ever-present reminder of your encouraging and effective assistance. In this context, my dear Dr. Jack, you will always remain a treasured part of my life.

"My blessings and good fortune to you and your loved ones; may your servanthood, in whatever manner, continue. And may many others continue to recognize you, as I have, as a servant who does justice, loves kindness, and walks humbly with their God.

"I will always hold you in highest regard, and now in sincerest appreciation I bid you farewell, sincerely, Roger Turner."

Gifted Persons

Customarily, we consider that a person who is gifted is a person who has outstanding intelligence and is extremely skilled in some field. Often, we attribute to them the capacity for exceptional achievement, especially in such fields as science, mathematics, or the performing arts. By no means is this an exclusive listing, however, as there are other fields where individuals can rightfully be considered as gifted. High on my list would be the ability to provide spiritual leadership. In the stories that follow I describe three such gifted people, each of whom I have had the privilege of meeting. One was a minister, one was a disgraced-politician, and the third was a prison inmate. Here are their stories.

The minister I refer to was Dr. Richard Halverson, who for 24 years was a Presbyterian minister to churches from California to Washington, DC. He was also a former Chairman of the Board of World Vision, an organization designed to help the needy and to spread the Christian message of good will throughout the world. Despite these marvelous accomplishments, Dr. Halverson received even greater praise for his 14 years of spiritual leadership as Chaplain to the United States Senate, 1981-1995. In his Senate office, I was privileged to discuss with him his views on the importance of one's faith.

During our meeting, Dr. Halverson described his belief as to why many successful politicians sought his spiritual counsel. He said, "At first it was surprising. Rightfully, they had gained wide public recognition. Despite this, they continued to experience a sense of emptiness or lack of meaning in their lives. They couldn't appreciate why their success had not translated into the sense of fulfillment they had anticipated." Dr. Halverson then described how he would try to encourage them.

Typically, he would begin by saying, "Consider yourself a zero. All zeros put together will still only equal zero. So instead, imagine yourself placing a one in front of the zero; then you have something. Make Jesus Christ number one in your life and then you have something in abundance." As he explained this approach, I immediately thought of how frequently today our culture uses a numerical scale of 1 to 10 to describe success, or even ultimate value. We equate 10 as being the ultimate number.

As Dr. Halverson's wisdom suggests, our human efforts are often blinded by a search for fame, fortune, and fun—the cares of the world if you will. Far too often, these goals draw us to a god of our own making rather than to the true Source, the God of Scripture. Spiritually, we remain at zero. It is only when we learn to put that one in front of our zero that we begin to experience the abundance Christ promised, "I came that they might have life and might have it abundantly."[3]

The second gifted person I will describe is Charles Colson, the disgraced politician. From my relationship with him I learned another lesson. True abundance in life sometimes

3   John 10:10

can only come through service to our Savior. Colson is often remembered as the hatchet man in the White House of former President Nixon. He conceived many of the "dirty tricks" designed to further Nixon's political agenda. But he was sent to prison in 1974 for his criminal break-in of Daniel Ellsberg's office. It was a dirty trick designed to discredit Ellsberg for having released the top-secret Pentagon Papers. When Colson was released from jail in 1975, he rededicated his life to Christian religious work, most famously, his founding of Prison Fellowship. Today, its volunteers are active in prisons and jails throughout the world, bringing the hope and good news of God's grace to thousands of lost men and women.

In 1993, it was my good fortune to travel with Colson and five successful businessmen to visit the state prisons in India, Indonesia, Taiwan, Hong Kong, and Portuguese Macao. During our amazing trip, Colson spoke to thousands of inmates and to hundreds of religious volunteers. He described how Christ can change lives as He had done for him.

Colson also confessed that from youth he had had three goals to lift him to political success in life: to get a good education, to become financially independent, and to gain influence in the highest corridors of power. He had succeeded. He was working for the most powerful man in the world, the President. But when the Watergate scandal erupted, the gods of Colson's success began to fail him.

One day, in the midst of the Watergate crisis, he said:

> "I was sitting in my White House office, gazing out the window, wondering why I felt such emptiness in my life. Here I was, near to the most powerful man

in the world, but my striving for success no longer had meaning for me. Why, I wondered, hadn't the achievement of my goals provided me with the sense of fulfillment I sought? In time, I began to realize that the answer was that I needed God in my life, but I didn't know where or how to find Him.

"A good friend urged me to begin my search by reading my Bible. He also loaned me his copy of C.S. Lewis' *Mere Christianity* to help me recognize why my pride and striving had turned me from the Source. I began to realize that I had been worshiping a god of my own making, my goals, rather than the God of Scripture. If I were to ever find the fulfillment I sought, it would have to be by turning my life over to His Son, Jesus Christ. Almost imperceptibly I began to do so, until I realized I had been born again. Then I began to realize that God was calling me to bring the good news of Christ to others. His call filled the spiritual void in my life."

During our 1993 trek through the Orient, Colson often would refer to the fact he had been a Marine. And occasionally, he spoke about a visit with a group of Marine officers at Camp Lejeune, North Carolina. The subject of his talk was ethics. At the end of his talk one officer stood up and asked the following question: "Mr. Colson, which is the greater quality, loyalty, or integrity?" Colson's response was, "The answer is easy, even by the Marine code of *simper fidelis*, always faithful. It is integrity, because without integrity, loyalty can mislead you." Colson had obviously learned this from his White House years.

Colson had been misled by his misguided loyalty to President Nixon, but that painful experience had finally taught him the true meaning of integrity. It is loyalty to the Father in Heaven. When that is one's standard, loyalty does not become an issue. Through his understanding of this truth Colson had changed his way of thinking. It had made him a gifted person.

Until his death in 2017, Colson was a highly sought-after speaker and evangelist, not solely to inmates, but others who needed Christ in their lives, especially students.

The prison inmate I mentioned earlier was Towanda, a 23-year-old African American woman. When I met her, she was in Arlington Jail for violation of her parole, having been convicted of credit card fraud. She had already served two years of her initial sentence in different jails, but having violated her parole, she was expecting to serve three additional years.

As we talked, I could see that she was angry. When I asked her why, she replied, "Because God has not answered my prayers, to gain early release to care for my two young boys." I described for her that there were different types of prayer, and that God knows what we need before we ask, although we don't always get our wishes.

The following week Towanda was scheduled for final sentencing. Consequently, I suggested that even though she might continue to pray for early release, I urged her to concentrate on the following gospel verse, *Do not become anxious about how or what you will speak … For it is not you who speak, but it is the Spirit of your Father who speaks in you.*[4] In this context I suggested she devote her daily prayer

---

4   Matthew 10:19-20

toward the Holy Spirit, asking Him for the right words to say to the judge and then to trust in God's faithfulness. At each of her two earlier jails, she had been housed in cells with nonbelievers. Yet by the time she was transferred, she had brought each of her former cellmates to accept Christ. "Clearly, God was using you," I said. As tears suddenly began to trickle from her eyes, she nodded in agreement.

A week later when I visited Towanda she was overjoyed. She explained, "I took your advice and each day prayed for the guidance of the Holy Spirit. When I repeated my prayer to the judge, she replied, 'Young lady, I was about to sentence you to the three more years. But after hearing your words today, I realize you have changed. Consequently, I am reducing your sentence to only nine months.' As I was being escorted from the courtroom, the prosecuting attorney suddenly walked up to me and apologized for having to send me back to jail. He was only fulfilling his required duties. He then admitted that, after listening to me, that I no longer belonged in jail. I was a changed person."

A month passed, during which time I had become a full-time Chaplain at Fairfax Jail. Out of curiosity, I called to find out what had happened to Towanda. A deputy informed me that she had been released. Yes, I think it fair to say that, like Dr. Halverson and Chuck Colson, Towanda was a gifted person.

Purposes of the Heart

As a boy it never occurred to me to be concerned about the purposes of my heart. I knew I had a heart. I could feel it beating faster when I was out of breath from running or jumping. However, that soon passed from my thoughts as I was busy exploring my world and getting into mischief; doing many things young boys customarily do. But as I have passed through the different seasons of life, from childhood to old age, I have gained increased respect for my heart's purposes. My reading of Scripture, as well as poetry, always seems to confirm that the heart has emotions.

Writers of poetry and novelists who write love stories consistently refer to the heart as the source of a person's emotions, especially where their love for others resides. At this point in life, I can certainly identify with such feelings. But when one comes right down to it or appreciates the heart's true purpose, it has but two functions: the physical and the spiritual.

Clearly, the physical aspect of the heart is essential to life itself. It supplies lifesaving oxygen to the rest of the body. When that ceases, a person must die. Speaking spiritually however, for those who believe in the transcendent, or God I consider one's heart is their lifeline to the Creator, the Source of all life itself. As it says in Scripture, *Watch over your heart with all diligence, for from it flow the springs of life.*[5]

---

5   Proverbs 4:33

When a person immerses themselves in the daily reading of Scripture, they discover that many of its most important passages consistently reference the heart. Consider the following:

(1) God hardened Pharaoh's heart before permitting Moses to free the Ancient Israelites;[6]

(2) The first Great Commandment begins by commanding that we love God with all our heart;[7]

(3) When God chose David to replace King Saul, he explained that He considered David's heart, not his appearance, in making the selection;[8]

(4) Jesus, when describing where the source of a person's real treasure in life is to be found, explains, *Where your treasure is there will your heart be also.*[9]

(5) In His Sermon on The Mount, Jesus blesses the pure in heart, promising that, "*They will see God.*"[10]

Yet Jesus also warns his disciples that the heart can be the source of spiritual decay. And on one occasion, He explained why the Pharisaic tradition of ritual hand washing exposed their hypocrisy. As He said, "This people honor Me with their lips, but their heart is far from Me."[11] He also warned that, "From within, out of the heart of men, proceed the evil thoughts of this world."[12]

I interpret His thoughts here to mean that such thinking will cause spiritual heart failure in a person, because the life-saving blood of Christ's sacrifice has ceased to carry the

6   Exodus 7:3
7   Deuteronomy 6:5
8   1 Samuel 16:7
9   Matthew 6:21
10 Matthew 5:8
11 Mark 7:6
12 Mark 7:21

essential oxygen required. At times, I have also wondered about similar failure in my own heart. When reaching that point, I find that it is only through prayer and obedience to God's commandments that my heart can be resuscitated.

To better recognize the parallel between spiritual and physical heart failure, we need to appreciate how theologians and ministers view the heart. They consider it the source of our will. In Jesus' day for example, little was known about the physical properties or the function of the heart. It was considered to be the center of a person's body, the seat of their life, and especially their will. In a theological context, this meant the heart was the primary influence over our mind, soul, and spirit. It was the source of our ability to reason, question, meditate, and to motivate.

Today, even though we know a great deal more about the heart, we need to be alert to Scripture's interpretation of its purposes. We need to put on Jesus' sandals so to speak. For example, we should not envision Him as saying, "You should love one another as your brain has loved you." Therefore, when it comes to avoiding spiritual heart failure, it would be wise to put away our medical books and look instead at how to succeed in fulfilling the heart's purposes, as reflected in Scripture.

Let me illustrate this thought. Years ago, when our children were nearing college age, I substituted for my wife at a PTA meeting on college admission procedures. Our speaker that evening advised on the utility of submitting letters of recommendation by using the following example. It was an amazing, moving story that concerned a rising high school senior and his school's janitor.

Apparently, right before school opened in the fall, the student learned that the janitor had lost his wife of 40 years.

Understandably, he was lonely and depressed, as he had no other family. The student made it a point to arrive 15 minutes early to school each morning, throughout the fall semester. He wanted to console and encourage the janitor. Then as time approached to apply for early college admission, the janitor wanted to help. Somehow, he had learned that his young friend wanted to go to Harvard. Although the young student had a good academic record, it was not outstanding; other applicants might look better by comparison.

So, upon learning of his young friend's desire, the janitor went to the school counselor and asked to help her prepare a letter of recommendation to the Harvard Admissions Office. Together, they drafted a letter and sent it forward. Several weeks passed until finally a reply came. And what an unusual reply it was. It included two free roundtrip airfare passages to Cambridge, one for the janitor and one for the student. When they arrived in Cambridge, Massachusetts, a special ceremony took place. First the janitor was given a humanitarian award and the student was given early admission to Harvard. Four years later, he graduated with honors. Clearly, the life-saving spirit of Jesus' blood flowed through the student's heart. For as Scripture has promised, *If we walk in (his) light ... the blood of Jesus ... cleanses us.*[13]

Another true story further emphasizes the spiritual importance of a person's heart. Our story concerns the great evangelist, Dr. Billy Graham, as well as America's most renowned theologian of the 20th century, Reinhold Niebuhr. When Niebuhr was asked to evaluate Billy's revivalism, he replied that it was too simplistic. Niebuhr's concern was that it would accentuate the anti-religious

---

13 1 John 1, 7

prejudices of enlightened people. The effect would be to divert public attention and resources from pressing social problems, including racial prejudice. Niebuhr opined that it was a mistake to claim that every human problem could be solved by a personal encounter or relationship with Jesus.

Dr. Graham made no attempt to defend himself or to directly justify his evangelistic approach. In fact, he thanked Niebuhr for helping him to better apply his Christian message to social problems. But he expressed an additional, important thought concerning his evangelistic views. He said, "I don't think you can change the world, with all its lusts and hatred and greed, until you change men's hearts. Men must love God before they can truly love their neighbors."

In closing, I will use one more true-life story. I believe it illustrates how a willful heart can ensure a person's faithfulness. The story concerns the great English runner and Olympic champion, Eric Liddell, who later became a missionary to China. It was during the 1924 Paris Olympics, where Liddell was one of the favorites to win the 100-meter dash. His faith compelled him to pull out of the race because he would have had to run qualifying heats on a Sunday, the Christian Sabbath Day, a day of rest for Christian believers like Liddell.

But he did eventually earn his gold medal in a different race when another member of the British track team gave up his place to Liddell in the 400-meter race. Liddell not only won his preliminary heat, but he captured the gold medal as well, twice breaking the world record for that distance. Liddell's explanation was, "When I run I believe I am pleasing Him." Yes, Liddell had a heart for God.

Responding to a Challenge

Conventional wisdom suggests that responding to a challenge requires our being called to confront or deal with changed circumstances. This can happen on any day, to any person. It can be a dramatic challenge requiring a response of great moral, spiritual, or physical courage. It can be a very mundane or routine challenge involving commonly experienced circumstances. Or it can even be caused by something we regret, or something we are not looking forward to, an exam for example. Regardless of the challenge, the critical issue is how do we respond? Are we able to meet it or will we permit it to overwhelm us? For some, just being able to live a fulfilling daily life is, in effect, a challenge.

In order to further explore these thoughts, I would like to begin with a very common challenge– being a good neighbor. The circumstances in question occurred recently and involved my wife and a next-door neighbor named Julia. She and her family had recently moved into a house across the street from ours. On a recent Saturday, she had been working in the yard most of the day with her husband. Soon it was dinner time, and she was running late. Dinner was to include brownies, a special treat for her husband. She rushed into her kitchen, and then realized that she had no egg with which to make the brownies. It was too late to get to the store and back. So, she walked across to our house and asked my wife for an egg. Ruth gladly obliged her.

Of course, borrowing an egg is not an unusual occurrence; it can happen in any neighborhood, on any day. Julia responded to that challenge. Actually, so did Ruth, by supplying Julia the egg. Now let's contrast this occurrence with a more unique example. It took place on the football field of Columbia University in the early 1930s. It involved a father, his son, and the great Columbia football coach, Lou Little. His team won the Rose Bowl in 1934 and was holding tryouts for the 1935 season.

One of the young men trying to make the team was a rising senior. We'll call him Jeff. He wasn't a terrific athlete, but he had tremendous enthusiasm and loved the game of football. When the coach made the final roster for the team, Jeff was included, but just barely. It was his enthusiasm that had convinced the coach to put him on the team, primarily to keep up team spirits.

Another characteristic of Jeff's was his devotion to his father. So, at almost every practice, Jeff brought him and introduced him to the coach and players. They all enjoyed meeting him. In time he became a fixture on the sidelines. Sadly, at mid-season Jeff's father died. Coach Little then called Jeff into his office to console him and promised that if there was anything he could do, Jeff only need ask.

A few more weeks passed, and Jeff had yet to play a single down. Then it was time for the final home game, with Columbia's traditional rival, West Point. Prior to the game Jeff went to see Coach Little and reminded him of his earlier promise. He then asked the coach to allow him to play in the game.

After consulting with his assistants, Coach Little agreed to put Jeff into the game for the opening kickoff and then planned to immediately remove him. The coach's thinking was that Jeff couldn't do much harm on a single play.

Not only did Jeff do no harm, on the opening kickoff, he made a touchdown-saving tackle. Surprisingly, he remained in the game the entire first half, playing with an ability that seemed to belie his limited skills. Jeff continued to be in the game during entire the second half and actually made a game-saving interception to preserve Columbia's victory. Once the referee's gun signaled the end of the game, Jeff's teammates swarmed around him, hoisting him to their shoulders and carrying him off the field.

In the locker room later, Coach Little congratulated Jeff. Then taking him aside, the coach asked, "Jeff how did you play the way you did today? I had no idea you had such hidden talent. What possessed you?" Jeff smiled and said, "Coach there is something I need to tell you. My father had been blind for several years. So, at today's game, it was the first time he ever got to see me play. I just wanted to do my best for him." Yes, Jeff certainly responded to his challenge; he rose above it.

Another example of responding to a challenge brings to mind the courageous leadership of Winston Churchill, Britain's Prime Minister during World War II. His nation faced a severe crisis shortly after the British and French armies were forced to evacuate the Continent of Europe at Dunkirk, in June 1940. This near disaster was followed in September by Hitler's order for the daily bombing of Britain. Hitler's hope was to persuade the British to sue for peace on Nazi terms.

During this period, Churchill chaired a hectic cabinet meeting at which Lord Fairfax rigorously tried to persuade the cabinet that Britain's cause was hopeless; that it should sue for peace. Churchill refused. Britain would fight on. His decision took great courage. Finally, America joined the war in December 1941, and the rest is history.

Earlier I mentioned that responding to a challenge could certainly occur in one's daily life. The following story is illustrative of just such a happening. It occurred during my junior year at Duke University, while I was playing in a touch football game for my fraternity. On the afternoon in question, an opposing player on the other team was raising havoc with our quarterback; nobody was blocking him out. Finally, our exasperated team captain asked me to switch from my normal end position to the blocking tackle position, in an effort to stop the opposing player. I agreed.

On the very next play after my change of positions, the opposing player rushed at me with great force, attempting to push me aside or knock me down. But I held my ground, determined not to let that happen. And so it continued for the remainder of the game. Although we were playing without any padding, our bodies continued to collide. The opposing player never got past me. But the next day, I could hardly move my shoulders and legs; they were so sore. When our captain came by to thank me, he said, "Boy, it was great to watch you two guys go at it yesterday. By the way, did you know that last year your opponent played freshman football on the Duke Team?" I replied, "No, but even if I had, it would only have made it a greater personal challenge to stop him."

By 2020, practically everyone became aware of the challenge presented by the COVID-19 pandemic. And eventually the TV newscasts made us aware of the many heroic tales of health care workers who responded to its challenges. Recently, I read an amazing tale[14] of how the State of Alaska's chief medical officer met the challenge. She had learned that almost one hundred years before, during the Spanish Flu Pandemic of 1918, hundreds of thousands had died. A tribal council chief recalled his grandmother's story of returning to her village after that pandemic and finding mainly children and dogs surviving and many smaller communities were nearly destroyed.

During the early days of the current pandemic, Alaska's largest hospital had only six testing swabs, and the state government had none. The medical officer described how they addressed the swab shortage by producing 3-D printed versions. Then when vaccines became available, health care workers traveled by bush plane, snow machine, and dog sled to deliver them to health care providers. With temperatures falling and indoor gatherings increasing, Alaska seemed like it would be overrun with the Delta variant. But then they were helped by almost 500 government-contracted health care workers from the lower forty-eight states. They were used to successfully dispense the vaccines throughout the state. Their efforts saved lives.

---

14 Anne Zink, "Alaska Did Well Early in the Pandemic. Then the Misinformation and Distrust Kicked In," *The Washington Post*, October 27, 2021, https://www.washingtonpost.com/opinions/2021/10/27/alaska-did-well-early-pandemic-then-misinformation-distrust-kicked/

The pandemic reminds Americans again of how we are all members of the same nation. This concept must continue to remind each of us that we need one another. This must continue to be the case if we are going to thrive as a nation. Regardless of political affiliation, religious belief, or race, we must remain willing to help one another in need. This remains true, even though we are also correct to subscribe to our traditional belief in the individual's right to life, liberty, and the pursuit of happiness. Our togetherness is equally vital. Therefore, when challenges like the pandemic arise, we need to follow Alaska's and America's example — out of many we are still one — *E Pluribus Unum*. The founding Fathers believed that this represented our strength as a nation. It still applies.

Good Bosses

Conventional wisdom interprets the noun *boss* to mean a person in charge, such as an employer, manager, supervisor, or even a president. However, by itself, the term boss is limited unless it incorporates the quality of being an effective leader. In the *Oxford Dictionary* a leader is one of the terms used to define a boss. And personal experience convinces me that a good boss is also a good leader. He has the ability to encourage others to perform at a high level.

Furthermore, the encouragement of a good boss correlates with the ability to demonstrate concern for the people under his or her supervision. In this context, I consider it correct to say that good leaders are also effective communicators; they are adroit in influencing others to perform at a high level. As a general proposition, I believe they can accomplish this because they are sensitive to the concerns of others and have mastered the art of being good listeners. Conversely, an ineffective boss lacks the leadership qualities to get high performance levels from their subordinates. An ineffective boss, even when he believes he or she is leading, may find that he has no real influence and no real followers. Such a boss is wasting everyone's time.

It was during a summer college internship that I first began to recognize the importance of effective leadership. At that time, I was working in the jungle of central Venezuela by the Orinoco River. My responsibilities included helping to clear the dense forestation in order to make way for a water line to our encampment. The U.S. Steel Corporation was building an iron ore crusher by the river to harvest the high-quality iron ore and load it into boats destined for its steel mills in North America. During my brief internship, I befriended Al, the boss of the iron ore workers who were building the crusher.

As the boss, Al no longer had to lift the fifty-pound riveting guns or hold the red-hot bolts needed to help secure the huge iron beams of the crusher. What impressed me most about Al was his obvious ability to direct and supervise the construction. One day as we were talking, I asked him for some advice. I asked him what lessons he had learned that enabled him to rise to leadership of his dangerous, demanding profession. What made him so successful?

Al thought for a moment and then said, "Always keep a watch over your men, to ensure they never get careless ... In iron working, it is not unusual for one or two men to be killed or seriously injured because of carelessness." He explained that sometimes heavy pieces of steel can slip or a cable holding them can break and crush the worker. The pay is certainly commensurate with the dangerous work, but one must be vigilant about these dangers. In addition, he advised I should never put off until tomorrow what I could do today.

There is another method of distinguishing a good boss from an ineffective one. Once again, I can relate an example of a boss from my own experience. His name was Calvin Berlin, the best boss I ever worked for. I got to know Cal during my first Foreign Service assignment to Santiago,

Chile, 1967-1970. He was an able, compassionate leader, respected by staff and peers alike. Yet despite his popularity, he was humble, considerate, and a good listener. Equally important, he was knowledgeable in how to deal with mistakes, and I made some. There were times when I was disappointed in my performance; the mere thought of them weighed heavily on me. But once Cal arrived in Chile as my boss, things began to change.

Almost immediately, we formed a bond of friendship and mutual respect. This was greatly facilitated by his willingness to treat me as a person. Occasionally when I became confused and got down on myself over mistakes of judgment, he encouraged me. He explained that he had also experienced growing pains. During our conversations he explained that he had to work as an apprentice to pay his way through college and graduate school. During those times, he often became frustrated by mistakes he made in trying to prepare or finish wood pieces. Ultimately his boss, a master carpenter, took him aside to encourage him.

As I have previously indicated, the master carpenter explained that everyone makes mistakes, but it is not the mistakes, it's the ability to repair them that counts. I greatly welcomed Cal's advice and became much more effective in my work as a result. After my tour in Chile ended, I tried to keep track of Cal. He continued to receive ever more important promotions in the Foreign Service, reflecting his professionalism and his leadership. Although Cal passed away around 2012, I will always remember our time together and especially the lessons of leadership that he modeled for me.

Earlier, I suggested that the quality of leadership should always be a key component in defining what makes a good boss. I believe this is true in any profession, including the ministry. In my next example I include our former minister, John Yates. I distinctly remember how impressed I was with his preaching. He seemed to be able to draw people of all ages and beliefs to our church. Prior to his arrival, our church was seldom full. You could almost pick your own pew on any given Sunday. But in the forty years that John was our minister, our church continued to grow. We had to construct two new church buildings during his tenure. While one would never think of John as a boss, he would certainly qualify as a leader. As he always used to say, "Leadership is influence, the ability of one person to influence others to follow their lead."

In America's relatively brief history, we have had many good presidents or bosses. They knew how to lead (for example, men like Washington, Lincoln, and the two Roosevelts, Teddy and FDR). We also have had great leaders in other fields, including Martin Luther King, Jr. and Billy Graham in the spiritual arena. And like all successful bosses, they understood that America's people are its greatest natural resource, an asset without which America will cease to thrive. Good leadership remains essential to sustaining our nation.

An Enlightening Summer

It was a summer job that provided me the educational and cultural experiences I was seeking to help prepare for a career in foreign affairs. The job would be in a foreign country, where I could perfect my Spanish and learn about a foreign culture. The year was 1953, and the country was Venezuela. For three months I would be working at the U.S. Steel encampment by the Orinoco River in the jungle of central Venezuela. As previously noted, the corporation had discovered a large iron ore deposit there and was building an iron ore crusher to harvest the ore and then ship it to their steel mills in Pittsburgh. I would be classed as a punk, the iron worker's term for rookie or trainee.

At the time, Venezuela was governed by a military dictator, Carlos Perez Jimenez, and there seemed to be soldiers everywhere as our plane touched down at Maricaibo Airport just outside Caracas, the Venezuelan capitol. There I would board a smaller plane that would take me to my Orinoco River destination. Previously, I had been warned that the attitude of Venezuelan officials toward Yankees was somewhat anti-American; we had apparently earned a reputation of unfairness in our dealings with Latin countries.

At the airport I got an immediate sense of this disapproving attitude toward North Americans. It happened when I went to present my ticket for clearance to my connecting flight to the Orinoco. Despite speaking in Spanish, and with great courtesy, and being on time for my flight, I was prevented from boarding until moments before the flight's departure. The few other passengers had already been cleared and boarded much earlier. It all seemed like my first lesson in foreign affairs. My education had begun. I made no complaint, as I realized that in a foreign country it is always wise to follow local customs, regardless of how unreasonable they may seem.

The U.S. Steel encampment was like a small town, filled with double occupancy cottages, large communal restrooms, an enclosed cold shower facility, a mess hall with an adjoining recreation room containing ping pong and pool tables, an outdoor movie theatre, and a baseball field. The other residents were mostly iron workers from the United States. Other non-specialized workers were native Venezuelans who were temporarily housed nearby. Some of the American workers had actually purchased exotic birds like macaws and parrots as well as three-toed sloths from the locals and kept them outside their cottages.

My first job had nothing to do with the actual construction of the ore crusher. Rather, I was attached to a team of young local Venezuelans to clear a path through the jungle for a water line to our encampment. The work required using machetes to cut a pathway. I had heard stories that panthers and even huge anaconda snakes had been seen in the area, but I never saw any. Insects and bugs were another matter, as all kinds seemed to follow us wherever we worked. Fortunately, the tropical heat made me perspire profusely, so that when they landed on my face or arms my sweat seemed to act as a repellent. At the end of work each day, my shirt often had several dead insects attached to it.

But one day I had an encounter with a different kind of insect that I was unaware of, until a fellow worker pointed it out to me. While I was cutting down some bush-like forestation, my machete cut in half a twelve-inch, poisonous centipede. It had been climbing up the reverse side of the bush near my leg. As I recall, I stopped to look at the large black creature, with its many sharp, curved tentacles and wondered how close I had come to being bitten. Somewhat startled, I nonetheless picked up my machete and continued cutting the pathway, although I became more vigilant in viewing what I was chopping. Later, there was another encounter with wild insects that I vividly remember, primarily because I was bitten. It happened in the following manner.

On the day in question, I was helping the native workers clear a path when suddenly they stepped away from me. For a moment or so they began gesturing toward a location nearby. Then they came up to me and excitedly pointed to what looked like a large, grassy tunnel running parallel to the ground. They urged me to kneel down and crawl into it. In Spanish they seemed to be saying it would be very interesting. Wanting to retain my friendly relationship with them, I obliged but didn't see anything. "No hay nada aqui," I replied. Nonetheless, they urged me to go further into the burrow, which I did. That was until I suddenly came face to face with a huge nest of wild jungle wasps. Needless to say, I crawled out quickly while being attacked and bitten from all sides. After my escape, I couldn't help but notice the hearty laughter of the workers over my predicament. I was beginning to learn something about Venezuelan humor.

Rather than showing anger, I smiled, saying to myself *Fool me once, the joke's on me*. Thereafter, we all seemed to bond more closely. In fact, on those occasions when we played softball at night, we were actually teammates. I was the only non-Venezuelan on the team. The opposing team was made up of iron workers. My teammates seemed to enjoy my prowess with a bat and in time began to call me Quixote, after the naïve knight in Cervantes' famous novel. My teammates spoke no English, so we communicated in Spanish. My language ability seemed to increase commensurately as we bonded.

One afternoon following work, I went into the recreation room to watch the iron workers shoot pool. After watching for a time, I said to Sam, one of the workers, "I bet you can't miss that shot." The cue ball was sitting within a quarter inch of the seven ball, as the latter faced the side pocket. Sam asked me how much I was willing to bet, and I told him a dollar. Sam agreed and then proceeded to teach me a valuable lesson. He picked up his cue stick, chalked the tip, and aimed it directly at the balls, and then intentionally muffed his shot. Next, he held out his hand and I gave him a dollar. He smiled and said, "Never bet on something you cannot control." The result wasn't the type of education experience I was seeking that summer, but it taught me an extra-valuable lesson.

On weekends, some of the iron workers went water skiing in the Orinoco and invited me to join them. At first, I reminded them of the man-eating piranha and crocodiles that were known to inhabit parts of the river. They assured me that these creatures usually did not venture out in the deep center of the river, so it would be safe to ski there. I then agreed to accompany them but had no intention of doing any skiing. In fact, I had never previously attempted this sport. Once we got out into the river I watched as the men took turns. Then they urged me to try my luck and explained how easy it was to do. Finally, I agreed, and eventually was able to stay upright for a few minutes. I was surprised at how much fun it was. But once my turn was over, as I waited in the water for the boat to pick me up, I must admit I was more than a little bit concerned for my safety. Fortunately, nothing in the river seemed interested in me that day so I am here to relate this story.

As August ended, it was time to return to college. When my Pan Am flight took off for New York's Idyllwild Airport, I sat back in my seat and reflected on a truly educational summer. My Spanish had improved; my exposure to some of Venezuela's culture had been challenging, but enjoyable, and like Cervantes' hero, I could dream of future worlds to defend and conquer after graduation.

Special Games with a Special Person

Sometimes our lives can be so influenced by another person it actually helps to shape our life for the better. And when the subject of games and youth is raised, I invariably think of how fortunate I was to have had a grandfather like Ludavick Anderson, or "Gramps," as I affectionately called him. When he visited, not only did he teach me how to play different games, but he also taught me an even more valuable lesson. He set an example of how important it is to convey a sincere interest in others. In this brief snapshot, I will provide some background on his life as I remember it, and the games he taught me.

He was born in 1874, in the small village of Halmstad, located near the southwestern coast of Sweden, directly across from Denmark. At the age of eleven, he, his parents, and ten other siblings migrated to America, eventually settling in Springfield, Illinois. When he grew to manhood, Gramps stood about 5'7" tall, had wavy blonde hair, loved to listen to classical music, possessed a marvelous tenor voice, made baseball a hobby, and had a jovial spirit. He always seemed to wear a broad smile and enjoyed greeting friends and strangers alike. As he would often say, "Smile and the world smiles with you."

Like many children of immigrants, even today, Gramps was unable to complete his high school education. I often recall him saying, "Roger, what a wonderful thing it is to get a college education. You are so fortunate to have had this training. It will open many opportunities for you." When he shared such thoughts with me, I sensed it made him feel a little sad, owing to his own lack of education. It definitely limited his ability in the workforce of mid-western America.

While he never had the benefit of a full high school education, he never stopped trying to learn. Quite easily he learned to speak English fluently, without even a trace of a Swedish accent, except when he was suddenly surprised. On those rare occasions, he would express his surprise by using Swedish words. I must confess I enjoyed hearing him speak in Swedish and actually attempted to mimic his words. Once I actually did this for a Swedish friend of mine who interpreted them for me. I was somewhat confused afterwards as to the words' meaning, so I considered it best to stick to my own native tongue.

At fifteen, Gramps began work initially on the Pennsylvania Railroad as a brakeman. In the latter part of the 19th century, railroad cars had to be individually braked as they came into a station, whereas today, the train engineer uses a hydraulic system to automatically brake the train as it glides slowly to a stop. Over the course of the ensuing sixty years, Gramps rose from being a brakeman to becoming a valued express messenger. Eventually, he was hired by the New York Central Railroad, where he worked until his retirement in his late seventies. He was always proud of his life of hard work and sometimes when we greeted each other he would say, "Shake the hand of an iron worker."

An express messenger is a mailman who delivers and receives mail and freight while traveling in the freight car of a train. In Gramps' day, the railroad was a primary source for delivering goods from one state to another. Federal Express, including air freight, had yet to surface. During the late 19th and early 20th centuries, a messenger would customarily begin his work at night, leaving from one major rail hub en route to another. Along its route, his train made intermediate stops in smaller cities until it reached its final destination where he would overnight. The following day, he reversed the trip and returned to his original starting point. Throughout this roundtrip, he would continue to deliver and receive all kinds of mail, boxes, foodstuffs, and even live animals to workers waiting for his train at each temporary stop. In railroad parlance, such travel was referred to as a run.

As a teenager, I was privileged to make a run with Gramps from Cincinnati to Chicago and back. Here are some episodes I remember from that occasion. At one stop in Kankakee, Illinois, we took on a large pig. Throughout the rest of our trip to Chicago, I occasionally played with the pig, although it wasn't really playing as such. Rather, I was trying to pet him. I had never petted a live pig before. Every time I would touch his bristly back, he squealed loudly, as only pigs can do. When this happened, Gramps would burst out laughing. Later during the run, I felt hungry. Fortunately, we had just taken on some large boxes of cherries. They were and still are one of my favorite fruits. I am ashamed to admit that I committed some petty larceny that night by scrounging a few cherries for myself.

When Gramps wasn't busy doing inventory, we talked. He described an earlier run when he carried a live bear for a zoo. Unfortunately, there were also live chickens in nearby crates. Once the bear smelled them, he eventually broke free and had chicken for dinner. This allowed Gramps time to barricade himself behind some boxes. At the next stop the police and fire departments were called and corralled the bear. While my grandfather carried a pistol on all his trips, he never had to use it. After listening to the bear story (not "*Goldilocks and The Three Bears*," of course), I finally fell asleep on some surprisingly comfortable cardboard boxes. It's amazing how soft cardboard can feel when one is truly sleepy.

After we arrived in Chicago that night, we had to exit through the freight section of the train depot to reach our hotel. In the process, Gramps had to check in his pistol with railroad officials. While I waited for him, I became distracted by a strange hissing sound. It was coming from a small, partially enclosed wooden box cage resting nearby on the floor. As I watched, I observed that every time someone walked by or accidentally hit the box with their shoe, a large weasel popped his head out from his enclosure, menacingly barring his teeth, while hissing. The speed with which the weasel popped in and out of his enclosure amazed me. It was like he was shot out of a canon. For the first time I finally understood how the well-known nursery rhyme came to be written. You probably remember the words to it as, *Pop goes the weasel*.

While the run to Chicago and back to Cincinnati was a once in a lifetime experience, it cannot really express how much I enjoyed being with Gramps. He thoughtfully taught all his grandchildren how to play different card games. Consequently, I learned how much fun card playing could be, especially when bad weather prevented our playing outside. The fun was not only in being able to win, but more importantly, in learning how to acquire a card sense or strategy as to how cards are played.

The game that we played most often was called casino. It can easily include both adults and children. The object of the game is to earn twenty-one points before your opponents do. It usually required the dealing of several card hands to win, especially when we played with my brother and cousins. We actually played for an hour or two at a time. While we never attempted to play the adult game of bridge, the techniques I learned playing casino ultimately aided me in becoming a good bridge player. Three such techniques were: to always play by the rules, to keep track of what cards had been played, and to plan ahead before your turn came. Gramps enjoyed every game. I can still remember his laughing loudly when my brother bluffed me into thinking he held the big casino.

Today, as a grandfather myself, I am amazed at how kind Gramps was to spend so much time with us. By comparison, where my own eight granddaughters are concerned, I am humbled to even think of matching the patience he demonstrated. I believe tic-tac-toe was probably as close as I ever came to finding a game they truly enjoyed. Most were not old enough to learn bridge. When they grew older, of course, card games with an old grandfather didn't interest them as much.

By the time I reached adulthood, Gramps could no longer play games. At 85, senility had affected his keen mind and warm heart. He had to live in a nursing home. On his last night with us, I visited him. Surprisingly, he proved to be somewhat lucid. So, I asked him if there was anything he wanted me to tell the family. His reply was, "Just tell them I love them." By the next morning he had passed away.

Before closing this family story, I would be remiss if I did not suggest that Gramps' entire family is grateful that he came to America. Quite likely, each of us can credit some of our patience and good nature to the examples he set. Thanks Gramps! We'll always love you.

Chapter VI

Patriots and Politicians

In a republic, it is generally understood that patriots are citizens devoted to their country and are willing to support or defend it. They take pride in the principles their country represents. In theory, a politician may also be a patriot. But until that interest becomes apparent, he or she is customarily considered as someone who seeks to achieve political power within a governing body, *viz.* the presidency or the Congress. Ideally, where the concept of patriot and politician conflate, their leadership is trusted by a majority of the electorate. Some leaders are revered for their quality of patriotism, like a Washington, a Lincoln, a Roosevelt, or even a Reagan. They place their love of country and concern for its welfare above personal ambition or a narcissistic desire for power.

John Locke, the 17th century Scottish political philosopher, espoused the concept that the purpose of a government was to protect the people. As he explained, "A government exists to promote the public good, and to protect people's life liberty and property. Those who govern, (i.e., the politicians), must be elected by the society they are supposed to protect, and that society must enable the people to install a new government when necessary." At America's founding, our Constitution reflected Locke's approach to governing. In fact, Thomas Jefferson's Declaration of Independence closely mirrors some of Locke's words, especially Jefferson's famous preamble in his Declaration: *We hold these truths to be self-evident, that all men are created equal, that they are endowed by their Creator with certain unalienable rights, that among these are life, liberty, and the pursuit of happiness.* Lincoln agreed.

The Founding Fathers, men like Washington, Franklin, Jefferson, and several others, were certainly patriots as well as politicians. However, their leadership can be distinguished from many failed politicians of today by their civic virtue. This was characterized by a willingness to compromise their political self-interests for the betterment of the public good. Without this character virtue, their efforts to establish a unique republic would have failed. Our nation is anchored by America's two greatest documents, the *Declaration of Independence* and the *Constitution*. In some respects, the Founders were similar to the Biblical prophets of old. They spoke not just to their current history, the times in which they lived, but they also had a positive vision for the future.

In America today there are two major political parties, Democrats and Republicans. To the extent the *Constitution* permits, the party in power is expected to deal with the business of governing. Sometimes the party out of power acts in a bi-partisan manner, sometimes it is obstructionist. In the latter instance the obstructionists seek to gain advantage over the governing authority. This remains true regardless of who resides in the White House. Ideally, when the party in control of the White House leads in a non-partisan manner, and within its *Constitutional* parameters, the American people should benefit. When this fails, as was the case on January 6, 2021, it not only attacks the *Constitution*, but it also weakens our political tradition of a peaceful transfer of power.

Mere partisanship limits the ability of the party in power to govern, witness today's frequent gridlock in the Congress, especially over such issues as the budget or economy, gun control, and immigration. Far too often, the reason for these difficulties is the politician(s) in charge have failed to place the electorate's concerns ahead of their party's political interests, especially its chances for reelection. When this happens, the politician(s) have shed their patriot's cloak for their partisan benefit. Admittedly, the issues facing politicians can be difficult, especially where strong opinions differ, such as in the cases of abortion and voting rights.

In February 2023, *The Washington Post* quoted retiring Congressman David Price of North Carolina, concerning difficult political issues. He had long recognized the difficulty in reaching accommodation involving difficult issues. He explained his politician's approach to addressing those issues. It is consistent with being both a patriot and a politician. He said, "Don't hesitate to advocate strongly for what you believe in, your morality, and principles. At the same time, understand that not every issue can be won on the first try and that politics is a matter of striking a balance between compromising and finding common ground where you can, and fighting where you must. You don't necessarily solve all problems at once." The politicians who follow the Price approach demonstrate they appreciate what it means to have been elected by and for the people. But if they lose sight of this truth, they neglect their responsibility, and our nation suffers.

The founding of the American Republic was truly unique in that it was not based upon race, religion, or language. Rather it was founded on ideas, such as equality, religious freedom, free speech, and individual rights. The Founders' beliefs, especially the freedoms they were and are designed to protect, have been a unifying force for all patriotic Americans. With the tragic exception of allowing slavery to continue, our nascent republic was fortunate; and slavery has been ended. Today, the principles set forth in the *Constitution* and the *Declaration* still provide a foundation around which all Americans can unite.

A politician's quest for unbridled power and disrespect for the *Constitution*, are antithetical to our freedoms. Yet they have been used by some politicians who have forgotten the need for patriotism. This has seemed to set our nation adrift. As President John F. Kennedy once warned: "A nation's character, like that of an individual, is elusive. It is produced partly by things we have done and partly by what has been done to us. It is the result of physical factors, intellectual factors, spiritual factors … In peace, as in war, we will survive or fail according to its measure."

The essays in this chapter were written to describe some of the crucial issues now facing our nation. I believe they present a call for all patriots to once again demonstrate their love of country over mere self-interest or lust for power.

What I Treasure about America

Regardless of its faults, I love America. I am proud to be an American. While I have lived or traveled in many countries around the world, I will always recall my father's words, "There has never been a nation like America. No other major country has ever offered the political freedoms, the economic opportunities, or the legal protections it offers. Yes, for even the lowliest of its citizens. Even the poorest individual can dream of becoming president." Beginning from my earliest memory of such thought, these were, and still are, the beliefs I embrace. They were the foundation upon which America's greatness was built. Time and experience have alerted us to the need for more improvements. They are essential to ensure our lofty goals continue to be upheld, regardless of a person's race, creed, or color.

In his famous speech following the Battle of Gettysburg, which was the turning point of the Civil War, Abraham Lincoln emphasized that he obviously felt similarly about these goals. A few months after that great battle, he proclaimed, "Our fathers brought forth on this continent a new nation, conceived in Liberty, and dedicated to the proposition that all men are created equal."[1] While Lincoln was referring to a quote from the Declaration of

---

1   Abraham Lincoln, The Gettysburg Address, November 19, 1863, https://www. abrahamlincolnonline.org/lincoln/speeches/gettysburg.htm

Independence, he was also relying on the ideals or principles of freedom embodied in our *Constitution* of 1788, including freedom of speech, the press, and most importantly, religion.

Our republic was the first in world history to use an entire written document to birth a new government. And unlike other nations, America was founded on a set of moral beliefs or principles and, I repeat, not upon a common ethnicity, language, or religion. Our *Constitution* has survived, unlike many imitations around the world, because it was democratically constructed and freely adopted by the people. It also remains a guidepost for individuals, the states, and our Federal government. It helps to ensure the rule of law is followed. I grew up believing that America was a government of laws not of men.

But today you may rightfully ask, *How do you overlook the racism that continues to exist? It has denied many citizens the right to benefit from their Constitutional rights. How do you reconcile America's faults, or failures, with its ideals?* If the reader will bear with me a few moments longer, I will try to address those issues, but first I want to explain what makes me still proud to be an American.

I grew up shortly after the close of World War II. In my studies in high school, I was thrilled to be living in a nation that had twice in the 20th century helped to save many parts of the world from dictatorship and tyranny. Further, I was living in a country that had stood up against the repression of communism. Ours was a country whose industrial might and technological capability have amazed the world. It has set an example of how to make life easier and more enjoyable under a capitalistic system. Yes, I had yet to appreciate that there were flaws in our nation's past, some of which still need to be rectified.

For example, I was unaware of the forced relocation of some 100,000 Native Americans from their homes in Georgia and North Carolina in mid-winter during the 1830s. This was done in spite of the fact that they were living peaceably in their native habitats in the Eastern United States. President Jackson, in sympathy with the forced removal, ignored a ruling of The United States Supreme Court by doing so. Thousands died as a result of this injustice, while the new white landowners profited.

I was also unaware that for 100 years after the end of the Civil War in 1865, Jim Crow policies in many parts of the South defied the 13th, 14th, and 15th Amendments to the *Constitution*; these had abolished slavery, given citizenship to the former slaves, and granted them the right to vote. Previously, I had always felt proud that we had ended slavery. Little did I realize that slavery by another name continued to exist in parts of our nation. Black families were literally tyrannized beginning with Reconstruction. Then Jim Crow was instituted and Reconstruction ended, but the tyranny continued.

Nor was I cognizant, until recent times, of how many Black communities throughout America are so constituted that children there cannot receive the quality of schooling and able teaching available to white people in nearby wealthy communities, especially in the South. The tax base (which largely funds education) in the poorer communities cannot afford these advantages. This is critical because education is one of the essential components to advancement in our nation. Today, owing to these and other societal failures, Black people are often justified when they believe they are not yet considered as worthy as whites, especially by police.

The Black community's frustration with the continuing racist treatment it has unfairly received was one of the reasons for the New York Times Project of 2017. It came out in support of the historically incorrect claim that the American Revolution was fought largely to protect American slave owners[2]. The project was further incorrect in alleging that plantation slavery was the foundation of American capitalism. Unfortunately, the project also tried to spin the Critical Race Theory concept as an explanation for America's founding; suggesting that America is a culture best understood as one where American Blacks struggle against white supremacy. The unfortunate truth underlying these claims is that there remains more that still needs doing to better ensure *all* citizens, regardless of their race, color, creed, or background share in their right to equality of treatment and opportunity. Still, we must not overlook the important civil rights advances that have been made.

In the process of addressing inequities, we must not enable overly activist liberals to cloud the truth of what America represents and its importance in the world where freedom is concerned. We must also remember that it was Samuel Adams who truly birthed The American Revolution, in Boston, Massachusetts. There, he sought to obtain freedom from British hegemony, not to preserve slavery. And as Oklahoma University Professor William M. McClay has noted, "The goal of Washington in crossing the Delaware had nothing to do with preserving slavery in America, but everything to do with fighting for the right to be free. This universally admired right and human desire held out great promise, a great example to peoples in nations throughout the world."

2   The 1619 Project, *New York Times*, 2019

By 1861, slavery had made cotton our largest export earner. Yet none of the significant industrial, transportation, communications, or other innovative advances in America owes its birth to the autocracy of slavery. Its autocracy lounged only in ill-gotten wealth and did nothing to advance our nation's basic infrastructure, industry, or inventions.

Yet, these truths concerning our origins as a nation of freedom loving people must not allow us to overlook the inequities that continue to exist. We must strive to eliminate them.

Whether it is government-inspired or private sector supported, no effort should be spared to eliminate the prejudice and inequity of the past where minorities, especially Blacks, are concerned. For only in this manner can the ideals preserved in our *Constitution* and the *Declaration* be fully realized. Only in this manner can every citizen and immigrant in America have an equal opportunity to thrive.

We must continue to fight the cultural poison of racism. To accomplish this, we need to recapture the patriotism and love of country that Lincoln held and believed in so deeply. As he so ably said, "So that this nation, under God shall have a new birth of freedom; and that government of the people, by the people, for the people, shall not perish from the earth."[3]

---

3   Abraham Lincoln, The Gettysburg Address, November 19, 1863, https://www.abrahamlincolnonline.org/lincoln/speeches/gettysburg.htm

Racism and America

Two destructive forces exist in America today that, like cancers, continue to eat away at the essential life cells of our nation's culture — "caste" and racism. They are not synonymous, but they serve to reinforce one another. As Pulitzer Prize winning author, Isabel Wilkerson, has explained, "Caste is a universal form of human division, as in India or the former Nazi Germany. But it exists in America as a race-based pyramid. It stigmatizes those deemed inferior because of their appearance, the color of their skin. What people look like is the visible cue to their caste."[4] It is my belief that caste will not disappear until racism is overcome.

Racism is best explained as the prejudicial belief that certain characteristics attributable to the white race somehow make it superior to races of color. Whether subtle or direct, since early in our nation's history, this corrosive attitude has caused suffering and disrespect for non-whites, be they Blacks, Asians, Latins, or Native Americans. For America to affirm the moral integrity of its founding precepts, especially in the words of the Declaration of Independence, this destructive force must be overcome. To accomplish such racial justice will require the respect for truth and accommodation that should rest in the heart of every patriotic American. As has

---

4   *Caste, The Origins of our Discontents*, pp 17-19, by Isabel Wilerson.

been said, *Go and learn what this means, for I desire compassion and not sacrifice.*[5]

In boyhood, I was raised in a small rural community a half-hour's drive outside New York City. Until high school, I did not experience racism. Rather, I was brought up to believe that America stood for freedom for all persons; for me this symbolized the greatness of our republic. During World War II, I recall President Roosevelt speaking of every citizen's right to the Four Freedoms — freedom from want, freedom to worship, freedom of speech, and freedom from fear.

I recall my father extolling America as a republic unique in the world, where anyone could dream of becoming president. How proud I felt that our nation tipped the scales toward victory, thus ensuring the defeat of tyranny in two world wars. Then I began to learn other truths that truly discouraged me. That our fighting men were segregated by color on the battlefield; that American Negroes had been enslaved; that an entire society of Native Americans had been forcibly removed from their native lands during the Trail of Tears; and that Asian Americans in a nearby community were denied the right to buy homes because of protective covenants or redlining.

Racist prejudice greatly disturbs me, especially for the following reasons. Foremost, it is culturally divisive; it not only elevates what is wrong with America but disparages what is good and right about our republic. Secondly, it tends to disavow the very principle upon which America was founded, the individual's right to freedom and opportunity. The immediately damaging effect of the first can be seen in some of our nation's schools and educational institutions

---

5   Matthew 9:13

today. Apparently, white youths there are now being urged to believe that they are racist by birth and thus guilty of the sins of their slave-owning forebears. Accordingly, Blacks are supposedly encouraged to believe they are living in a terribly repressive nation and will remain permanently oppressed simply because of their race.

Unquestionably, our youth need to know the full truth of our past failures as a nation, warts and all, along with our achievements. But such truth should not be employed to create antagonism between and among the races or to misrepresent the truth concerning our founding purposes as a nation.

Tragically, two of our original thirteen colonies, where slavery was pervasive, prevented its complete eradication from the *Constitution* at our founding. They and possibly neighboring colonies would have refused to approve the document had slavery been totally banned. An unfortunate compromise had to be reached, for nine colonies had to ratify the *Constitution* if our republic was to be birthed. Consequently, slavery was permitted to continue. Many of our founders, men like John Adams, George Washington, Roger Sherman, Benjamin Franklin, George Mason, Thomas Jefferson, Gouverneur Morris, Alexander Hamilton, and James Madison acknowledged that slavery was morally wrong, even though several were slave owners. Many of them believed slavery would die out of its own accord. History has proven they were witnesses against themselves. It was a tragic miscalculation of human nature.

These facts seem to encourage those who misguidedly claim that America was founded to protect slavery. On the contrary, the truth concerning our historical purpose was to create a unique republic designed to protect hallowed rights, especially freedom of religion, speech, and the press; and to break away from the yoke of English sovereignty. Once this context is recognized, it is clear that our founding was inspired by and designed for adherence to a set of ideals that were not based upon ethnicity. Thomas Jefferson outlined these ideals in his Declaration of Independence, in 1776, when he wrote: "[All men] are endowed by our Creator with certain unalienable rights, the right to life, liberty and the pursuit of happiness." Dumas Malone, Jefferson's major biographer, and President Abraham Lincoln believed that these ideals were intended to set forth a universal principle, inclusive for all mankind, not just whites.

It took America until 1865 to abolish slavery. Partly because of this, the *Constitution* is often cast as a cynical exercise in subjugation. Today, a chorus of concerted liberals are claiming, incorrectly, that the document is repressive, undemocratic, and in need of an overhaul. But two of the greatest Black figures in our history, Frederick Douglas and Dr. Martin Luther King, Jr. disagreed. They honored the documents' purposes but decried the lack of enforcement.

Respected historians concur that despite America's failures, it has advanced far toward achieving the ideals of Jefferson's *Declaration*. As historian Mary Grabar recently explained, "Prior to the American Revolution, there were few abolitionist movements to contemplate … But when blacks filed suits for freedom, as they did for example in Connecticut in 1779, they used the language of the Declaration. Its words helped to set in motion a new philosophy that had worldwide repercussions." Yet until racism is effectively confronted, vital work remains to be done. Justice, not prejudice, must prevail.

Why did it take until 1865 to correct our founding document, following the great Civil War of 1861-1865? Correction began with the 13th, 14th, and 15th Amendments; respectively, they outlawed slavery, granted citizenship, and the right to vote to former slaves. Unfortunately, history demonstrates that you cannot change cultural attitudes of a people simply by enacting new laws that bestow new rights, especially when racial prejudice has been the norm. Critical to the effectiveness of such legislation, on both moral and political grounds, is that the hearts of a nation must demand such change. Unfortunately, when the desire for it is lacking, enactment of legislation is ineffective.

At our founding, the hearts in many sections of America were not morally constituted for the changes that freedom from racism requires. Thus, even allowing for the Civil War Amendments, it took 100 years to effect positive change and to quash Jim Crow practices. In 1954, Constitutional change outlawed segregation in schools (Brown v. Board of Education); and Civil Rights legislation of 1964 and 1965 helped to implement earlier Constitutional Amendments, especially protection of voting rights. Additional civil rights protection has followed.

Unfortunately, it required the tragic death of George Floyd, in 2020, to dramatically reawaken the American conscience to the destructive practice of racism. The need for greater vigilance to end this social menace, a potential cancer to us all, has become paramount. To accomplish this, we must take to heart the wise words of Dr. Martin Luther King, Jr., who in 1963 so eloquently expressed his awareness of the need for such justice. As he said:

"When the architects of our republic wrote the magnificent words of the Constitution and the Declaration of Independence, they were signing a promissory note to which each American was to fall heir … We refuse to believe that there are insufficient funds in the great vaults of opportunity of this nation … that will give us upon demand the voices of freedom and the security of justice." (8/28/1963)

At Gettysburg in 1863, Lincoln acknowledged America's future role in protecting freedom: "We here highly resolve that these dead shall not have died in vain — that this nation, under God, shall have a new birth of freedom — and that government of the people, by the people, for the people, shall not perish from the earth." Influenced by both the *Declaration* and the *Constitution*, Lincoln reaffirmed the ideals inscribed in these great documents.

The desire to ensure such freedom must continually be demanded and reinforced by the hearts of every American who loves our nation and abhors racism. If America is to remain a light for freedom to the world, its luminance must remain fired by the Divine will of the Creator of whom Jefferson wrote. For in that Creator's great command from Scripture, He warned what He expected of human kind: *I have told you, O man, what is good; and what does the Lord require of you, but to do justice, to love kindness, and to walk humbly with your God.*[6]

---

6   Micah 6:8

Wartime Memories

She is like a voice from the past, my past. It might sound surprising to some, but to me it is reassuring. For at times, I seem to hear the loving counsel of my mother from almost 80 years ago. Invariably, it arises at mealtime, just before I take a large helping of broccoli, scoop out a potato skin, or cut into a piece of meat. Her message or proclamation was always the same, "You boys must clean your plates or there will be no dessert. Remember there is a war on; think of the starving people in Europe and just how much they would enjoy having your meal." It made no difference to her whether the food in question happened to be weird-tasting broccoli, soggy spinach, burnt potato skins, or Spam®, the so-called ham what am. She believed in what she was saying.

Mom was born in October 1904, and the war she believed that she was referring to was the Second World War, which was at its mid-point in early 1943. Actually, she was somewhat mistaken. For embedded in her conscientious mind was her recall of a similar proclamation her own mother had made to her and her siblings during and immediately following the close of World War I, in 1918. This earlier war had claimed the lives of nearly nine million combatants, and literally left millions of people starving and displaced throughout Europe — until American aid came to their rescue, mass starvation threatened. War always causes hunger for the innocent. It is one of the great tragedies of war.

While I have studied the history of both the aforementioned wars, I only experienced, indirectly, World War II, from 1939 to 1945. At the time, I was in my late boyhood years and my brother's and my life seemed to be pretty much unaffected by it. We were protected by two oceans, and other than the attacks on Pearl Harbor and Alaska's Aleutian Islands, there was no real concern of Japan or Germany ever reaching our shores. The only significant changes we faced were rationing and a slight change of diet.

Where food items were concerned, I distinctly remember the disappearance of butter. At first, we substituted margarine, often putting a dye in it to make it resemble butter in color. Later, however, we actually made our own butter, by skimming off the cream from the top of our milk bottles, adding a little salt, and then whipping it into butter the old-fashioned way.

As mentioned in Chapter III, I distinctly remember helping my father dig a large victory garden, possibly a quarter acre, in our back yard; it included potatoes, corn, asparagus, lettuce, and other vegetables. Unfortunately, it took two years to harvest the asparagus, so we never had very much. Overall, our gardening was reasonably successful, except that the squirrels usually ate much of the corn. My mother grew fresh tomatoes in a separate plot. I loved them so much that I have continued to grow them to this day whenever I can.

Meat was rationed and fresh oranges were so scarce that our orange juice squeezer was no longer used. When veal was no longer available to make veal cutlet, Mom occasionally switched to a canned meat concoction branded as Spam®. It wasn't very tasty. If memory serves me correctly, it actually had the smell of ham but tasted like a mixture of luncheon meat and dog food.

Gasoline was also rationed, so car trips were restricted mostly to local errands or the doctor. Vacation trips were limited. Before gas rationing began, my father had filled a ten-gallon can with gasoline for emergencies, but it was soon emptied. Obviously, our troops throughout the world needed food and fuel to fight the enemy.

Before the war, we could always hear the day's weather reports on the radio, much like we do on TV today. (TV was unknown commercially until the late 1940s.) Once the war began, weather reports were no longer given on the radio. Our military and security officials believed that to provide them might be of aid to the enemy, should they ever attempt to attack the States.

I frequently asked my father for reassurance that America was winning the war. He always assured me that we were. He was constantly traveling to Washington, DC, working with the War Production Board on supplying our troops. Our weaponry was continually being upgraded, including guns, tanks, and bombs. It wasn't until August 6, 1945, that the first atomic bomb was dropped on Hiroshima, Japan, followed by a second one on Nagasaki, three days later. On August 15, Japan finally surrendered. I remember after the second bomb my father told me that a unique weapon had been used that might end all wars.

Unfortunately, that did not prove to be the case. The use of atomic bombs on Japan was and still is a subject of controversy. Our military had advised President Truman that its use could save the lives of as many as a million servicemen. They would probably be lost if we had to invade Japan. And that did not include the many, many thousands of Japanese soldiers and civilians who would also perish. As former Civil War General Sherman once said, "War is hell."

Concerning wartime and atomic weapons, this seems like the appropriate moment to share with you an article from the *Washington Post* of November 2, 2011. It concerns a Japanese survivor of Hiroshima. His name was Akihiro Takahashi. His experience began at 8:15 a.m., August 6, 1945. The fourteen-year-old Takahashi was about a mile away from where the bomb exploded, making a tremendous roar that suddenly pierced his ears.

According to Takahashi, this is what happened next. "Everything went black and the blast knocked me some 30 feet from where I stood. My back, legs, and arms were severely burned, and my ears nearly melted off. I then walked to a nearby river to cool my body. En route, I passed several injured people who looked to me like ghosts walking in procession. I also passed a baby crying for its mother, but all that remained of her lay in front of the child in a charred lump." When interviewed in 2002, Mr. Takashi said, "It is my belief that those of us who were saved should continue to talk of our experiences. We live to hand down awful memories … of those who died in misery and terror."

It is striking how such memories have an affinity with all wars. While there is joy in victory and the welcoming home of loved ones, there is always sorrow in defeat, destruction, starvation, and the loss of life. Unfortunately, the sad reality is that humankind appears unable to avoid war.

During World War I, Oswald Chambers, a chaplain to the British troops in Egypt, in one of his sermons said, "Life without war is impossible in the natural or the supernatural realm, because of the continuing struggle for balance in the physical, moral, and spiritual areas of life."[7] Even our Savior, the Prince of Peace, understood this reality, as he prophesied, "For nation will rise against nation."[8]

Christ also proclaimed, "Blessed are the peacemakers, for they shall be called sons of God."[9] Let us hope that eventually followers of our Lord and their posterity can do a better job of emphasizing His proclamation. Our track record to date has been quite poor.

---

7   Oswald Chambers, My Utmost for His Highest (New York: Dodd, Mead & Company, Inc., 1935) December 4th entry

8   Matthew 24:7

9   Matthew 5:9

Cousins

It is common for families to have one or more cousins in their family tree, including those from different generations. In my case, there are four who immediately come to mind. They include three men, now deceased, and one woman, Delsa Wilson, who is still very much alive at age 90. I begin with background on each of the men. Their lives were dramatically changed on December 7, 1941. Here are their stories.

Harry Schmidt was born in 1886 in Holdrege, Nebraska, where he grew up on his father's farm. He was my mother's first cousin, eighteen years older than Mom. Even as a young girl she remembered him as being very stoic or almost Buddha-like, a typical old-line marine. In 1909, after attending two years at a local college, at twenty-three years of age, he enlisted in the United States Marine Corps as a Second Lieutenant. For the next thirty-two years, he served in conflicts in Latin America, the Philippines and China, with several assignments in the Washington, DC area, including the War College.

When Japan attacked Pearl Harbor, it was almost noon on the eastern seaboard and Harry and his wife, Doris, had just returned from church. They were discussing plans to entertain family members over Christmas when they suddenly learned the news. Harry, after thirty-two years of distinguished service, was now a general officer, planning for retirement. But suddenly those plans were put on hold. It would be another seven years before he could fulfill them.

In early January 1942, he was appointed Assistant to the Commandant of the Marine Corps and promoted to the rank of major general. By July 1944, he had been given command of the 5th Amphibious Corps, which he led during the successful capture of Iwo Jima. Once Japan surrendered, in August 1945, Harry participated in the occupation of the Japanese mainland until ordered back to Washington in February 1946. He was then promoted to the rank of Lieutenant General, acclaimed for his tactical skill, sound judgment, and administrative ability. He eventually retired in July 1948, at which time he was advanced to the rank of a four-star general. He died in 1968, at age 82.

Kling Shank Anderson was born in 1911, in Fort Wayne, Indiana, but grew up in Cincinnati, Ohio. He was my mother's younger brother and also a first cousin to Harry Schmidt. After college, he had begun law school at New York University at the time of Japan's attack. He attempted to enlist in the U.S. Navy but was turned down because of an ulcer. But by 1942, it had healed and he was drafted by the U.S. Army as a private.

After finishing his basic training, Kling was scheduled for assignment to the Pacific theater. But within a few weeks of being shipped out, he was selected for Officer's Candidate School. After finishing, he was commissioned a Second Lieutenant and assigned to Fortress Monroe, Virginia. Initially, he was tasked with strategically sighting the fort's powerful 16-inch guns against possible German

U-boat attacks. On one occasion his calculations resulted in the disabling of a German U-boat in U.S. territorial waters. At the time, however, details of this action were kept secret, lest Americans grow alarmed that Germany could invade our shores.

Once I asked him how he acquired his first name, and he told me the following: "My father, your grandfather, was a longtime fan of the Chicago Cubs baseball team when they had Tinker, Evers, and Chance. Their great catcher was Johnny Kling, who happened to have met and talked with my father. He then promised Johnny that he was going to name his newborn son after him. And that's what he did."

Kling retired from the army in 1946 with the rank of captain. Although offered a permanent commission in the Army, he decided to go into business for himself. He settled in Atlanta, Georgia, where 40 years later he turned his multi-million-dollar dry goods business over to his son, Wayne. Kling died in 1997 at age 86.

Duncan Buist Dowling was born in December 1911, in Columbia, South Carolina. He was my father's first cousin and thus my first cousin once removed. He had graduated from the United States Military Academy at West Point, Class of 1936. He planned for an Army career.

Five years later, at 7:55 a.m., on the morning of December 7, 1941, in Oahu, Hawaii, the Japanese were bombing Pearl Harbor. First Lieutenant Duncan had just finished shaving and was dressing for breakfast. He had plans to join some of his buddies at Wheeler, the main Army Air Force Base there. But that was not to be.

One of the Japanese bombs exploded near Duncan's quarters, its force knocking him to the floor. As quickly as he could, he sprang to his feet, threw on a shirt and pants, and ran to help resist the Japanese attack. As a result of his and others' heroic efforts, a few Japanese planes were actually shot down. By 1944, Duncan had become a Lieutenant Colonel and Battalion Commander for the 28th Division in France. They landed at Normandy on D-day, June 6, 1944, as part of the allied effort to retake Europe from the Nazis.

Five days later they had advanced into the Mortain-Vire sector of Normandy. It was there that a sniper's bullet ended Duncan's life. He and nearly his entire battalion were almost wiped out. Later action in the U.S. advance would effectively prove that the men in Duncan's battalion had played an important role in enabling General Patton to complete encircling movements around the German line. Eventually almost all of the German forces in Western France were either captured or pushed back toward Germany. Posthumously, Duncan received the Bronze Star and the Purple Heart. Sadly, he never got home to meet his newly born son, Duncan Buist Dowling Jr., who had been named for him.

I met Duncan at West Point in 1934, when I was two years old. While I was too young to remember him, I do recall seeing a home movie taken during our family's visit to the Point. My parents lived about an hour's drive away and my father enjoyed visiting with his cousin. I will always feel proud when viewing this film, specifically of Duncan in his full cadet uniform, holding me in his arms and smiling at the camera.

The fourth cousin, Delsa Walsh Wilson was born in Minneapolis, Minnesota on December 13, 1932. Our mothers were sisters, so we were first cousins, born within four months of each other that same year. Over our 90 years of life, we have remained close. In earlier years, our families regularly celebrated Christmas and Thanksgiving together. We both went off to college at the same time and graduated the same month: May 1954. When I want off to law school, she married a man who was in law school at the University of Virginia. She raised three boys; a fourth died in his youth. She also worked for many years at a home for orphan boys.

Today, Delsa is the only person still living who has known me since my birth and we still communicate. An example of this would be the following birthday card I sent her last week. It read:

> *Dear Delsa, rumor has it that today is your 89th birthday. As an ardent admirer, I just wanted to wish you a happy one.*
>
> *The fact that you are now heading into your ninth decade shouldn't be a problem, provided you are willing to make a few adjustments. Don't be concerned about them! They are a natural occurrence of old age, or a time of natural maturity. While I don't mean to alarm you, I do believe that I should mention three of the more common adjustments you must consider. They are:(1) learning how to get sufficient sleep; (2) finding a way to compensate for your loss of hearing; and (3) overcoming a tendency to forget things you want to remember. Concerning sleep, I suggest you try five minutes of deep breathing before turning out your light at night. This may have the added benefit of reducing snoring. My only fallback would be to suggest a few half-hour naps in the afternoon. Unfortunately my doctor tells me that longer naps tend to detract from a good night's sleep.*

Concerning hearing loss, I suggest you read a good book, rather than continue to listen to your favorite soap operas on TV. Should you remain determined to watch them, use Medicare and get a set of hearing aids; no charge up to $2,400.00; you'll only miss out on things you don't hear.

On forgetfulness, I'm not certain I can offer much help; I have already forgotten what I was going to recommend. Watching Jeopardy might help us both. Just remember, with old age comes wisdom, provided one can remember how to take advantage of it.

Love and kisses,
Cousin Roger

Was Lincoln a Racist?

Is it historically accurate to claim that Abraham Lincoln, probably our greatest president, was a racist? Possibly some such naysayers of history who claim this were aroused by George Floyd's tragic death in May 2020. Until recently, I would have enthusiastically rejected any such claim as a false reading of history. Such claims I believed were merely intended to tarnish Lincoln's legacy. I reasoned that his leadership enabled our nation to defeat the Confederacy's slave autocracy. His political efforts were instrumental in persuading the Congress to carry forth ultimate passage of the Thirteenth Amendment, outlawing slavery in America. And he consistently maintained that Jefferson's *Declaration* included Negroes as being entitled to life, liberty, and the pursuit of happiness. To resolve the conflict between my belief and the protestations of his naysayers, I determined to explore the truth of the matter by embarking on a review of the historical record. Here is what I learned:

Historians agree that Lincoln's parents were adamantly opposed to slavery. So, from Lincoln's childhood their attitude likely influenced him. He was seven when his father moved their family from Kentucky to Indiana, therefore Lincoln had no clear opportunity to interrelate with slaves, although he occasionally had contact with free Blacks. And in his late teens and early twenties, he took two flatboat marketing trips to New Orleans, then America's largest slave market. The cruelty he observed being inflicted on Black slaves in the marketplace greatly distressed him.

In the future he would consistently share this disapproval with others. He was quoted as saying, "By God boys let's get away from this. If ever I get a chance to hit that (slavery) thing, I'll hit it hard … Something must be done or slavery will overrun the whole country."[10] Historians are generally agreed that, based upon these and similar comments over the years to family and friends, three things increasingly influenced Lincoln's abhorrence of slavery. He viewed it as a violation of natural rights and fairness, he considered it as dehumanizing and brutalizing Black human beings, and, like his parents, he considered its economic institution created an uneven playing field for laboring whites.

Born in 1809, Lincoln began his political career in the Illinois State legislature by the time he was 25. Between 1834 and 1847, he was elected four times. As a pragmatist, and follower of Henry Clay, he focused on internal improvements. The first time he addressed the issue of slavery in the state legislator he maintained, "The institution of slavery is founded on both injustice and bad policy." At that time, disapproval of slavery in Illinois was not a significant political issue.

Like the Founding Fathers, he recognized that the *Constitution* protected slavery, and hoped that the institution would soon die out. Nonetheless, he was adamantly opposed to its potential for expansion. When serving in the United States Congress (1847-1849), he voted for the Wilmot

---

10 *Journal of The Abraham Lincoln Association,* Vol 7, Issue 2.

Proviso. It proposed keeping territory acquired during the Mexican War free from slavery. He also sought to have the Washington, DC slave market eliminated. He outlined a special procedure for that very purpose, but his proposal could not gain support for its passage.

By 1854, the issue of slavery's expansion had become of increasing national concern. The 1820 Missouri Compromise, which prohibited slavery in the Louisiana Territory north of the 36-30 latitude, was superseded by passage of the Kansas-Nebraska Act. Rather than limit slavery it authorized new states to decide for themselves whether or not to allow it. Lincoln rightly saw this as potentially an unlimited expansion of slavery throughout the states and federal territories.

In an 1854 speech in Peoria, he referred to slavery as a "monstrous injustice, a vast moral evil, and odious institution, a cancer capable of destroying the republic." Further, in 1857, he disparaged the infamous Dred Scott decision, by which the Supreme Court had held that Congress had no right to restrict slavery. The Court also held that the *Constitution* had recognized Black persons as beings of an inferior order with no rights, which the white man was bound to respect. Individual states could make Blacks citizens within their jurisdictions, but the federal government and other states were not required to recognize them as such.

In rebuttal against the Court's racist decision, Lincoln maintained that Jefferson's *Declaration* did include equality for Black people. He explained that this did not mean all men were equal in all respects, such as color, size, intellect, moral development, or social capacity. But it did mean that all people were equal with respect to the inalienable rights to life, liberty, and the pursuit of happiness, especially the right to enjoy the fruits of their own labor. Nevertheless, such distinctions did imply a racist inequality.

Then, in his 1858 Springfield speech, he qualified his earlier remarks by saying he did not claim Blacks were entitled to all the civil and political rights that white Americans took for granted, e.g. like voting rights. But he still considered that the *Declaration* applied to every human being, regardless of color.

Yet, in his famous house divided speech that same year he said, "A house divided against itself cannot stand. I believe this government cannot endure permanently half slave and half free ... it will become all one thing or all the other."

A subsequent remark muddied the waters on Lincoln's attitude, especially where racism is concerned, when he said, "The two races could never coexist in the same country on the basis of equality, because of physical, (but) not (necessarily) moral or intellectual differences."[11] Clearly, by today's standard, this suggests racism on Lincoln's part. But was it really?

In 1860, Lincoln was elected president and Southern States began to secede from the Union. In February 1861, Congress, in its desperation to appease the South, passed a Thirteenth Amendment that, had it ultimately been fully ratified, prohibited Congress from ever having the Constitutional authority to abolish slavery. Only Ohio, Maryland, and Illinois ever ratified it. Even in March 1861, at his inauguration as President, he claimed that while he had not read the proposed amendment, he had no objection to its "being made express and irrevocable." Clearly this also suggests a tint of racism by today's standards.

11 *Lincoln on Race and Slavery*, by Henry Louis Gates, Jr., pp. 236-241.

He went on to say, "I have no purpose, directly or indirectly, to interfere with the institution of slavery in the States where it exists. I have no lawful right to do so, and I have no inclination to do so." Realistically, his primary responsibility as President had to be to save the Union. Two years later he said, "If I could save the union without freeing any slaves I would do it." His statements, while damning, were, I believe, politically motivated. He was trying to focus on this primary responsibility as President, which was to preserve the Union. For a divided Union meant slavery/racism would continue in the South.

What naysayers also tend to forget is that almost simultaneously, he had been drafting a version of the *Emancipation Proclamation*, to begin freeing the slaves in the Confederacy. Upon its issuance in January 1, 1863, it also authorized the use of Black troops. Heretofore, such a step was not politically viable, owing to Northern prejudice against it. But Lincoln's thinking was changing. He had begun to appreciate that he could never fully restore the Union unless that restoration included ending slavery and providing a path for Negro people to have their rights under the *Declaration*. Colonization of the slaves was not a viable option.

Approximately four million slaves had been born in America and had no desire to immigrate to Africa. Colonization was merely a thinly veiled form of Negrophobia. And he was aware that Black troops had proved to be heroic during the final two years of the Civil War. He saw the significance of this and said,

> *Negroes, in fighting to save the Union, have fought themselves out of slavery. They are people, just as we are; and just like us, they are motivated by what is best for them. We have entered into a contract with them. There is no turning back; the promise being made must be kept.*

Does this suggest racism on his part, or wise and compassionate presidential leadership?

The Black author Henry Louis Gates, Jr. has written, "I believe that Lincoln honestly felt, for both humanitarian and economic reasons, that all men should be free. Lincoln had remade himself as a proponent of black freedom, fully aware of how far he had come in doing so. His commitment to his elite group of warriors was impressively total and absolute."

Until an assassin's bullet took his life, I am convinced that whatever seemingly racist theories Lincoln had once espoused had now been overtaken by a deeper appreciation of the principles embodied in the *Declaration. We hold these truths to be self-evident* … You can fill in the remaining words yourselves. Racism is clearly prejudice, something I do not believe that we can accuse Lincoln of being at the time of his death. He was a man of compassion, reason, and great leadership.

Concerning prejudice, I like what the popular writer and scholar Deborah Lipstadt, has written. She recognized that the force against prejudice in a free culture must be ongoing, "All forms of prejudice are impervious to reason, they cannot be disproved. Therefore, in every generation they must be fought."[12] Lincoln recognized this, and I believe he would have fought racism had he lived longer.

---

12   Deborah E. Lipstadt, *Denial* (New York: Harper Collins Ecco, 2016), p 206

The Rule of Law

Respect for the "rule of law" is understood to be adherence to a series of constitutionally accepted laws and procedures. It is far more than a mere expression of the need for law and order, as essential as that is. While laws and procedures naturally evolve, respect for the rule of law continues to mean that all laws and procedures must be: (1) publicly promulgated, (2) equally enforced, (3) independently adjudicated, and (4) consistent with the moral precepts inherent in our *Constitution*.

The rule of law is one of the major pillars upon which our Republic was founded. Without rigid adherence to it, our free culture, and especially an efficient judicial system, cannot expect to survive. Respect for the rule of law is designed to ensure equal protection of the laws embodied in the American *Constitution*. It must be applied equitably regardless of an individual's social, political, or economic status. As the *Washington Post* correctly noted, "Respect for the rule of law depends on peacefully complying with both its substantive and procedural processes," even when you may dislike or disagree with them.[13]

In the March of 1953, I had my first occasion to be confronted by the rule of law, although on an exceedingly

---

13 Editorial by David French, April 1, 2023.

modest scale. I was caught for exceeding the speed limit en route to my return to college. I was doing 35 mph in a 20 mile zone, while driving through the City of Colonial Heights, Virginia. As a result, I was taken before a local magistrate and forced to pay a fine or have my car impounded. I paid. Many have had similar experiences, but if there were no traffic regulations, driving could become chaotic. Even traffic laws have to be obeyed if public safety is to be protected.

If we fast forward several years to late March 2023, we learn that a former president claimed he was about to be indicted by a grand jury for alleged crimes in the State of New York. His immediate response was to threaten "potential death and destruction" if he was indicted. This attitude was certainly not consistent with respect for the rule of law. Fortunately, on April 4, the former president surrendered to the court in New York City and was arraigned. He thereby complied with the procedural requirements necessary to uphold the rule of law. Now it is up to the New York Court to decide whether to dismiss the indictment or to uphold it and set a date for trial.

The genesis for the rule of law can be traced to England's King John signing the *Magna Carta*, in 1215. This result was caused by a group of English barons, forcing the king to reduce his absolute power by recognizing their several rights. These included many of the rights protected by the United States *Constitution* today, including the right to a fair trial, protection of right to inherit private property, and avoidance of unreasonable taxation. It also marked a significant challenge to the concept of the Divine right of kings, by ushering in the concept that no one is above the law, including the king. Hence originated, the concept now embedded in our *Constitution*, that all are equal before the law, and thus subject to it, regardless of their social, political, or economic status.

In Federalist Letter 78, Alexander Hamilton explained that America's judiciary was being established to ensure that rights of the individual would be guaranteed to the people under the *Constitution*. To carry out this responsibility, he said: "[The Courts are] to declare all acts contrary to the manifest tenor of the Constitution void."[14] The Founding Fathers sought to enshrine the rule of law by establishing a government of limited powers, so that in all its actions it would be bound by rules that were fixed and announced beforehand. As future president John Adams opined in 1780, "[The *Constitution*] makes us a government of laws not of men."

When the precepts and traditions supportive of our rights under the *Constitution* are incorrectly applied, redress under our judicial system is available. The 1982 Supreme Court case of *Plyler v. Doe* is a case in point. In that case the Texas legislature had revised its education laws to deny enrollment in its public schools to children of illegal immigrants, and to withhold any state funds for the education of such children. The United States Supreme Court correctly held the Texas statute unconstitutional because it violated the Equal Protection Clause of the 14th Amendment to the Constitution.

That Amendment reads: *No state shall make or enforce any law which shall abridge the privileges or immunities of citizens of the United States, nor shall any state deprive any*

14 *THE FEDERALIST, A Commentary on the Constitution of the United States*, by Alexander Hamilton.

person of life, liberty or property without due process of law, nor deny to any person within its jurisdiction the equal protection of the laws. The Court ruled that denying undocumented children of illegal immigrants to attend public schools was discriminatory. It was inconsistent with the fairness required in observance of the rule of law. The state had directed the onus of the parents' misconduct onto their children; this did not comport with the fundamental concepts of justice guaranteed under our *Constitution*.

In another case before the Supreme Court, *Batson v Kentucky*, in 1986, a black defendant was convicted of stealing and related crimes. During jury selection, however, the prosecutor had removed all potential black jurors from the jury pool. The defendant appealed his conviction on the grounds that it violated the Equal Protection Clause of the 14th Amendment as well as Article VI. The latter reads that: *In all criminal prosecutions, the accused shall enjoy the right to a speedy and public trial, by an impartial jury.* The Supreme Court held that the removal of Black jurors simply because of their race was unconstitutional. It was based upon the false assumption that members of the Black race, as a group, were not entitled to serve as jurors. Such conduct on the prosecution's part undermined public confidence in the fairness of our system of justice; clearly it was an inappropriate application of the rule of law.

In *Brown v. Board of Education*, May 1954, the High Court ruled that segregation in public schools was unconstitutional. African American children throughout the South could no longer be denied admission to public schools attended by Whites. The Brown decision also held that segregation *per se* is illegal. This decision effectively overturned the 1896

Supreme Court holding, *Plessey v. Ferguson*, which had permitted segregation in public accommodations, provided substantially equal facilities were available, even though separate. The doctrine of separate but equal was no longer constitutional.

In his decision, Chief Justice Earl Warren reasoned that, "Separate educational facilities are inherently unequal. That to separate students on the basis of race creates a feeling in the student of inferiority as to their status in the community that may affect their hearts and minds in a way that may never be undone."

As indicated in the above, failure to abide by the rule of law is a threat to the smooth functioning of our constitutional system of government. Any such failure weakens it. In 2020, following the November Presidential Election, a defeated candidate sought to remain in the presidency. To accomplish this, he claimed his re-election had been stolen and sought to have the decision reversed. Provided he could substantiate this alleged fraud or illegality had actually occurred, his seeking of court relief was his Constitutional right. However, his suits were all rejected, save one, and that decision was reversed upon appeal. He was unable to establish a *prima facie* case, sufficient for the courts to accept his suit for trial.

In our judicial system, a litigating party is said to have a *prima facie* case when the evidence in his favor is sufficiently strong for his opponent to be called on to answer it. In other words, the evidence presented will suffice unless contradicted and overcome by other evidence. But *prima facie* evidence must be good and sufficient on its face to establish a given fact or chain of facts, until it is rebutted or overcome by other evidence. However, the defeated candidate failed to present such evidence. Instead, his representatives merely made a series of allegations or rumors about improper election processes, vote counting and vote certification, none of which on their face could be shown to be true. Going to court and merely laying claim to facts not in evidence does not make a *prima facie* case.

Failing in the courts, the defeated candidate devised a plan inconsistent with the rule of law. The plan was to prevent the duly elected president-elect from taking office on January 20, 2021, under our duly prescribed Constitutional procedures. Under the 20th Amendment to the *Constitution* that date is the date upon which a duly elected president takes office. My reasons for objecting to the candidate's plan are set forth in the following essay, Disrespect for The Constitution.

The failure of the candidate to abide by the rule of law disturbed many people. And, his efforts to remain in office were in violation of our nations observance, over two centuries, of respect for the rule of law. One U.S. Senator expressed his strong disagreement with the candidate's efforts, claiming, "Such efforts were a serious crime against democracy and against our country."[15]

---

15 Sen. Mitt Romney, (R. of Utah)

Disrespect for the Constitution

The United States *Constitution* is the central pillar upon which our American republic was founded. For over two centuries, its stability has withstood the political trials confronting our nation, especially slavery, the Civil War, and civil rights. In doing so, it has remained the bedrock of American democracy and the linchpin around which all Americans can rally. Moreover, adherence to it has sustained sanctity for the rule of law, freedom of religion, speech, and individual rights.

Rightly, the *Constitution* has protected Americans from the potential tyranny of an insurrection designed to subvert the will of the people. For this, it deserves our continued respect. But on January 6, 2021, the *Constitution* was challenged by a defeated president. Was this challenge justified or was it a sign of disrespect for the *Constitution*? Here are some pertinent facts.

On January 6, 2021, a mob of some 2,500 supporters of defeated President Donald Trump were encouraged by him to protest and obstruct the constitutionally-authorized certification of the Electoral College results from the November 3, 2020 presidential election. Those authentic results were the voice of the American electorate voting their preferences for president. Their votes clearly confirmed that Joseph Biden had been elected our 47th president. Had the mob accomplished its purpose by delaying or preventing certification, it would have been a clear violation of Article II of our *Constitution*. (And it must be noted that there is no constitutional provision authorizing the President of the Senate to challenge Article II, Paragraph 3, or otherwise disrupt the orderly counting of Electoral College votes.)

Article II, Paragraph 3, requires that, "the President of the U.S. Senate … shall, in the presence of (a joint session) of the Senate and House of Representatives, open (the votes of the Electoral College) … and the votes shall then be counted. The person having the greatest number of votes shall be the President." There is no provision in the *Constitution* that would authorize a defeated presidential candidate to overturn a national election once the people have voted and electors have been legally selected.

Where electors are concerned, there is no constitutional mandate or federal statute that requires legally appointed presidential electors to follow the popular vote in their state, unless, of course, the state in which they are selected so requires, as some now do. However, with one or two minor, individual exceptions, properly chosen presidential electors traditionally have voted for the winner of their state's popular vote in all presidential elections.

Clearly, the attempt by some Trump partisans to generate the submission of alternate lists of presidential electors to the Vice President was improper, unauthorized, and inconsistent with the spirit of the *Constitution*. Therefore, prior to the January 6 certification date for submission of electors, the only recourse available to a defeated candidate would be to challenge the election in the courts. This, of course, is what Trump and his partisans did. And the following is a summary of their failed efforts.

Following the 2020 election, Trump, or his supporters, in an effort to invalidate the 2020 election results, brought some 50-60 lawsuits in state and federal courts, including the U.S. Supreme Court. The fraud alleged by the plaintiffs centered on election processes, vote counting, and vote certification. Major legal action was concentrated in Arizona, Georgia, Michigan, Nevada, Pennsylvania, and Wisconsin. Trump supporters lost every case but one. The latter had to do with reducing the amount of time Pennsylvania voters had to fix errors on their mail-in ballots; it was overturned upon appeal by the Pennsylvania Supreme Court. Further, at President Trump's request, the Departments of Justice and Homeland Security were tasked with investigating the election. Each determined that no serious fraud altered the election results.

In all cases, the Trump plaintiffs clearly failed to meet a standard of proof required to bring a lawsuit. To succeed, it must be a *prima facie* case. That means that the complainant or plaintiff must show credible evidence that their complaint is based upon fact, not speculation, rumors, or hearsay. For example, in some instances, Trump supporters alleged that voting machines had transferred thousands of Trump votes into Biden votes, but a subsequent hand count both affirmed the earlier results and demonstrated that, even if their claim had merit, the number of votes was insufficient to have altered the election. In Arizona and Georgia, subsequent hand counts not only confirmed earlier results, but also uncovered additional votes for Biden. In several of these suits, judges appointed by Trump or earlier Republican presidents ruled against the plaintiffs.

The U.S. Supreme Court refused to hear a suit brought in December 2020, by the State of Texas, because Texas lacked legal standing. Texas wanted to void the votes of Georgia, Pennsylvania, Wisconsin, and Michigan. The Texas suit claimed the states were in violation of Article II, Section 1, Clause 2, of the *Constitution*. It requires that, *Each state shall appoint, in such manner as the legislature thereof may direct, a number of electors, equal to the whole number of senators and representatives to which the state may be entitled in the Congress… .*

Apparently, owing to the COVID-19 pandemic, the executive branches in these four states, not their legislatures, had changed their voting laws prior to the 2020 election. Their rationale for the change was to make postal voting easier, primarily due to fears that in-person voting exposed people to the pandemic. But under Article III, Sec. 2, Paragraph 2 of the *Constitution*, only the Supreme Court has original jurisdiction to bring such a case, specifically, *In all cases in which a state shall be a party.* These cases could not be brought, so whether the health care concern would have been considered an insignificant violation of Article II, or *de minimus,* was not ruled upon by the courts.

Certainly, Trump and his supporters were entitled to make legal court appeals, but not on January 6, 2021. So, on that date, President Trump violated both his oath of office and the spirit of the *Constitution*. At his inauguration as President in 2016, (in accord with *Article II, Section 1, Clause 8*) he took the following oath, "I do solemnly swear that I will faithfully execute the office of president of the United States and will, to the best of my ability, preserve, protect, and defend the Constitution of the United States."

Yet, in spite of his sworn oath, and from a podium within view of the White House, he urged his supporters to void a constitutionally mandated procedure. Later, despite urging by members of his family, his staff, and Congress, Trump purposely delayed nearly two hours before calling off the rioters. Instead, he elected to watch them on TV from his White House residence. His attitude toward his oath under the *Constitution* was not only disrespectful; it demonstrated his shallowness as a leader.

Evidence of such failed leadership should have been apparent from earlier Trump statements to the press. For instance, during both the 2016 and 2020 presidential election campaigns, Trump claimed that he could only lose if the election was rigged against him. Campaign rhetoric, yes, but wasn't he also trying to shield himself against his fear of losing and admitting defeat? Earlier presidential candidates had respected what the *Constitution* required and accepted defeat.

For example, during Andrew Jackson's run for the presidency in 1821, he was defeated in the House of Representatives owing to the so-called "corrupt bargain" between John Quincy Adams and Henry Clay, whereby Clay gave Adams his electoral votes, apparently in return for the promise to be appointed Secretary of State. Jackson took his defeat gracefully; he ran again in 1824 and won. There was also the case of Richard Nixon. In 1960, he narrowly lost to John F. Kennedy, when he clearly could have claimed voter fraud in Chicago, Illinois. Political analysts agree that thousands of illegal votes were cast for Kennedy. However, instead of appealing to the courts, Nixon avoided a court battle he might well have won. He thereby saved the nation from the political chaos that could have resulted in attempting to invalidate a presidential election. In 1968, he ran again and won.

It has been argued that Trump's remarks on January 6 were not unconstitutional, but merely an exercise of his right to freedom of speech. But clearly, he was in violation of America's sacred tradition of a peaceful transfer of power. George Washington established that tradition in 1796. Until the 22nd Constitutional Amendment of March 21, 1947, a president was not limited to two four-year terms.

Trump's disrespect for the *Constitution* caused me to remember another inauguration, that of our 41st president, George H.W. Bush, some thirty-three years earlier, on January 20, 1989. At that time, I was filled with pride to be an American. One of our nation's greatest demonstrations of freedom was on display before the world on television — the peaceful transfer of political power.

What made the scene so memorable was the departure of retiring President, Ronald Reagan. After he mounted the steps to board a waiting helicopter that would soon take him into his retirement, he suddenly turned, stood erect and then saluted the incoming president. Immediately, President Bush returned his salute. At that moment, as I watched this display of America's greatness, tears of joy filled my eyes.

Speaking of the *Constitution* and inaugurations, I also recall that of January, 1960, when incoming President Kennedy said, "Ask not what your country can do for you. Ask what you can do for your country." Trump's disrespect on January 6, for our nation and for the *Constitution*, dramatically demonstrated that he was incapable of entertaining such a question.

Effective Leadership

Former Supreme Court Justice Potter Stewart, in a 1964 Court decision, acknowledged that he could not define precisely what constituted pornography, yet he felt confident in claiming, "But I know it when I see it." When attempting to define various unique styles of effective leadership, much the same lack of precision is understandable. Still, we do know it when we see it. And despite varying degrees of uniqueness, effective leaders invariably convey the following in some manner. In each instance, the order of their importance will depend upon the circumstances:

(1) The ability to influence others;
(2) The wisdom to project a vision beyond mere self-interest;
(3) The skill to earn and sustain the trust of others;
(4) The courage to learn from failure and disappointment; and
(5) The acuity to recognize the importance of using a moral compass to identify difficult decisions.

In the following essay, I will cite two instances of how effective leaders successfully employed them.

The first concerns a true story about a church I attend in Falls Church, Virginia, now referred to as The Falls Church Anglican (TFCA). Churches are understandably one of the most leadership-dependent enterprises in our culture. This explains why highly successful churches inevitably have spiritual leaders with an outstanding ability to influence, along with a vision that is not limited by mere self-interest. Where such leadership is lacking, however, a church will find its growth stymied. Or as one writer explains, "If you can't influence others, they won't follow you. And if you think you are leading but have no followers, you're merely out for a walk."[16]

The circumstances affecting our church began to arise in the late 1970s. It had been without a permanent rector for some time; its small congregation was aging and attendance declining. On most Sundays you could literally pick your own pew. Accordingly, pledges were low and all but a few of the younger congregation had left. There was an informal woman's group, but no organized men's group, a tiny Sunday school, and few youth attended, except at the behest of their parents. The church resembled a ship mired in the shoals, with neither wind nor sail enabling it to come about. It was devoid of effective leadership.

Finally, a search committee identified a promising young minister, John Yates, to become its rector. He soon demonstrated his ability to influence and to envision change. Over the next few years many positive changes occurred. Accordingly, the size of the congregation expanded rapidly, causing the need to build a larger church annex. A younger congregation soon began to fill the pews, so additional clergy were hired. A youth ministry was established, and

16 John C. Maxwell, *The Laws of Leadership*, p. 20

outreach to the community was greatly increased. Today, well over forty years later, TFCA has become a dynamic, spiritual force in Northern Virginia. Its influence is felt even beyond. Had it not been for the young rector's ability to influence and envision future needs, it is unlikely the TFCA would be what it is today.

Effective leadership, of course, is not limited to the field of religion. In truth, is it is essential to the success of every major human endeavor, especially in the political arena. And it was America's good fortune that one of its greatest presidents and most effective leaders came to prominence during the critical days before, during, and after the birth of our nation. He was George Washington of Virginia.

As one noted biographer has claimed, "Washington was never a perfect man and had the familiar cravings for money, status, and fame. Yet he learned to subordinate his personal wants to the service of a larger cause … he had an unwavering sense of America's future greatness."[17] This enabled him to learn from his early mistakes and disappointments, enabling his great leadership capability to emerge.

By the time Washington was in his early twenties, in the 1750s, he had learned how to accept and profit from disappointment and personal failure. His father had died when he was a child and his much older half-brother, Lawrence, who acted as a second father to Washington, died unexpectedly. Then, as a young Colonial military officer, he was an active participant in the French and Indian War, where he was twice defeated in battle. The latter events likely contributed to his failure to attain his dream of obtaining a British regular army commission.

---

17 *Washington — A Life*, by Ron Chernow, p. 812

Yet these failures, although not entirely his fault, actually highlighted his impressive qualities, including his courage, dignity, fearlessness in battle, and his capacity for unrelenting self-criticism and improvement. It was the latter capacity especially that enabled him to profit from difficult experiences. The effect was, his reputation as a military leader increased. So, when the Revolution was about to begin, in 1775, he was selected as the commanding general of America's colonial troops.

Throughout the nearly eight years of war, Washington lost more battles than he won, yet he continued to retain the trust of his undersupplied, underpaid, and underfed troops. The trust was abetted by his concern for his men, his courage in battle, and a firm patriotism that inspired them. Finally, in 1781, with assistance of French soldiers and the French fleet, Washington and the French won the decisive battle of Yorktown and the British soon ceased their efforts to defeat the thirteen colonies. Yet, before the peace treaty was even signed in 1783, Washington had a final military encounter to surmount. It involved many of his officers and members of the Continental Congress. It had failed to provide the promised back pay and half pensions owed our soldiers.

Initially, communications with the Continental Congress on the payment issue proved futile. Finally, the situation worsened, to the point where it appeared that the military might take action against the civil authority of the Congress. The threat of a *coup d'état* arose. Washington understood the potential dangers, especially the possible loss of everything the American colonists had fought for. At an appropriate time, he called a meeting of his officers and appealed to their patriotism.

His earlier ability to influence had earned their trust. He purposely avoided elevating himself above his men. His moral compass enabled him to portray himself as their friend and fellow soldier, which he was. He, too, had suffered during the war. At one critical point in his remarks, he appeared unable to read until he put on his glasses and said, "I have grown gray in your service and find myself growing blind."[18] His presentation effectively broke the potential revolt of the officers, bringing many of them to tears. He then worked with Congress to persuade it to grant five years full pay for all soldiers who had served. Washington's ability to influence carried the day. He also prevailed because of his skill in getting both solders and the Congress to trust him. And he used his moral suasion with Congress to ensure his soldiers received what was due them.

Once Washington had led our young nation to victory and independence, he retired. But his greatest accomplishments were yet to come. He and other Founding Fathers recognized that improvements would have to be made if our nascent republic was to survive. Each of the thirteen colonies would have to sacrifice a degree of its independence. Washington recognized that he would have to participate in this process. Rising above mere self-interest, he agreed to come out of retirement to become the acting head of the Constitutional Convention of 1787. This resulted in the creation and eventual adoption of our *Constitution* in 1788, one of the most honored and effective political documents ever written.

When it came time to choose our first president, our young nation's trust in Washington's courage, patriotism, and honesty made him the unanimous choice. So once more

---

18 George Washington, *Newburgh Address*, March 15, 1783

Washington agreed to come out of retirement and was elected unanimously. During his eight years as president, Washington's ability to envision the future caused him to work persistently at establishing administrative precedents and political traditions designed to preserve our young republic. One such tradition still speaks to rulers throughout the world. It was his refusal to run for a third term. By doing so, he emphasized the importance of a peaceful transfer of power. This tradition was unsuccessfully challenged on January 6, 2021 by a defeated president, failing in his illegal attempt to remain in office.

Yes, Washington had his flaws. To his credit, and our good fortune, he definitely also had the ability to influence others, to rise above mere self-interest, to earn the trust of the American people, and to learn from his failures. Yet, probably the one leadership quality that influenced all others was that he always sensed when and how to factor in his moral compass when difficult decisions had to be made. He understood the importance of civic virtue; a talent few politicians are adroit at practicing today.

Chapter VII

Failure, Faith, and Fulfillment

In life we must expect that there will be tribulation as well as joy. None of us is perfect; we all make mistakes, and those mistakes have consequences. As the renowned biographer and historian, David McCullough once noted, "Nothing happens in isolation. Everything that happens has consequences."[1] Because of mistakes we sometimes fail in our efforts, yet sometimes we succeed beyond our wildest dreams. I believe there is also another reality. Regardless of our achievements, everyone seeks a sense of meaning for their lives, a realization that their birth has had a purpose, that their existence is justified. As a young man, Abraham Lincoln was often troubled by his frequent concern that no one would remember that he had ever lived. History certainly proved him to be mistaken.

Understandably, it is not always easy to find one's sense of meaning; initially that was my experience. Many of us come from different walks of life, harboring distinct and often unique experiences. Some have to struggle mightily to find their sense of meaning or worth. Certainly, poor and minority groups have often been disadvantaged in our culture. Others may have been more fortunate.

It wasn't until I accepted the need for God in my life

1   David McCullough, *The American Spirit: Who We Are and What We Stand For* (New York: Simon and Schuster, 2017)

that my understanding of meaning and purpose changed. I realized that until I ceased equating these goals with mere self-interest, I could never find myself as a person. I needed to humble myself before the source of all life, our Father in Heaven, through belief in His Son. Once this began to occur my life experienced a compelling need to serve something far greater than self.

I respect that there are many who will strongly differ with this spiritual belief. Some may consider it unrealistic. And in some instances, they may claim to have found their meaning in life by their impressive achievements. And they deserve praise for all such efforts. The real question is, have they truly found their meaning in life or are they merely allowing success, by itself, to substitute for spiritual fulfillment?

It wasn't until late in mid-life, my 50s, when these changes began. And the essays in this chapter will relate how my transformation took place. I must confess that it was difficult at first to realize that success by itself, regardless of how pleasing, was insufficient to fully define me. In other words, I learned that when the thrill of success no longer fully satisfies, it is definitely time to reassess one's sense of meaning. Eventually, I had to undertake that reassessment.

In summary, let me be clear. I have found that to live a fulfilling life, even if one is extremely successful by world standards, does not fully define an individual's sense of meaning. Of course, I respect a person's desire to accomplish or achieve success. I have sought it myself. In fact, Scripture-wise, use of one's talents is consistently heralded, (see Luke 19:12-26). But eventually I realized worldly efforts, by themselves, are but a part of who a person is. For as has been said: *For even when one has an abundance their life does not consist of their possessions.*[2]

Accordingly, I feel the need to give thanks to our Divine Creator for the gift of life itself and for the forgiveness of my sins. It has caused me to recognize the need to contribute to life and not merely to take from it. I believe this is essential, regardless of the manner by which we accomplish it. In my case there was the call to prison ministry. It enabled me to realize that in some small manner I could give to the world rather than merely take from it. Surprisingly, in the process my secular accomplishments became more meaningful to me, primarily because I had finally learned how to weigh the secular with the spiritual.

As the following essays will convey, I learned a great deal more than I anticipated.

---

2   Luke 12:15

In Good Hands

It is a comforting, confident feeling during times of adversity to believe you are in good hands. Whether it is family, friends, or national leaders, you believe your needs or concerns are understood. Politicians certainly recognize this. It is why one of the most important skills a successful politician develops is to discern how to shake hands with their constituents, enabling them to make a connection with people they may have never met before. Certainly, during times of national crises Americans hope for a president who projects a reliable air of confidence. If so, we can believe that his leadership is competent to securely lead our ship of state. Then, we believe we are in good hands. Two of our former presidents stand out in this regard, Abraham Lincoln and Lyndon Baines Johnson. Here is why I believe this.

With Lincoln, it occurred during the Civil War, on New Year's Day in 1863. At the annual White House reception on that New Year's Day, Lincoln shook hands with hundreds of visitors over a four-hour period. He then returned to his office, his hand literally shaking from the strain of shaking so many hands of constituents and strangers. He briefly rested it before officially signing, and thereby activating, the *Emancipation Proclamation*. By doing so, he freed the slaves in each of the eleven rebellious Confederate States.

Its political significance practically ensured that neither the French nor the British would recognize the Confederate States as a nation. It also authorized the use of Negroes, most of them free blacks, to participate as soldiers in the Union Army. This enabled the Union Army to enlist two hundred thousand badly needed men. Yes, history has confirmed that America was in good hands.

While I certainly wasn't present in 1863, I was definitely alive in November 1963, and, like millions of Americans, emotionally saddened by the Kennedy assassination. Tragically, but fortuitously, our nation was placed in the hands of a leader whom I had actually met and supported. It all began one February evening in 1956, while I was attending law school at the University of Texas in Austin, Texas.

The law school was hosting a private reception for the then Leader of the United States Senate, Lyndon Baines Johnson. Lloyd Hand, a law school classmate of mine, guided Johnson around so that he met everyone in attendance. When it came my turn, I suddenly realized what a large man Johnson really was, standing around 6' 3" and easily weighing well over 230 pounds. As Lloyd presented him, Johnson stuck out his large hand and smiled, saying, "How nice it is to meet you, Mr. Turner." Then as I attempted to release my hand, Johnson held onto it, while clasping his other hand over the top of mine. I was somewhat startled by this unusual gesture, but managed to ask him whether his wife, Lady Byrd, was going to join us. He said no because she was attending another function. Several seconds later, he released my hand and we parted. I did not meet him again until eight years later, in the fall of 1964, when he was running for a full term as president.

The occasion was a visit to the White House with our group of Young Citizens for Johnson, from New York City. I had been working there as a volunteer when we were invited to Washington to meet with the President. Upon arriving at the White House, we were escorted to the Rose Garden. A few moments later he appeared. As requested, we formed a line so the President could greet each person as they walked by. When it came my turn, I mentioned that we had met before and said it was good to see him again. He smiled right away and acknowledged my greeting.

Obviously, this was mere courtesy on his part, as I am confident he didn't remember me. Still, it sounded nice coming from a President. He then offered his hand and immediately I remembered our previous hand shake eight years earlier. When I attempted to release my grip, he once again held on, placing his other hand over my right. As I mentioned earlier, Johnson's hands were somewhat larger than mine, and seemed to be soft or puffy. But the impression he left after his greeting was a sense that he enjoyed meeting me. In between our two handshakes Johnson's unique way of shaking hands had been extremely important to Americans, especially following the assassination of former President John F. Kennedy.

It was November 25, 1963, the day of Kennedy's funeral procession at Arlington National Cemetery. Following that, Johnson met with or was introduced to hundreds of foreign officials, royalty, and diplomats who had come to pay their respects. Robert Caro, in his five-volume biography of Johnson, describes these proceedings and why the famous

Johnson handshake may have been so significant, "As each dignitary came up to him, Johnson shook his hand. But then that hand wasn't released. While still holding it, Johnson would grin — and in almost every case, the dignitary would grin back … The average handclasp was held for minutes, if necessary, until condolences and wishes had been expressed. Older acquaintances were clasped for longer periods. It almost seemed as if each such meeting allowed foreign leaders to gain a sense of respect for America's new leader," to feel him out, so to speak. Despite the peaceful transfer of power, few of these visiting dignitaries really knew much about the former Vice President, or whether America was in good hands.

> *The State Department Officials supervising the greetings saw that Johnson understood what was at stake … how he was being measured by these important visitors, many of whom he would be dealing with in the near future. And they realized that foreign leaders were being impressed … As one State Department official said, 'The visitors came away with a good… deal of respect.' These included the Russian Foreign Minister and French President Charles de Gaulle, each of whom, at times, had been antagonistic toward America. Johnson had his photograph taken with each of the two, but there were no smiles or recriminations apparent on Johnson's part. His visitors seemed to express positive feelings about their brief meetings. America was in good hands.*[3]

---

3   Robert Caro, *The Years of Lyndon Johnson* (New York: Alfred A. Knopf, four-volume series published 1982-2012), fifth and final volume not yet published.

I find it interesting that despite the apparent usefulness of these meetings very few historians, other than Caro, have ever mentioned the Johnson handshake, nor how it may have left the right impression that America was in still in good hands, especially after Kennedy's tragic death. Of course, handshakes do not make a presidency any more than kissing babies. A president's influence has to rise or fall based upon his accomplishments, and his mistakes. Certainly, Johnson made a tremendous contribution to our nation by pushing through the 1964 and 1965 civil rights legislation. But his nadir was Viet Nam, a story for another day.

In closing I guess I should add that I offered some minor assistance to Johnson's future presidency. For example, I did travel to Los Angeles in the summer of 1960, when Johnson sought the nomination, but lost to Kennedy. As Johnson's name was being placed in nomination, the President of Braniff Airlines and I led the entire demonstration onto the convention floor. We each held up one side of a huge Texas cowboy hat, approximate forty inches in circumference and weighing several pounds. At the time my mother, back at home in New York, happened to be watching on television. I was later informed that when she recognized me, she said, "Oh my God, there's Roger!" Subsequently at the convention, I was talking to a reporter about who the next vice president might be. The reporter claimed that Lady Byrd had said to him, "We're happy where we are now, in the Senate, and we don't want anything to change." But the next day Kennedy selected Johnson for his running mate. So much for "fake news."

Satisfying a Need at Christmas

For many in America, belief in the Biblical Christmas story presupposes they have the capacity to identify with their spiritual needs. Unfortunately, that requirement was a problem for me for several years, even though I didn't consider it as such. Simply put, I was unable to discern the need to internalize, spiritually the Christmas story. Its relevance had little impact on my thinking. The result was that Christmas was just an enjoyable season of the year for me, much like New Years Eve.

Yes, I knew the Christmas story from early in my Sunday school years; and I did accept that God had sent his Son to earth for some reason. Still, I believed, as some still do, that all good things come from outside the self, not from within. So, for me, good things at Christmas continued to mean gifts, decorated Christmas trees, delicious desserts, lovely carols, and family gatherings, all of which were enjoyable. And when it snowed, I could also look forward to a sled ride, a snowball fight, or making angel wings. All such pleasures were sufficient unto themselves to make Christmas a special and exciting time of year. A relationship with the Divine didn't seem to matter much to me as a child. Yet, as the Christmas years rolled by, increasingly I had an inner sense that Christmas was supposed to mean more than just experiencing pleasure. These feelings began to surface in 1950, as I was enjoying a Christmas vacation at home during my first year in college.

At that time, commercial TV as we know it today was in its infancy. My college, in Durham, North Carolina, had only one channel, so I seldom watched any. At home on vacation, I compensated by watching as many boxing matches and late movies as I could. One movie in particular caught my attention. It was the impressive 1951 British adaptation of Charles Dickens' *Christmas Carol*, featuring Alastair Sym as Scrooge. As I watched the cinema story unfold, strong emotions surged within me. I was stunned that anyone could have such a lack of compassion as Scrooge. I was also amazed at how his lack of compassion was not only shrinking his personal nature but hurting good people in the process. I saw how Scrooge's selfish, money-grubbing attitude adversely affected the lives and families of others around him.

When the sequences of the three spirits of Christmases past, present, and future were shown, they caused me to choke up to the point of tears. The lack of sensitivity Scrooge showed for his clerk, Bob Cratchit, his indifference to the death of his partner, Jacob Marley, and his loss of his fiancée because he idolized money more than her love, tugged at my heart strings. I began thinking about my own thoughtless dealings with others. It even got to the point where I could almost identify with Scrooge's inconsiderate nature. Today, as I try to recall my feelings of years ago, I am reminded of what our Lord once said, *For what does it profit a man to gain the whole world and forfeit his soul?*[4] In

---

4   Mark 8:36

the movie, I also remember how my spirits improved greatly when Scrooge changed his way of thinking and helped to ensure that Tiny Tim would live. There it was in front of me, proof that a change in one's way of thinking, a change of heart, can rebirth a soul. At home, for the next few days, I felt the need for such change; I tried to be a more loving, more considerate, and a more helpful son and brother. But once I returned to college, the same old self-centered person resurfaced.

Sadly, I must confess, this continued to be the pattern of my life for nearly the next thirty years. During that period there was success, and such wonderful additions to my life as marriage, children, challenging career opportunities, and wonderful new experiences. Yet I was still burdened by my inability to identify with and to understand the spiritual meaning of Christmas. Believe it or not, over those next thirty Christmas seasons, whenever I was able to watch the Scrooge movie, the same tug at my emotions surfaced. I continued to have increasing guilt feelings of remorse, shame, and sadness. It was as though I once again identified with Scrooge's nature. This made me feel even greater remorse about my own selfish life. While I was not a Scrooge clone, I still felt guilty about the person I saw in the mirror each morning while shaving.

Then early one morning in February 1991, my mind seemed restless, and I was unable to sleep. I went into another room so as not to wake my wife and tried to get back to sleep by finishing a biography of the great Supreme Court Justice, Oliver Wendell Holmes, Jr. He was raised a Unitarian but was not a believer. Holmes was highly respected for his patriotism in the Civil War where he was wounded three times, and for his legal excellence. But in his 94th year, in response to a friend's question, he showed that his spiritual tendencies had not changed. When his friend asked him how he felt about his long life, he replied with the following thought:

"Life reminds me of a picture, which one's imagination does not allow to end with the margin. Man aims at the infinite but when his arrow falls to earth it is in flames. In other words, death is final. There is nothing more."[5] As I finished reading his words, I immediately began to reflect back on my own life and became filled with a tremendous sense of regret. As mentioned in earlier essays, I considered that I had failed others, especially my family. My guilt caused me to consider that I likely had wasted the most import years of my life by believing in the myth of self-sufficiency. Had I lost my soul, I wondered? Whatever the purpose of my life might have been, it might be too late to make any changes.

Feeling worthless and lost, I knelt beside the bed, instinctively raising my arms in the form of a cross, something I had never done, before or since. Then with tears streaming down my cheeks, I literally cried out to God, "Lord God, please help me. I know I cannot ask you to keep me from dying. But please help me, Lord! I truly do not even know how to pray to you." A few agonizing moments passed in that quiet, early morning darkness, and my mind seemed devoid of all thought, as my head slumped to my chest.

Yet, in the quiet darkness of my despair, I heard a commanding voice repeating the two great commandments. My lips were still and there was no other sound. Yet I was

5   *The Justice From Beacon Hill*, by Liva Baker, p. 635.

experiencing the most electric moment of my life. I knew my desperate prayer had been heard. I understood that the answer for me was to love God with all my heart, and to serve His people. In that moment my acceptance of God's love, and belief in His Son's birth finally became real. It was almost as if St. Paul had described just such a moment two thousand years before, *For we do not know how to pray as we should, but the Spirit Himself intercedes for us with groaning too deep for words.*[6]

It has been just over 30 years since that morning of February 1991. Since then, my life has been filled with challenge, joy, and thanksgiving as I have sought to serve Christ at church, in jails and prisons, and in the other byways of my world. In the interim, while I have seen the *Scrooge* movie several more times, it no longer leaves me confused about my need at Christmas. That need has become the same every day, the maintenance of my relationship with our Lord. For me it is now the meaning of Christmas. So, each day I attempt to remind myself of this, as I thank our Lord for His great Christmas gift — the birth of His Son, Jesus Christ.

In closing, I am reminded of a cartoon on *Dennis the Menace* concerning Christmas, in the *Washington Post.* In it, poor Dennis has a problem. He is depicted with a little friend standing before their next-door neighbor, Mrs. Wilson, at her doorstep. He looks confused, almost desperate for an answer, as he exclaims, "Your husband, Mr. Wilson said Christmas is just around the corner … But we can't find it." If Mrs. Wilson is a believer, she probably told Dennis, "Not to worry boys, Christmas is right here, every day of the year. Just be patient and one day you'll understand."

6   Romans 8:26

A Spiritual Marker

Scripture says, *A person is not justified by the works of the law but through faith in Christ.*[7] Some thirty years ago, such thought held no real meaning for me. I had only a marginal concept of what it meant to have spiritual faith, much less to believe that I was loved by a Heavenly Father, and by His Son who died on the cross. But, as recounted in the preceding essay, my life changed in the early morning darkness of February 1991. I had heard and accepted the words of the two great commandments.

As I knelt emotionally helpless in prayer, either God or His messenger had made clear what would be required of me — to love God and my neighbor. This wonderful moment was an answer to prayer that I took to heart. As a result, my life began to change. It was the beginning of my spiritual rebirth. At last, I understood my essential need, to form a relationship with God through my personal relationship with his Son, Jesus Christ. No longer was my world to be centered solely on my self-interest. As the following background

---

7   Galatians 2:16

will indicate, the road I had been traveling had been leading me astray.

I had neither understood nor felt any need to forge a relationship with Jesus. Instead, as I have earlier described, I was focused on worldly concerns, including career, pleasure, and my future. Consequently, I often faced disappointment until, at age fifty-nine, it seemed as if my life was essentially over. It was too late for me to make amends for my past failures and sins. I was convinced that I had thrown my life away, wedded to my belief in the myth of self-sufficiency.

I vividly recall many of the events inexorably leading up to that February morning. I was a man lost in the darkness of his world of self-absorption. Some of my readers may have been there. It's a condition that doesn't lend much encouragement. No matter what task one undertakes, it seems as if life suddenly has no real meaning or purpose.

What I had yet to accept, however, was that the spiritual seeds of a relationship with Christ had been planted in my youth. In time they would bear fruit. In Sunday school I first learned about the Biblical Jesus. And I marveled at the fact He had risen from the dead. I believed it was true. But otherwise, the Christian message seemed to have no application for me. I was entirely focused on the secular aspects of life.

I was raised by kind, loving parents who tried to satisfy my every material need. That added to my problem. This enabled me to believe that my world was centered on my needs. As a consequence, I often ignored parental advice. My parents had joined the Episcopal Church more as a community endeavor than the result of any religious fervor. My mother participated in some church activities, including the altar guild, and my father occasionally delivered a few sermons. The latter activity was at the request of his good friend, the part time minister at our small, suburban St. Andrews Episcopal Church, 30 miles outside New York City.

In our home there was never any discussion of faith or religion, or the importance of prayer. Yet, my father did make certain that I attended Sunday school and was baptized when I was twelve, and later confirmed. My father purposely held up my baptism until I had reached an age when I would remember it. Thereafter, I was often assigned to read a Sunday lesson during regular worship service; I was also volunteered to sing in the choir. Apparently, the choir director considered I had a good voice. None of this activity interested me. It all seemed so pointless. It was merely a way to keep me involved with the church, rather than enjoying myself playing with friends. What I didn't recognize was that, despite my indifference, the seeds of faith were being planted, and in time they would bear fruit.

Truly, I had no appreciation that I was in the process of being introduced to the spiritual world, which I would eventually come to embrace for over thirty years. In college, I joined the large Duke Chapel Choir, which I sang in for four years. Unfortunately, the sermons I heard in the chapel often seemed bland and without meaning. But at least I was going to church. It seemed like the proper thing to do. I also recall one mid-week occasion in 1953 when Billy Graham spoke in our chapel. I went, hoping that I would learn how to become a good person. But his words had no effect.

While in law school, I actually spent a semester living in a Christian religious community. Somehow, I felt drawn to it. I believed the community would help me to be a more thoughtful person. I met many good people and made friends, but nothing really strengthened or awakened any personal desire for a relationship with Christ. Following graduation and passing the bar exam, my first full-time job was in New York City with General Motors, at that time the largest corporation in the world. I drove a new sports car, lived as a contented bachelor in Greenwich Village, and dated many attractive young women. I sensed that I was on a fast track leading to success and satisfaction.

Yes, occasionally there were signs that the seeds of faith had actually grown. Increasingly, I felt I should be doing something for God, if only to show Him that I wasn't completely self-absorbed. Such thoughts would usually occur in the morning, following an evening of pleasure the night before. I would suffer pangs of guilt at my lifestyle, although I was never, ever involved with drugs. But I convinced myself that there would be ample time to serve God after I had finished my professional career and retired. Such naiveté is literally shocking to me today. As I look back at such an attitude, I shudder to think what our Lord must have thought of my ignorance.

After working in LBJ's presidential campaign of 1964, I found employment in Washington with the U. S. Government. My desire had always been to make a career overseas, helping our nation do good in the world. This messianic goal was probably influenced by my father's desire for wanting his two sons to make a contribution to the world. The Cold War was at its height, and this influenced me to want to show other nations that America was their friend and wanted to help them. It was around this time in the early 1960s that one of the best-selling books on the market was *The Ugly American*.[8] Naively, I wanted to change that perception by working abroad and showing my interest in other cultures. I was accepted by the Peace Corps but chose an overseas assignment with the State Department instead.

The next quarter-century of my life was a roller coaster ride, as I experienced both success and failure. But all that began to change after that February morning in 1991. One of the most important changes occurred in 2001, after hearing Charles Colson describe his spiritual conversion at the Columbia Baptist Church. Elsewhere in this book I have already mentioned how my introduction to Colson aided my walk of faith. As earlier noted, two years later I actually accompanied him and some businessmen on a visit to several prisons in Southeast Asia. Upon my retirement from government, I became a full-time prison chaplain, at the jail where I had previously been a weekly volunteer. The spiritual seeds in my walk to faith had finally shown mature growth. Thanks to God's grace, I had at last learned how to yield my will to His. My relationship with Christ had truly given me a sense of meaning and purpose. I began to see the light of life of which Jesus spoke when He said, "I am the light of the world. He who follows me shall not walk in darkness, but shall have the light of life."[9]

Recalling the events that followed that early February morning in 1991, I have come to believe the following. In some manner, all humankind has an innate desire for a relationship with the transcendent, the Divine, regardless

---

8   *The Ugly American*, by William J. Lederer & Ugene Burdick, 1958.

9   John 8:12

of their national origin or previous secular beliefs. If left unmet, however, this may leave the individual with a sense of emptiness or incompleteness, no matter how successful their secular life may be. It is only when this desire is accepted, and then fulfilled, that the person has a sense of completeness or wholeness. It becomes their spiritual marker.

The National Prayer Breakfast

The Washington Post of January 22, 2023, reported that the National Prayer Breakfast would be held the first week in February. This annual event was started in February 1953, shortly after Dwight D. Eisenhower became President. Several Congressmen had been urging him to speak on our nation's need for spiritual renewal. But he was reluctant to participate because of his concern it would violate the Constitution's First Amendments prohibition against Federal Government interference with religious practices. Finally, the Rev. Billy Graham persuaded him to change his mind and participate. But it wasn't until January 1979, that the event attracted my attention. The reason was the featured speaker, Archbishop Fulton J. Sheen, had referred to President Jimmy Carter as a sinner. Once this accusation hit the evening news it became a real attention-grabber. Here's what happened.

Bishop Sheen began his remarks in an unexpected fashion. He said, "Mrs. Carter, Mr. President and fellow sinners. We Americans are not very much given to the thought of sin. We excuse our anti-social behavior because we were fed Grade B milk as children, or because of insufficient playgrounds, or because we were loved too much by a mother or too little by a father. The clergy dropped sin lest they offend their congregation; jurists then picked it up and turned sin into crime; and finally psychiatrists converted it into a complex. The result is that no one is a sinner." National TV jumped at the chance to cover the occasion.

While I wasn't present on the occasion of Bishop Sheen's remarks, I did attend the breakfast when Billy Graham last spoke to the group. At the time he told the following, amusing story. "There is a popular hunt club in South Carolina that my friend Johnny goes to every fall. Once there, he always requested a superb hunting dog called Jackson. It was a perfect match. Johnny was completely satisfied with his canine companion, and their hunt went well. But later in the fall a Harvard man came to the hunt club and asked for Jackson as his guide dog, having heard of his excellent reputation for bonding with hunters. Apparently, they got on well together. Shortly afterwards Johnny made his annual pilgrimage and again asked for his favorite dog Jackson.

Surprisingly, Jackson no longer responded to Johnny's commands and their hunt that day was unsuccessful. Upon returning from their unsuccessful outing, Johnny complained to the kennel custodian. "Oh," said the custodian, "Jackson hasn't been the same dog since that Harvard man took him out and began calling him Dr. Jackson. He just won't respond to any other command."

Most of the participants at the February Prayer breakfast attended a large luncheon. It was there where I heard a less amusing story from one of the guests. But it made the event an even more memorable one for me.

As we sat down to our roundtable luncheon that day, I felt quite emotionally moved. I had just come from listening to Joseph Girzone's marvelous story of a miracle. As some of you may recall, he is the former Roman Catholic priest who authored the 1983 best-seller, *Joshua*. Almost immediately I felt compelled to repeat the story to the distinguished gentleman sitting next to me, on my left, to explain to him why I was filled with tears of joy. He was a complete stranger to me but that didn't matter.

He seemed to understand my emotions and introduced himself in an effort to calm me. I could see from his badge that he was President of Compassion International or CI, an American child sponsorship and Christian humanitarian aid organization. Their mission is to influence the long-term development of children globally who live in poverty. And to accomplish this, CI often sends out individual clergy to foreign countries. I do not recall the President's name, but to encourage me he said, "Girzone's story is certainly a moving one. It actually reminds me of a similar miracle that happened to the young priest we recently sent to Colombia, to help the young homeless river children there. Let me share it with you."

He then proceeded to relate the following story. Apparently, CI had assigned the young priest to Bogota, Colombia. His work there would be to minister to the young children who daily come to beg along the Tunjuelo River, a tributary of the Colombia River. Unfortunately, they were being used by local drug lords to run errands, for which they would receive small tips. Eventually many of the young boys, mainly from the Muisca tribe, ended up either being arrested, killed, or, if they survived, serving the local drug cartel. The priest's mission was to persuade the young men to change their lifestyle, get some education, and get away from drug running.

After approximately a year the young priest had become amazingly successful. Many of the boys had left the riverbanks and taken advantage of CI's assistance. The latter included food and clean water, medical care, life skills training, and spiritual guidance. In many instances the long-term benefits of their changed lifestyle were greatly improved. Unfortunately, the local drug lords were not pleased; they no longer had the help they needed to further their local drug operations. As a result, they tried to eliminate their CI competition.

The young priest had two young children of his own, whom each day he drove to a local school. The local drug lord had been monitoring this practice. He planned to kidnap the two children, holding them until the priest ceased his efforts. But on the very day such an attempt was planned, the priest's car wouldn't start; so the children were taken to school by taxi. The kidnap failed. The next day his car started easily; nothing proved wrong with it. (The priest only learned of this failed attempt many months later.) Not to be dissuaded, the drug lord put a funeral notice in the local newspaper announcing the death of the priest. When CI officials were informed of this, they immediately transferred the priest and his family to another locale in Colombia, I believe it was Medellin.

At his new location the priest continued to be successful in helping young boys, much to the dismay of another local drug dealer. Something had to be done, so he hired their top assassin. He was tasked with killing the priest when he walked to lunch, the same route each day. Fortunately, after many hours of waiting, the assassin gave up. He could never get a clear shot at the priest, even though he followed him each day for over a month. Several weeks later the priest received the following letter in the mail.

"We are no longer going to try to eliminate you. Despite our best efforts, none has succeeded." The letter then proceeded to outline the ongoing efforts to kill the priest, most of which he had been unaware of previously. The letter then closed with the following confession, "For the past several weeks we have put our top marksman/assassin to follow you to lunch, but he can never get a clear shot at you. You are always surrounded by several tall men." When the priest first read the letter, he said, "I don't understand, I always go to lunch and back alone. No one ever accompanies me." Soon he realized the protection he had received had been designed by a "Planner" far more effective than any assassin.

When the President of CI finished telling me this story, I turned to him and said, "Wow! That's amazing grace; God is in control." He said yes, as we shook hands and then parted. Lunch was finished and it was time to go to our respective afternoon programs. But what a luncheon it had been. While I never had another opportunity to communicate with my luncheon partner again, there was no need. He had told me all I needed to hear. It would be a prayer breakfast I would always remember.

The Path To Virtue

It is likely that many of us would define virtue as a type of moral excellence or right conduct that conforms to an elevated standard. In this context, virtue has innumerable traits, including compassion for others, honesty, and faith. Yet, no trait is necessarily superior to any other. And certainly, we recognize virtue when we see it practiced. The value of virtue is often determined by circumstances. Possibly, St. Augustine was the most perceptive in describing virtue when he wrote, *The path to virtue starts from humility and rises to higher things.*[10] In the following essay I will venture to describe instances of virtuous conduct, including its effect on a person when it may be in decline. I begin with a story involving my wife Ruth, and some good neighbors.

Late one evening in 1987, I suddenly had to rush Ruth to Fairfax hospital for an emergency operation. Fortunately, it went well, and she recovered fully. During the following week, she remained hospitalized. Somehow word of her difficulty got out to her circle of friends, so for the next several days, alternately, the children and I received ready-made dinners from one of them. Today, as I recall that challenging period, I am reminded of St. Paul's letter to the Philippians: *If there is any virtue and if anything worthy of*

---

10 St. Augustine, *City of God, Book II*, (early 5th century), Chap. 17, p. 71

praise, let your mind dwell on these things.[11] Since that time, my thoughts often remind me of the compassion of our neighbors and how their virtue rose to higher levels.

In recalling my neighbors' compassion, I am reminded of my dear mother, Clara. In 1904 she became the second of four children born to a relatively poor family in central Ohio. Her father had to travel long distances and work long hours for the Pennsylvania Railroad to make ends meet. In addition, her mother brought in added income by renting out rooms in their home to boarders. Clara grew to be a beautiful young woman, characterized by her love of people, laughter, and music. After college and marriage, she raised two sons, of whom I was the eldest. As I grew into young adulthood, I became increasingly impressed by her ability to meet and enjoy others, to take a sincere interest in them.

Numerous times, she and my successful father would meet many new people, at both business and social gatherings. On such occasions she easily made new friends. Those she met always seemed to enjoy her, especially her humility and considerate nature. It was as if complete strangers were captivated by her invariably taking a sincere interest in them. She enjoyed putting them at their ease, and never making her interests the center of their conversation. Often, I discerned this truth from the fact she would remember interesting things to tell me about her new friends, and how they were looking forward to socializing together in future. As I fondly think back about her gracious life, I think of how her humility continued to raise her virtue in the eyes of others.

Mom was not alone. My father also enabled me to have a good understanding of virtue, including the need for honesty.

---

11 Philippians 4:8

On one occasion, he clearly helped to convey its importance to me. At the time I was about fourteen, and he and I were enjoying a brief chat over some coffee and donuts at a local ice cream parlor. A few days prior to our get-together, he had given me one of his speeches to read so I could then give him some feedback. During our conversation, he reminded me of this and asked what I had thought of it. At once I felt guilty, because I hadn't read it — possibly because the subject was technical and related to his work.

In answering his question, I responded in the only manner I thought I could. I said, "Dad, I'm sorry, but I haven't read it." He smiled and said, "I'm proud of you. You told me the truth and that's more important to me than any speech I might write." Immediately, I felt elated; my feelings of guilt disappeared. My sudden surge of relief was mixed with an equally strong feeling of love for him.

In the future, I would never forget the lesson learned that day. It had reinforced my belief in the essential virtue of honesty, and how its path frequently begins with humility.

The lesson I learned from Dad has had more than one application. As a jail chaplain many years later, I have had many occasions with inmates to reinforce the vital importance of honesty. I found this application essential to their understanding the meaning of humility and faith. Some inmates found these virtues difficult to apply, especially when recognizing their need for repentance. My use of a real life example, which conveyed my own vulnerability, sometimes helped the inmates to better interpret Scripture, such as the following passage, *You younger men ... clothe yourselves with humility toward one another, for God is opposed to the proud ... Humble yourselves therefore ... that He may exalt you at the proper time.*[12] My willingness to confess my own failures usually helped the inmate to see how he could apply the authority of God's word.

At the beginning of this essay, it was suggested that the decline of virtue can be harmful. This is certainly a risk if a culture and its people hope to endure and prosper, to avoid corruption and lying. I suggest this because a nation's civic virtue acts as a firewall against the temptations of corruption, especially the temptation to endorse greed and immorality. In our culture today, crimes of various kinds are increasing. While the need for improved policing is often called for, so are the moral virtues, which help to undergird the need for lasting protection against crime. These virtues stem from our religious and political heritage and thus embody the concept of civic virtue.

If our culture is to sustain such virtue, it will require more fellow Americans to accept the responsibility for being a good neighbor. Even where differences exist, it is imperative for good neighbors to acknowledge the importance of others' interests, rather than merely focusing on their own. Our first president, George Washington, grasped the dangers inherent in a culture where lack of concern for corruption and immorality exists. As president, he was meticulous in his efforts to put the needs of our nascent nation before his own interests.

We saw this truth expressed in the 1993 best-seller, Bill Bennett's *The Book of Virtues*.[13] It included several categories of admired virtues, including compassion, honesty, and faith. In the chapter on faith, Bennett described Washington's

---

12 1 Peter 5:5-6

13 William Bennett, *The Book of Virtues* (New York: Simon & Schuster, 1993)

farewell address to the American people. In it, Washington expressed his belief in the correlation between faith-based virtue, religious belief, and the success of the future course of the American republic. Such a symbiotic relationship has increasing significance for our nation today.

In Washington's view, the lack of religious belief, and the immorality that accompanies it, could weaken our nascent republic's belief in the need for virtue. He expressed his concern as follows,

> *Of all the dispositions and habits which lead to political prosperity, religion, and morality are indispensable supports … Whatever may be conceded to the influence of refined education … reason and experience both forbid us to expect that national morality can prevail in exclusion of religious principle.*

The words of our first president addressed an important concern of the Founding Fathers during the framing of the *Constitution* — the need to avoid a despotic monarchy or a privileged, ecclesiastical class.

The Founders also considered virtue to be a natural condition of freedom and good citizenship. Consistent with this belief was that they considered freedom, like nature, was naturally good. And they held that freedom in conformity with virtue enabled a people to choose the good, while avoiding corruption and licentiousness. Tragically, slavery was a cancer that had to be exorcised, but the *Constitution* had made a good start. Witness the First Amendment's protection of religion and speech from government coercion.

As Catherine Drinker Bower has written:

> *While the Federal Constitution did not discuss religion, the relationship of church and state was already well established ... yet there sat no delegate whose ideas of government or political philosophy were not profoundly influenced by his religious beliefs and training.*[14]

St. Augustine was correct, "The path of virtue starts from humility and rises to higher things." To sustain virtue in our culture, we need to remember to think higher.

---

14 Catherine Drinker Bowen, *Miracle at Philadelphia* (Boston: Little, Brown & Company, 1966) p. 215

Church Retreats

Where church retreats are concerned, there are so many fond memories it is hard to know where or how to begin. In no particular order, I would classify them as fun, fellowship, faith, food, and frost. I might add that I had never been on a church retreat of any kind until Ruth and I joined the Falls Church, in 1991. Over the ensuing years, we were to have many surprises and treats in store.

You might wonder why I list frost as a memory. It is because on our first October night at Shrine Mont, a small mountain retreat owned by the Episcopal Church, and located in the western hills of Virginia. We shared a bath and open-air salon in one of the clapboard cabins on the hillside at Mt. Jackson. Unfortunately, we had not brought any extra comforters or blankets with us. Even though by Texas standards, Mt. Jackson is more of a foothill than a mountain, it can get quite cold at night. And it frosted at thirty degrees that night.

That first night, unbeknownst to us, a member of the Sierra Club had joined our party. He was the six foot seven inches, 275-pound son of Dennis Crawford and his wife. I discovered him the next morning when I went downstairs for breakfast. He was still asleep on a sofa, but during the night he had managed to open both windows. The door was also slightly ajar in order for him to breathe in the gentle wind that circulated throughout our un-insulated cabin. He was wearing only trousers and a tee-shirt, so I had to look twice to make certain that he wasn't suffering from hypothermia.

He was an amazing specimen of young manhood, as well as an accomplished scholar and athlete. Only a few years later, he went on to become an All-American football player at UVA. And a few years later, he was a star defensive end on the Super Bowl champion Tampa Bay Buccaneers. It's amazing what cold air can do for the body. Ben Franklin was also a strong advocate of cold air baths when he traveled.

Switching from frost to food, reminds me of those Shrine Mont breakfasts of delicious bacon with hot cakes and the scrumptious fried chicken at dinner. But most of all, I remember the lunches of meatloaf and stewed tomatoes. The reason is they reminded me of a good high school friend, named Joe Livergood. His father was a local butcher in nearby White Plains, New York. Joe always brought Dagwood-sized meat sandwiches for lunch in the school cafeteria. Often, they were meatloaf and looked so delicious. Especially when compared to my peanut butter and jelly fare.

While I didn't particularly care for hot meatloaf at home, when my mother made a cold sandwich of it for me I became hooked. I have loved them ever since, especially when made on Jewish rye bread with lettuce and plenty of mayonnaise. At home, I often cook the loaf myself, flavoring it with two eggs and plenty of stale bread. While I did come to enjoy the meatloaf at Shrine Mont, it always reminded me of Joe and his sandwiches. By the way, Joe dreamt of becoming a doctor and became a good one.

Where fun and Shrine Mont are concerned, I truly enjoyed the Saturday night square dancing. It brought back memories of when I was serving at the American Embassy in Santiago, Chile. There was a large group of second-generation Scots living in Chile. Annually they would host a night of Scottish dancing. One of their featured dances was called the Duke and Duchesses of York.

After dancing it a few times I realized that the steps in the dance are exactly the same as those we do at square dances in America. However, we call it the Virginia Reel. My guess is the Virginians likely changed the original name of the dance, inherited from the Brits, after our Revolution. It probably coincided with the lives of Washington and Jefferson. Historians claim that both Founding Fathers enjoyed dancing, especially with attractive women.

The fellowship I enjoyed at Shrine Mont was important to Ruth and me. It enabled us to meet and make friends with many in the Falls Church congregation. Just listening to the stories of fellow believers was a treat that was entirely new to us. In addition, at Shrine Mont we always had such good guest speakers.

I distinctly remember talking privately with one such speaker, in response to a comment he made during his talk. He had confessed privately, to my surprise, that his wife had been abused by her father. Apparently, this sometimes affected her confidence, even though she and he had a good marriage. During his remarks to the entire Congregation, he shared with us a thought that I wrote down and still keep in my Bible, it was: "The best way to glorify God is to make Him your greatest source of pleasure." Over the last thirty years I have often shared this same thought with many of the prison inmates I counseled.

Faith is certainly a major element of any Christian retreat. And the fact that it is mixed with celebrations and festivities in no way diminishes that truth. I saw this again when I traveled with Charles Colson, founder of Prison Fellowship, throughout Southeast Asia in the summer of 1993. At each stop we made, in India, Indonesia, Hong Kong, Portuguese Macao, and Taiwan, local celebrations and worship were held. At these large gatherings of new Christians, the extensive singing and prayer dramatically reminded me of the joys of Shrine Mont.

I also saw this truth in our own family, after our youngest teenage daughter, Sarah, had attended a youth retreat with her sister, Anne. Both daughters were and are believers, but for my youngest daughter that particular church retreat made a significant difference for her. Previously she had attended church, but after the youth retreat Christ became fully real to her. Today, she is Director of Youth Ministry for the children in the church she attends near Stamford, Connecticut. I am also reminded that Jesus performed his first miracle at a wedding celebration, turning water into wine at Cana.[15]

Of course, God is not limited by time or occasion in bringing about His miracles. And individuals may experience them at any retreat, at any location. It is wonderful to see how such events enable a person to make Christ their greatest source of pleasure.

---

15 John 2:6-11

Receiving A Call

It is characteristic of our human nature to want to have a life filled with meaning, a life with purpose. This is an instinctive desire in almost all of us. It makes many of us inclined to focus on the readily available idols of success, achievement, recognition, wealth, power, or pleasure. Consequently, one or more of such idols has heretofore likely played a prominent role, at some point, in many people's lives. It is difficult to believe otherwise unless we consider the following exception: The circumstances where an individual believes they have received a Divine call.

The obvious question then arises, how does a person realize they have been called? And if that is their honest belief, how do they distinguish it from mere personal ambition? Oswald Chambers has suggested one answer. He opines that a Divine call, "is the expression of God's nature; that a person can only recognize such a call if that same nature is in them."[16] What Chambers is suggesting is that when a person believes they have been called, that person's nature and God's purpose become as one.

From my own experience, I must confess that it took me several years in prison ministry before I could appreciate that I had been called. The reason for my tardiness was I

---

16 *My Utmost for His Highest*, by Oswald Chambers, January 16.

had failed to distinguish between merely doing something religious that I considered might please God, from believing that God had planned for me to act on His behalf. It was not my initiative but His that had brought me to prison ministry; something that I previously never even considered. My realization enabled me to internalize what Christ meant when He said: "No one can come to Me unless the Father who sent Me draws him."*[17]*

Of course, responding to a Divine call is never routine. Quite the contrary, it is likely to be disruptive of one's previous routine. Scripture certainly reminds us there are numerous instances where individuals were called. They range from Abram, Moses, and Isaiah, in the Old Testament, to the New Testament's St. Peter, to that of St. Paul, called while on the road to Damascus.

Early in the Book of Isaiah we read of him worshiping at the Temple in Jerusalem, when suddenly the Biblical God appears before him, surrounded by angelic figures. Immediately, a trembling, startled Isaiah acknowledges that he is a sinner. He has seen the living God and expects to suffer severe punishment; for no human is permitted to lay eyes on the Biblical God. As Isaiah helplessly ponders his fate, one of the Seraphim suddenly takes a burning coal from the Temple altar, touches it to Isaiah's lips, assuring Isaiah that his sin, his iniquity has been forgiven.

In the following verse we read of God issuing a Divine call asking, "Whom shall I send and who will go for us?"[18] God is asking Isaiah whom can He send to warn the ancient Israelites of their sinful ways: that unless they change they

---

17 John 6:44
18 Isaiah 6:7

face exile. Immediately, Isaiah responds, offering to carry God's warning to Israel, even though he has no idea of what this will mean for his own future. By answering God's call Isaiah's life is forever changed. But the initiative for this change belonged to God, not Isaiah.

In Acts 9 of the New Testament, we can read how Saul, an influential Pharisee, and technically a citizen of Rome, is traveling to Damascus to persecute Christians. Suddenly he is called out by the risen Christ and challenged because of his persecution of Christ's followers. This challenge is followed by Saul being called to preach the Christian Gospel to the Gentiles.

After his encounter with Christ, Saul begins to use his Roman name of Paul, beginning in Acts 13:9. For the next 30 years of his life, or until his in martyrdom in Rome, St. Paul will devote his life to preaching the gospel to the Gentiles. As was the case with Isaiah, God's call changed Paul's life. Since St. Paul, many thousands of followers of Christ have been called to serve, although few are specifically mentioned in Scripture. The following example is a personal recollection of one of those.

I was in my early fifties and had almost never read the Bible. I attended church primarily because it seemed the right thing to do, a practice that had been ingrained in me from childhood. Later, after marriage and children, my wife and I made certain they attended Sunday school. As I explained elsewhere in this text, I did believe in the resurrection of Christ, but failed to see how it was relevant to my ambition for a successful career in the Federal Government. But as I approached middle age my indifference toward faith and the Christian God began to weigh on me. Career by itself no longer provided me with the sense of meaning I sought. In an attempt to change this way of thinking I began volunteering at a nearby Episcopal church.

I even read the Sunday lesson in church on occasion. As a young teenager I had been cajoled by my parents into doing such readings, so I had some sense of how it should be done. Later, as an adult and a member of the Episcopal Church, I was assigned to read the call of Isaiah. To be prepared, I practiced at home. Yet for some reason I began having difficulty reading verses seven and eight from Chapter VI, despite my repeated efforts. I couldn't understand why.

The aforementioned verse seven gave me particular difficulty, especially where Isaiah is told, "Your iniquity is taken away." As I recited the verse my voice seemed to choke up, possibly because the words made me identify with Isaiah's sense of guilt. It almost seemed as if I were admitting my past sins before God Himself. Even when I tried reading verse eight, where God says, "Whom shall I send, and who will go for us?" I continued to falter. Only through repeated efforts was my voice able to read the verses to my satisfaction. Finally, I was prepared, or so I thought.

When Sunday arrived, there were approximately 200 worshipers in the congregation. Finally, my turn came, and I walked to the altar and began my assigned reading. It started off well enough, but when I reached verse seven my voice completely stopped. I couldn't finish the sentence. There was nothing I could do but stand there and try to gather my thoughts. In a few moments my voice returned, and I completed the assigned passage, finishing with the words, "Here I am send me." The moment I finished a strange idea flashed through my mind. "Has God been calling me?" Immediately thereafter another disconcerting thought flashed through my mind, "What would God want with a jerk like me?" Then I closed the Bible and returned to my seat. Could it be that my sins had been forgiven?

After the service ended, our minister asked me if I was okay. When I nodded yes, he replied that the Isaiah passage was one of the most profound in Scripture. Over the following weeks I continued to become more active in the church and was even chosen to lead the brothers in our Fellowship of St. Andrews. Clearly something had changed my attitude. And I began visiting other churches to gain a better sense of what it meant to live a life of faith. Owing to the advice of a close friend, I visited the Colombia Baptist Church in Falls Church, Virginia.

On one particular Sunday, Charles Colson, the disgraced former White House aide, was the guest speaker. Because of his association with former President Nixon and the scandal of the Pentagon Papers, I felt ambivalent toward him. I almost left the church. Fortunately, curiosity caused me to remain. I had wondered what a convicted felon had to say that could be of interest. The answer was: a lot. Over an hour later the service ended with the final hymn, "How Great Thou Art", as tears filled my eyes.

Colson had dramatically described his recent trip to India where he had preached to several thousand inmates at a large prison. Listening to him made me wish that I had been with him. So, as I left the church that Sunday, I was determined that somehow, someway, I would become involved with prison ministry. Previously, I would never have entertained such a change to my life. To me, prison was for the lost. Surprisingly, I now felt a tremendous surge of enthusiasm to aid the lost. Here was my opportunity to give unselfish meaning to my life through service to Christ.

Surprisingly, only a few years after listening to Colson I was invited to accompany him on a similar mission to India and Southeast Asia. Then, following my retirement from government, I was offered a full-time chaplaincy at the Fairfax Jail. Clearly, God has His own unique way of calling people. And if I am correct, I had been called. Gradually, my nature became one with the Source of my call.

Finding Our True Identity

The everyday secular world in which we live considers a person's true identity to be how that person defines themselves, who they believe they are. This identity is customarily conveyed by the uniqueness of a person's character, their personal beliefs, and other traits. It also largely distinguishes that person from all others. And because true identity has its own internal source or uniqueness, it cannot be duplicated. As St. Paul said, "Who ... knows the thoughts of a man, except the spirit of the man which is in him?"[19]

Yet no matter how fixed our true identity may initially appear, it can be transformed, provided our belief in who we are, or how we choose to think of ourselves, is altered. Most often this occurs when the person discovers their need for the world of the spiritual or the sacred. While remnants of any earlier secular identity can still be recognized, they are united within a much more unique identity. Such a transformation occurs when the individual recognizes the authority of a source greater than their mere secular self. Such a transformation is surprising, especially in view of the person's earlier rejection of any religious belief or even their previous indifference toward it.

In the following essay I will elaborate further on the uniqueness of a person's true identity; suggesting how it

---

19 1 Corinthians 2:11

begins, is molded, and can remarkably be transformed, but never stolen. Concerning the latter, it may be true that a skillful thief can steal another's name and credentials, so-called identify theft. Nonetheless, no thief can steal or duplicate the true internal self of another. *For as a person thinketh in his heart, so is he.*[20]

In considering these viewpoints, initial questions might be: How does a person's true identity develop? When does it begin to emerge? I consider it begins at birth, although Scripture suggests it may be earlier.[21] At birth, however, a young child is further influenced by the characteristics, beliefs, and values patterned and conveyed by its parents; especially where the parents' love and affection are present.

As the child becomes increasingly cognizant of its surroundings, it begins to develop and express specific responses to such phenomena as pleasure, pain, fear, joy, desire, and sadness. By the time the youth matures, their responses have formed an internal pattern, a psyche if you will, that identifies the uniqueness of the person. It becomes who they believe themselves to be. For better or worse the person's identity has crystallized. The following brief stories indicate how this may or may not occur.

Consider the case of 19-year-old Joshua Cooke, of Fairfax, Virginia, who in August 2003 bought a 12-gauge shot gun and two days later murdered both his adoptive parents. At the time, Joshua said he felt like a zombie, and was filled with rage at the emotional and physical abuse he had suffered at the hands of his parents, along with his continued failures in school and rejections outside it. At his trial, he admitted

---

20 Proverbs 23:7
21 Psalm 139:15

that if he could have afforded an assault rifle, he would have attempted to kill more people. The influence of abuse and failure had molded a youthful identity in him of a sullen and resentful nature, completely removed from spiritual thought. At the moment of his horrendous crime, his identity with the darkness of evil was all that mattered to him.

Three months later while awaiting trial, and not knowing whether he would eventually face the death penalty, I met with Joshua in the Chaplain's Office at Fairfax Jail. He explained how the religious counseling he had received since his confinement had powerfully awakened him to the terrible acts he had committed, his need for sincere repentance, and his belief that Christ had forgiven him. Any belief in his being made in God's image[22] had previously been buried beneath parental abuse. Nonetheless, his unexpected spiritual awakening had begun to change his way of thinking about himself and his life. A new identity was emerging. The effect was that months later, at the time of his being sentenced to forty years imprisonment, he confessed that, "Upon my eventual release, and for the remainder of my life, I want only to serve others, to show them, in whatever way I can, the love and compassion Christ has shown me." Joshua's true spiritual identity had transformed his view of himself. He had begun to identify with his Savior.

Unfortunately, not all whose lives have been affected by a tragic death are able to surmount its damaging effect on their true identity. Instead, their image of themselves can become twisted and they are resentful toward the world. Such was the case of Ty Cobb, one of the greatest baseball players of all time, and one of the first five entrants into

---

22 Genesis 1:27

the Baseball Hall of Fame. In August 1917, he received a telegram telling him of his father's murder. His father, a highly respected Georgia politician and teacher, had been murdered by his wife, Ty's mother. The circumstances are still somewhat clouded in mystery, but their lasting impact on Ty's identity was apparent. Ty was 18 years old at the time of his father's death, but admitted he never recovered. He told reporters and teammates, "I didn't get over it. I've never gotten over it."

His ability on the baseball field did not suffer, as he went on to win batting titles and set other records. But the anger that he harbored crystallized into a resentful identity. Former teammates agreed that he was completely unable to get along with them. He became an alcoholic; was accused of abuse in his marriages, which both ended in divorce; he was also estranged from his children and did not attend his mother's funeral. Only three people attended his own funeral — the groundskeeper and two attendants. His true emotional identity remained darkened.

Such was not the case of former White House aide, Charles 'Chuck' Colson, initially known as the hatchet man of the 1970s Nixon White House. Colson's colleagues in the White House were well aware of his true identity; they sometimes remarked that he would cheat his own grandmother if it enabled him to gain an advantage. His attitude was to do whatever it took to defeat those who opposed him.

Nominally, Colson was raised a Christian, but in reality, his religion played no real part in shaping his early identity or his early political success. He admitted that his father had instilled in him the belief that political influence could best be gained by receiving a good education, earning a large amount of money, and then placing himself near the center of political power. Colson confessed that, "I had accomplished these three objectives and was sitting in an office next to the most powerful man in the world, yet I felt empty and depressed." And during the Watergate scandal in 1974, Colson pleaded guilty to the crime of obstruction of justice and served seven months in a federal penitentiary.

Prior to going to prison, however, Colson's identity underwent a transformation, aided by the help of good friends. He experienced a religious conversion. Soon after his release from prison, he founded Prison Fellowship, believing that God had put him in prison for a purpose: to help inmates turn their lives around. Over the next 36 years, he wrote many well-received books on faith and religion, received numerous awards, and became a sought-after speaker. His true identity had emerged.

As explained earlier, it was the winter of 1993 when I first heard Colson speak at the Columbia Baptist Church, in Falls Church, Virginia. At the time I was quite ambivalent as to the truth of his conversion, being well aware of his past political identity. At that time, I was on my own path to having my self-centered identity undergo a transformation. But after listening to Colson describe his earlier visit to a large prison in India, I was determined to get involved in prison ministry myself. In fact, two years later I was invited to join Colson and a small group of businessmen on a similar mission. During our travels, I asked Colson why so few ministers choose prison ministry as a vocation. He replied that, "One has to be called to it; a mere desire to do good deeds is usually insufficient." Looking back on my last thirty years, I do believe I was called to prison ministry, to serve Christ.

Going to Jail

Many worshipers are familiar with the Scriptural passage that reads, *I was in prison and you came to me.*[23] However, not many are acquainted with the efforts undertaken by those who see it as a mission to visit our jails and prisons. Consequently, few are apprised of how these volunteers try to bring Christ's message of repentance and forgiveness to the seemingly lost. In the following essay, therefore, I will sketch a few illustrations of how I have shared the gospel with individual inmates, all of whom were initially strangers to me. And I will close by describing an unusual blessing.

Let me begin by noting that each inmate is different; there is no magic formula to communicating with them. There is only God's word itself. Accordingly, my approach has always been to convey a message of forgiveness, encouragement, and hope. To accomplish this, I have frequently shared with each inmate spiritual thoughts that I considered had universal application. One of these I referred to as *The Three Options*, or, what Jesus said we could do with our lives.

The Three Options

At some point, we all ask ourselves what we should do with our life to find fulfillment. In Scripture, Jesus relates three

---

23 Matthew 25:36

options from which we can choose. One option explains how we can market or sell our life to the acquisition of money, wealth, or material things — thereby making them our idols. The second option describes a person who throws their life away by merely seeking to enjoy life's pleasures, such as parties and other indulgences. Once again, this option becomes an idol, separating us from God. The third option, the one which Jesus recommended, was to give our life to Him; in other words, to put God first in our life.

If we choose the first option, selling our life to attain material things, we risk losing the thing we crave most — salvation. For Jesus said, "What does it profit a man if he gains the whole world, but loses or forfeits his soul?"[24] We see Jesus' point illustrated in Scripture when a wealthy young ruler comes to Him and explains that he has kept the Ten Commandments, and wants to know if that is sufficient to enable him to get to Heaven. Jesus praises the man's faithfulness, but when the man hears Jesus' recommendation, he walks away, saddened. He is unable to follow Jesus' request: to sell all he had, give it to the poor, and follow Him. Jesus uses this example to emphasize why it is difficult for the wealthy to enter Heaven. It is not simply because of their wealth, but because material things have become their idols. This prevents them from putting God first in their life.

The second option, throwing one's life away in self-indulgent living, is certainly relevant to our world of today. We often read of people turning to drugs or drink as an escape to find fulfillment. In Scripture, Jesus uses the "Parable of

---

24 Luke 9:25

The Prodigal Son"[25] to illustrate this second option. He gives the example of how a young son squanders his inheritance on loose living until he loses it all and has to eat with pigs to survive. Left with nothing with which to sustain himself and filled with shame, he has to return home, with little hope of re-establishing his earlier life. While a loving father helps to restore the youth, the option Jesus is addressing is that the youth nearly threw his life away because he solely worshiped the idol of pleasure, leaving no room for God.

The third option, and the one Jesus recommends, is, "Whoever wishes to save his life shall lose it, but whoever loses his life for my sake shall save it."[26] In effect, He is explaining to those who wish to follow Him that they must re-order their way of thinking and doing. No longer can worldly idols take precedence in their lives. Instead, Christ and one's love for God must come first. We must live lives consistent with the example Jesus set — obedience to God's word. The question for many is how to do this, especially in view of the distractions, temptations, and difficulties that we all, at some point, confront.

On one occasion, Jesus explains how this can be done during his meeting with the Nicodemus, a Pharisee and a respected leader of the Jews. When Nicodemus questions Jesus as to how God enables Him to perform His many miracles, Jesus gives an unusual answer. He replies that no one can enter the Kingdom of Heaven unless they are born again. This term was almost entirely unique to *The New Testament*, which was first written in *Koine* Greek. And the closest Greek word to such rebirth was *metanoia*. It suggests

---

25 Luke 15:13-14
26 Luke 9:24

a person has had a change of mind, and thus, a change in their way of thinking and doing. And this is exactly what is required if we are to give our life to Christ. No longer can the cares of the world take precedence. God's precepts, as related to us by His Son, must take precedence. No longer are we inclined to worship gods or idols of our own making.

A Dangerous Detour

Jesus warned of the danger of the detour to Hell for those who continued to turn away from God's precepts merely to satisfy their own desires. In speaking to His disciples, He said, "Fear Him who is able to destroy both soul and body in hell."[27] The message was clear. Jesus was warning them of the penalty one faces upon taking the detour to Hell. He realized that at some point anyone can be tempted by evil thoughts or actions. But such temptations come with a price. This could mean the loss of one's sense of self-worth, the loss of any hope of God's forgiveness, and most importantly, the loss of any hope for salvation. He emphasized these dangers when He said, "For what will a man be profited, if he gains the whole world and forfeits his soul?"[28]

Christian believers have long been warned how dangerous it can be to ignore God's precepts, thereby enabling our hearts to succumb to evil thoughts or actions. The Great Russian novelist, Christian believer, and Nobel Prize winner Aleksandr Solzhenitsyn, addressed this phenomenon in his book, *The Gulag Archipelago:* "Gradually it was disclosed to me that the line separating good and evil passes not through states, nor between classes, nor between political parties either, but right through every human heart ... And even

27 Matthew 10:28
28 Matthew 16:26

in the best of hearts there remains an un-uprooted small corner of evil."[29]

Solzhenitsyn was certainly expressing what Jesus had earlier proclaimed when he challenged the hypocrisy of the Pharisees by saying, "For from within, out of the heart of men, proceed the evil thoughts ... and defile the man."[30] Jesus' emphasis on the heart was significant because in Scripture, the heart represents the will of a person. So, when one's heart is pure, evil can be resisted. But when evil thoughts are allowed to cloud our will, they turn us away from God and lead to a dangerous detour.

Even before Christianity existed, humankind was warned of this detour. For example, the famous Roman poet, Virgil, warned how easy it was for a person to embark on evil purposes, to stray from righteous behavior. He expressed this concern with the following thought, "The gates of hell are open night and day; smooth the descent, and easy is the way ... But to return, and view the cheerful skies — in this the task of mighty labor lies."[31] When Jesus ministered to His disciples, He often spoke of the danger or detour to hell. Nonetheless, He reassured them that God's church cannot be defeated by evil. As He said to Peter, "The gates of Hell cannot prevail against it."[32]

An Unusual Blessing

The first jail inmate assigned me was named Tremell, a powerfully built young man in his early twenties. He was in jail because of drug use. At the time I met him, our family

29 Alexandr Solzhenitsyn, *The Gulag Archipelago* (1973)
30 Mark 7: 21, 23
31 *Virgil, The Aeneid Book VI* (19 BC)
32 Matthew 16:18

had yet to join the Falls Church, although we were attending services there. With Easter approaching, Terrell asked me if he could attend church with me; his being on work release entitled him to do this. I agreed, as I felt like God was calling upon me to truly live the meaning of Matthew 25:36 about visiting those in prison, although I had yet to ask my wife or the Rector. Once I told Ruth what I planned, she reminded me that we were not yet members of the Falls Church and that our children, home from college, would be attending service with us. To ease her concerns, I promised to sit apart from them. When I spoke to the Rector he agreed to my plan, but suggested I attend services in the annex, Nicholson Hall.

When Easter Sunday arrived, I felt called to have Tremell sit with me in the main sanctuary, to experience an actual worship service. And what a service it turned out to be. As we walked into a packed church, Ruth suddenly motioned to me to join her and our children. Once we did, and until the service ended, every moment, every word, every prayer, every song, seemed to envelop me in a rapture-like significance. Of the many wonderful church services I have attended throughout my life, never before or since that amazing Easter Sunday, have I ever felt so completely attuned to the power of God's spirit. Afterwards, on the way back to the jail I shared my feelings with Tremell. He smiled and said, "Yes, we've been to the mountain top." What a blessing!

New Year's Day and Making the Right Choice

The last day of December every year is traditionally a time of great anticipation, expectation, and excitement. The holiday of January first is only a few hours away and it will soon be time to start celebrating the first day of another New Year. Conventional wisdom suggests it is also a time to forget about any past failures or disappointments, while looking forward to the improvements and new challenges of the coming year. As Oswald Chambers once claimed, "God's hand reaches back to the past, settling all the claims against our conscience." And at that point I consider His hand reassures us, especially when we have made the right choice.

While I certainly accept Chambers' wisdom concerning the past, I am also inclined to the belief that New Year's Day is vastly overrated as a holiday, as well as occasionally misunderstood. Based upon my experience, I consider New Year's Eve to be the real holiday and New Year's Day a badly needed day off work to watch football games. My reasons for suggesting this are several, but they begin with the meaning of the term holiday itself. What is the origin of the term?

In the old English vernacular, the word for holiday was comprised of two words; they were *hali* and *daeg*, meaning *holy* and *day*. Originally it was intended to refer to a holy day, a special religious day much like we consider Christmas and Easter. However, through modern usage the meaning of a holy day has been greatly expanded. Today a holiday can mean any day set aside for or dedicated for a celebration, whether it's for Martin Luther King, Jr.'s birthday or the Fourth of July. Of course, if there is also a religious purpose behind it, any holiday can still be considered to be a holy day.

In the distant past, depending upon which calendar was in use, the date for New Year's Day was different from today. In medieval times for example, most of Christian Europe regarded March 25th as the beginning of the New Year. Some likely reasons for this choice were that the March date coincided with the spring equinox as well as the Feast of the Annunciation. But in 1582 this changed. Pope Gregory XIII issued the Gregorian calendar which officially established January 1 as New Year's Day. The calendar change was evidence of the Christian Church electing to celebrate Christ's birth on December 25th, rather than March 25th.

Even leaving aside the issue of ancient calendars, I consider it questionable whether we should consider New Year's Day to be a holiday or even a holy day. Instead, it would seem more appropriate to consider it a day set aside for badly needed rest and reflection. My reason for emphasizing this is that most of the real celebrating, and I use that term in its broadest sense, actually occurs the night before the holiday actually arrives. Unfortunately, when it is actually time to celebrate the New Year's arrival, we find a great many celebrants either indisposed or far too tired to continue celebrating, suffering bodily from their excesses of the night before.

For those readers who are inclined to agree that the real holiday is not New Year's Day but New Year's Eve, I urge you to read further. Possibly you will learn some things about New Year's Eve celebrations that you hadn't considered before. For those who disagree, I also urge you to read further; so you will then see how my youthful experiences helped to mature me, to the point where New Year's Eve became far more special than New Year's Day; and how this attitude led me to make the right choice for my life.

The first New Year's Day that I can remember occurred when I was fourteen. I remember it not because of any special celebration, but because I attended my first New Year's Eve party the night before. My Uncle Dill and Aunt Sally had hosted the party for their old friends and relatives. They, along with their guests, were dressed in formal attire. While the food, champagne, and other beverages seemed to flow freely, I only imbibed a couple of ginger ales and ate a large piece of cake. At midnight I remember a lot of yelling, singing, and clicking of glasses as the radio indicated the clock in New York's Times' Square counted the final seconds of 1947. All things considered, the most exciting part of the event for me was staying up until four o'clock in the morning. I had never stayed up that late before, nor would I want to do so today. Age, and hard learned experience has taught me to value the comfort of a good night's sleep.

As was earlier explained, I had grown up near the greater New York City area, and soon become familiar with hearing of how one million people jammed together in Times Square to count the last few seconds of an old year, as they loudly welcomed in the New Year. Unless one has been there and experienced the roar of a million people yelling and cheering it is hard to imagine the booming sound they create. In future years, when I watched the event on TV, I realized I could not fully appreciate the sensational sound of a million voices shouting and cheering in unison. So, on New Year's Eve in 1953, I experienced this sound for myself. On that night, I made the half hour ride from my family's home in Hartsdale to New York City. Then I parked a few blocks away from Times Square and began running to get there before twelve midnight. I was only a few paces from the crowd when the clock hit twelve. Wow! What an experience. The vibrations from the crowd's sudden cry of pleasure almost seemed to shake the surrounding buildings; it sounded as if a huge bomb had exploded.

The following New Year's Eve I was determined to be in the middle of the crowd before midnight, so I could be part of the explosion; and I was successful. But the excitement that I had anticipated quickly changed to concern at midnight. Yes, again there was a huge roar. But along with it was the unique experience of a million people excitedly pushing and shoving against one another, and I was in the center. In order to stay upright during this unusual mêlée and avoid being trampled, I had to continue to push against hundreds of others, not knowing when the pushing would stop or whether I could stay upright.

Fortunately, the crowd began to disperse after several minutes, as people went on their way to various celebrations elsewhere. Within half an hour Times Square was only filled with a few thousand people, and I could walk largely unhindered along the street. Gradually I made my way to the sidewalk and headed for my car. My curiosity had been satisfied and in future I determined I would watch the Times Square celebration on TV from the safety of my home, with ginger ale and slippers nearby, a wise choice.

By no means do I mean to mislead the reader into believing that during my ensuing bachelor years I did not celebrate New Year's Eve. Even after marriage it took a while before my wife and I wisely learned to forget New Year's parties. And for many years now we have avoided that excitement and merely went for an early dinner at a nice restaurant, often with another couple. Then we came home, watched some TV, and went to bed well before midnight. I must also confess, however, that one of my early bachelor outings proved to be well spent, a right choice if you will.

At the time I was working in the U.S. Embassy in Santiago, Chile. Through my social contacts I had learned that an attractive young woman from England would be attending a New Year's Eve party that I had yet to be invited to. Still, I was quite interested in meeting her. My friends at the British Embassy said that she was delightful and that I should meet her. Unfortunately, I had not been issued an invitation to the party, and New Year's Eve was only a few days away. So, I devised a plan. Rather than leave my invitation to chance, I went to our embassy commissary and purchased two large bottles of excellent Scotch and delivered it to the party's host, a Chilean acquaintance named Eduardo. The very next day he called me and invited me to his party. I gratefully accepted.

Still, I had an important decision to make. I had already scheduled a dinner date with a young Chilean lady for that evening. So, my dilemma was how to gracefully fulfill my commitment to her and still get to meet the young English lady later that evening. My solution was to carry through with my dinner date and then take her home. Since she lived with her parents, I am certain they felt relieved and appreciated my thoughtfulness for her care. Afterward, I hurried to Eduardo's party and arrived before midnight. It proved to be the right choice — the best I ever made, as a few years later the young English lady and I were married. Her name is Ruth, and we are now into our 53rd year of marriage.

Now you know why I consider New Year's Eve will always be a real holiday for me, not January first. I continue to reflect on my good fortune and happily leave the celebrating to younger heroes.

The Afterword

Few, outside of my family and possibly a few friends, are likely to read this book, and maybe that is just as well, for I am mindful that a word misspoken can never be withdrawn. And opinions do tend to differ. I also accept that old age may not have made me wiser, but simply older. So, to those who may disagree with these, my final thoughts, or to those who believe I may have said either too little or too much, spoken foolishly, or self-righteously, I ask your forgiveness. Yet for those who are satisfied, I ask not to credit me, but to join me in rejoicing and in thanking God for His grace.

www.ingramcontent.com/pod-product-compliance
Lightning Source LLC
Chambersburg PA
CBHW021610120626
46545CB00001B/161